Early Praise for *Rails Scales!*

Rails Scales! is a must-read for building a scalable Rails application—this book distills the wisdom of an expert who has worked for many years on one of the largest Rails apps in production into a practical, on-point primer for the most common "gotchas" you'll encounter. Highly recommended!

➤ Ciaran Archer
   Lead Architect, Zendesk

Ruby on Rails has a record of rapidly launching successful startups. However, even the best idea is doomed if you can't keep up with the traffic. *Rails Scales!* gives an insider's view to the techniques we've used to scale one of the world's highest-traffic Rails applications.

➤ Gabe Martin-Dempesy
   Architect, Zendesk

I have worked with Ruby On Rails since 2007 and found Cristian's writing easy to read and the narrative very well constructed. What I like the most is that the focus remains on the key subject throughout hundreds of pages. A reader won't be distracted by unnecessary controversial tools or arguments; the book has a clear focus and brings the reader through the journey step by step. Engineers who have worked with Rails extensively will find that Cristian uses the best and most commonly used tools and libraries for the test project he develops to show it in action.

➤ Anatoly Mikhaylov
   Principal Software Engineer

Cristian does a great job covering the topics that will help developers with different backgrounds and experiences make their applications faster. I'm proud to say we worked together in the past!

➤ **Albert Bellonch**
  Founder and Former CTO, Quipu

Cristian, who is a beloved colleague, has been a strong source of Rails knowledge, with key contributions to several high-scale features we worked on together. I rely on him to solve complex feature requirements using Ruby on Rails.

➤ **Vancheswaran Koduvayur**
  Technical Leader

Rails Scales!

Practical Techniques for Performance and Growth

Cristian Planas

The Pragmatic Bookshelf

Dallas, Texas

Pragmatic
Bookshelf

See our complete catalog of hands-on, practical,
and Pragmatic content for software developers:
https://pragprog.com

Sales, volume licensing, and support:
support@pragprog.com

Derivative works, AI training and testing,
international translations, and other rights:
rights@pragprog.com

The team that produced this book includes:

Publisher:	Dave Thomas
COO:	Janet Furlow
Executive Editor:	Susannah Davidson
Series Editor:	Noel Rappin
Development Editor:	Michael Swaine
Copy Editor:	Karen Galle
Indexing:	Potomac Indexing, LLC
Layout:	Gilson Graphics

ISBN-13: 979-8-88865-102-5
Book version: P1.0—May 2025

For Jolanta. T'estimo. Aš tave myliu.

Cristian Planas

Contents

Acknowledgments xi

Introduction xiii

1. Setting Up Your Machine 1
   Understanding the Application Database Setup   2
   Downloading the Application   3
   Setting Up Ruby   4
   Installing the Database(s) and the Caching Stores   5
   Setting Up Rails   6
   Loading the Example Dataset   7
   Summing Up   9

2. Optimizing Data Access with ActiveRecord 11
   Managing Data the Rails Way   12
   Removing n+1s and Preloading Data   13
   Discovering Wide Fetching and Narrow Fetching   21
   Explaining EXPLAIN   30
   Indexing   38
   Summing Up   45

3. Understanding All the Faces of Caching 47
   Caching and Denormalizing   47
   Using counter_cache in Rails   50
   Setting Up Your Caching   55
   Using Fragment Caching   58
   Using Russian Doll Caching   61

Writing Your Own Caching   63
Using Write-Through Caching   70
Implementing Fan-Out Writing   72
Using Action Caching and Page Caching   75
Adding a Cache Layer to ActiveRecord   80
Choosing a Storage System for Your Cache   83
Using Denormalization   86
Summing Up   88

4.   **Designing a Scalable API** **89**
Paginating Your Endpoints   89
Discovering Cursor-Based Pagination   94
Splitting Your Model Data   100
Implementing Sideloads   105
Using GraphQL   106
Summing Up   112

5.   **Tracking the Lifecycle of a Request** **113**
Crossing the Internet with One Request   113
Using HTTP Headers to Speed Up Your Application   114
Introducing CDNs   122
Summing Up   124

6.   **Thinking Architecture for Performance** **127**
Discovering Sharding   127
Improving Your Response Time with Asynchronous
Processing   138
Getting Started with Event-Driven Microservice Architectures   151
Summing Up   160

7.   **Designing Product for Performance** **161**
Setting Product Limits   161
Managing the Life of Your Data   168
Doing Things That Don't Scale   180
Increasing Your Usability Time   182
Summing Up   188

8. Monitoring Performance to Build Scalable Systems . . . 191
    Choosing and Installing Your Observability Platform   191
    Monitoring (Almost) All the Things!   193
    Building Your Own Dashboards   203
    Setting Up Performance Error Budgets   206
    Being Wary of How Much You Spend   210
    Summing Up   210

9. Scaling, Beyond Performance 213
    Setting Up Ownership for Your Application   214
    Modularizing Your Application   217
    Using Feature Flags for Better Rollouts   227
    Summing Up   234

10. The Next 20 Years with Rails 237
    Scaling with Human-First Technology   237

    Index 239

Acknowledgments

Rails Scales! is the product of a professional journey spanning many years working with Ruby on Rails. I could not have embarked on this path nor written this book without the help of many wonderful people. This is my (admittedly small) token of gratitude to them.

My career with Ruby began at the Universitat Politècnica de Catalunya, where I discovered the language alongside my friends Pere Joan Martorell and Bernat Farrero. I would also like to thank David Morcillo, Albert Bellonch, and Josep Martins, who were important people in my early career.

Later, I was incredibly lucky to join Zendesk and live through many years of growth and challenges. I would like to thank some of the people who worked with me during this time. I will mention some of them, but not all. From my Copenhagen years: Libo Francesco Cannici, Bastien Vaucher, and Spyros Livathinos. From the Search team: Stefan Will, Shyam Sundar, Atul Purohit, and Di Xu. From the Authentication team, Swati Krishnan, Lisa Friedman, Gavri Fernandes, and Dolan Murphy. From FANG: Steve Curd, Preeti Dhiman, Wilfried Hounyo, David Cheng, Margarita Phuong, and Harley Herrell. Finally, as Group Tech Lead, I interacted with many people. I particularly want to thank David Henner, Adam Hart, Ryan Davis, Manjiri Deshpande, Daisy Itty, Shajith Chacko, and Jonathan Wilson.

Of course, I also have to thank my incredible reviewers, who devoted some of their very valuable time to helping me with this book. They are Gabe Martin-Dempesy, Ciaran Archer, Vanchi Koduvayur-Anantha, Albert Bellonch, and Anatoly Mikhaylov. Special thanks to Anatoly, who has also been my partner in crime at many conferences.

Given that I have already started talking about conferences, I would like to thank some of the figures of the Ruby community who have inspired me. The first one I would like to thank is Paolo Perrotta, whose speaking style and his book *Metaprogramming Ruby* have become sort of a north star in my career. Other people that have inspired me would be Yukihiro Matsumoto, David

Heinemeier Hansson, Aaron Patterson, Xavier Noria, Eileen Uchitelle, Charles Oliver Nutter, Sandi Metz, Jose Valim, and Brandon Weaver.

This book wouldn't exist without Pragmatic Bookshelf. In particular, I would like to thank my editor, Michael Swaine, who has been a constant support during the years that it has taken me to write this book. Another important person from Pragmatic is Noel Rappin, who I would like to thank for believing in me and giving me the opportunity to write this book for my favorite publisher. I extend my gratitude to everyone involved in the process of making this book a reality: Janet Furlow, Margaret Eldridge, Susannah Davidson, and the copyeditor, Karen Galle.

I also would like to thank my family. In particular, my parents, Emilia and Xavier, and my grandparents, Pilar and Antonio.

And finally, the person to whom I owe the most. Ačiū, Jolanta.

Introduction

This book has a superhero origin story. Let me tell it to you.

I started writing Ruby in the late 2000s while I was still in college. Those days, I was surrounded by fellow students who were becoming entrepreneurs, and soon, I decided to try my luck. In 2012, I became one of the co-founders and the chief technical officer of PlayfulGaming, a company that supported only one product: a game called Playfulbet. Playfulbet quickly became *very* popular. Within two years, the game had over half a million registered users.

This was a huge challenge for a 25-year-old CTO—especially considering that I was also the *only* engineer and the only technical person on the team. I took care of everything: from infrastructure to front end, from the Android app to database management, from writing Ruby wrappers around third-party APIs to the management of the iOS account for our iPhone app...which I also created.

All this was a titanic effort for one developer, only made possible by Ruby on Rails. Our web app had an extremely simple front end, and the mobile apps just rendered the mobile version of the web app. In this way, I was able to spend most of my time coding Ruby, the language that prioritizes developer productivity and happiness. And I *was* reasonably happy...and also crazily productive.

Still, Playfulbet suffered from very intense growing pains. We had a lot of trouble making it scale. The game became unplayable at peak hours when the Rails app was just unable to respond to so many simultaneous requests. I learned a lot during that period, and many of the techniques that I will share with you in this book were used to keep Playfulbet afloat during those years of rapid growth. Still, our growth was just too spectacular; my Rails application couldn't manage it. This was the beginning of my fascination with scalability problems and the reason why I decided to write this book. Was it possible that Rails just didn't scale?

We Need to Talk About the Rails Learning Curve

The idea that "Rails does not scale" is, unfortunately, quite common. A couple of months ago, while talking with the founder of a startup about this book, he told me, "The only thing I have heard about Rails is that it doesn't scale!" That this idea is around obviously does not make anybody happy in the Rails (and by extension, Ruby) community. But is it a fair assessment?

In short, no, it's not a fair assessment. Benchmarks[1] show that Rails does basically the same as similar technologies like Django (Python) or Laravel (PHP). Rails *does* scale. In truth, Rails is a battle-tested technology that has proven itself in enabling the growth of companies with planetary-scale needs, like Shopify, GitHub, and Zendesk.

So, if Rails has the demonstrable capacity to scale, where does the myth of "Rails does not scale" come from? I have a theory.

Rails famously follows the design paradigm of "convention over configuration." With it, Rails reduces the cognitive workload in projects by providing sensible defaults. This reduces complexity and helps increase productivity. Other concepts embraced by Rails nudge in the same direction: "batteries included" means Rails developers have access to many tools that bring a rich set of functionalities to their applications with a very low implementation and/or integration cost. On top of that, there's the famous (or infamous, depending on who you ask) Rails "magic": the fact Rails sets a series of implicit behaviors, conventions, and dependencies that increase development efficiency by abstracting away much of the complexity—and they may also prove obscure when the time comes to debug or when you need to go against the implicit convention.

While other successful web frameworks have also followed this path, Rails has been the most firmly committed to it and also the most successful. This success meant that many inexperienced developers (like I was when I worked in my startup) had much success—thanks to the Rails "magic" and supported by Rails' extremely smooth learning curve.

That is, until the time arrived to scale the application. At a talk at RailsConf 2022,[2] I joked that what the community seemed to be asking for is active_scale, a gem that would do the whole job for them. You just create a new initializer file and write:

```
ActiveScale::Rails.scale!(:sufficient_but_not_too_much)
```

---

1. https://www.techempower.com/benchmarks/#hw=ph&test=composite&section=data-r22
2. https://www.youtube.com/watch?v=mJw3al4Ms2o

And that's it. You can go back to writing business logic!

Regrettably, active_scale does not exist. It can't exist. There are multiple reasons for this: a lot of the scaling work is done outside of the scope of the Rails application itself, like database indexing and product design. Moreover, scaling is also highly context-specific, and the performance bottlenecks vary.

Fortunately, while it's true that we can't create active_scale, there are a number of techniques that can be used to scale web applications, including practices that are completely applicable to Rails applications.

Techniques for a Rails Renaissance

Getting back to my story, I eventually realized that the best way of learning how to scale would be to join a company that had managed to do it. That's why I joined Zendesk. It was a dramatic change moving from an organization in which I was the only engineer to one that had a product development team comprising over a thousand professionals.

This proved to be a smarter plan than I even realized. I now believe that an engineer needs three things to develop into a great professional. The first is a strong sense of ownership and responsibility, which you will definitely get working in a start12up. The second is being mentored by experts in different areas, which is something that can best be achieved by working in a big company. The third is time. You can be a great coder very early in your career, but you can't be an effective engineering leader without experience.

In my opinion, many debates in software architecture tend to be highly dependent on the broader social and economic context. Only experience can show you that there is not a general best solution, but only a best solution for these particular circumstances. A successful engineering leader needs not only a broad knowledge of the options to satisfy the requirements but also wisdom to separate the wheat from the chaff and pick the solution that will best fit the needs of the organization.

In the last 15 years, we have seen a great rise in the popularity of microservice architectures. While they have obvious upsides for scalability, flexibility, and autonomy, I cannot help thinking that their popularity has benefitted from the financial environment of the last decade. In other words, it might be partly a zero-interest rate phenomenon. Having so much money injected into tech allowed the hiring of very big teams for comparatively simple products, which helped to cover some of the trade-offs of microservices, like the higher complexity and increased cognitive load needed to manage them. If we are headed into more frugal times, this will have to change.

Still, the requirements and expectations as this book is published in 2025 are different from those in 2012. Modern applications are expected to be able to serve more users and have better performance than they had 13 years ago. If we are going to have a Rails renaissance, we are going to have to write Rails applications in which performance is a first-class feature from day one. Hopefully, this book can help.

About This Book

Before starting this trip together, I wanted to briefly introduce the content so you know what to expect from this book. When I was writing it, I had an ideal target audience: engineers who were in the same situation I was in 2012, when I founded my company. This means someone with a few years of experience under his or her belt and relatively familiar with the structure of a Rails application but not used to the peculiar issues that come with the need to scale an application. Still, my hope is that the vast majority of Rails developers will find something to learn from this book. Maybe you are an ace of SQL query finetuning and general database performance, but you may have never implemented write-through caching. Maybe you are incredibly knowledgeable about API design, but you may have never played around with the Cache-Control headers. I have this hope because, in this book, we will discuss a very wide array of ideas. A non-exhaustive list of the topics that you will read about in this book are:

- N+1s
- Customizing the size of database fetches
- Using EXPLAIN
- Database indexes
- counter_cache
- Fragment and Russian doll caching
- Write-through caching and fan-out writing
- Action and page caching
- Different storage systems you can use for your cache layer
- API pagination
- Adding sideloads to your API
- GraphQL
- Cache-Control and expires headers
- 304s and ETags
- CDNs
- Sharding your database
- Asynchronous processing
- Event-driven architectures

- Product limits
- Data archiving
- Performance dashboards and alerts
- Performance error budgets
- Application ownership
- Modularizing your application
- Feature flags

As you can see, we have plenty of stuff to discuss! Hopefully, you have already found something in this list that you are curious about. While I recommend reading the book from the beginning to the end, you can also go directly to a chapter you are particularly interested in; the problems and examples used in the book are sufficiently isolated for you to do so.

There are some resources I want to share with you before starting with the content of the book. The first one is the page dedicated to the book in DevTalk.[3] It's a great space if you want to share with others your opinion of the book or give feedback to me, the author. Another one is the repository[4] of the book; you will learn more about it in our first chapter, "Setting up Your Machine." Finally, remember that on the book page on the Pragmatic Bookshelf website,[5] you can find the errata page and download the code. This is a code-heavy book; if you have purchased the ebook, clicking the little gray box above the code extracts will directly download the extract for you.

And now, let's go for it!

---

3.   https://forum.devtalk.com/t/rails-scales-pragprog/162323
4.   https://github.com/Gawyn/rails-performance-book
5.   https://pragprog.com/titles/cprpo/rails-scales/

## CHAPTER 1

Setting Up Your Machine

Theoretical knowledge is important, and acquiring it is fun. However, when you read a technical book, often it's because you want to learn how to *do* something; it's a reasonable assumption that you, my reader, expect the same from this book. This is why this book has been written as a hands-on experience. You will find demonstrations for each and every explained subject, and this book comes with a companion application.[1] In this chapter, tools and libraries will be presented; they are the ones that you will use during the course of the book. You will also find help to install them. If you are an experienced Ruby developer, feel free to skip and only come back if you face any difficulty when using the application. Still, I'd recommend that you read the next section, "Understanding the Application Database Setup," as it explains certain peculiarities of the example app.

Engineering: Definition and Ethos

According to the Merriam-Webster dictionary of English, engineering is defined as "the *application* of science and mathematics by which the properties of matter and the sources of energy in nature are made useful to people" and also "the design and manufacture of complex products." Software engineering is given as an example of this second definition. Still, the first definition includes the word *application*, and that is the key word to understand the discipline of engineering. As engineers, our goal is to solve real-life problems, not to humor ourselves with theoretical questions (something we can totally do, but it's just not our professional purpose!).

---

1. https://github.com/Gawyn/rails-performance-book

Understanding the Application Database Setup

When writing a book on Rails performance, the database picked for the demonstration is a very significant choice. Of course, a relational database needs to be featured in the book, but it is not clear which one to pick. For "planetary-scale" applications, there are two main choices: MySQL and PostgreSQL. MySQL has been the dominating implementation of SQL for decades now; PostgreSQL has been its main challenger for a long time, with the difference in popularity getting smaller and smaller. If you are an experienced developer in the Rails space, it's probable that you have used both at one point in your career. Which one to go with? The answer was found in a popular meme: *Why not both?* Both implementations are popular enough to suggest that commenting on their specifics is worth our time.

Of course, this adds complexity to the application. The book mitigates this a bit by making it easy to switch the running database. Changing the database that the application will use is as easy as setting an ENV variable: DB_MODE. For example, running DB_MODE=postgres rails c will start the Rails console connecting our application to the PostgreSQL database; executing DB_MODE=mysql rails c will do the same with the MySQL database. The default is MySQL, so not defining that ENV variable will get you an application running on MySQL. You can change the default in config/database.yml. Just replace this:

```
development:
  <<: <%= ENV['DB_MODE'] ? "*#{ENV['DB_MODE']}" : "*mysql" %>
  database: moviestore_development

test:
  <<: *mysql
  database: moviestore_test

production:
  <<: *mysql
  database: moviestore_production
```

With this:

```
development:
  <<: <%= ENV['DB_MODE'] ? "*#{ENV['DB_MODE']}" : "*postgres" %>
  database: moviestore_development

test:
  <<: *postgres
  database: moviestore_test

production:
  <<: *postgres
  database: moviestore_production
```

Using MySQL or Postgres to run the application does not matter for the majority of the chapters in this book, except for the chapter in which you will work on database access, Chapter 2, Optimizing Data Access with ActiveRecord, on page 11. For that chapter, we recommend you install both and move back and forth to test the different characteristics and techniques enabled by each of the databases.

Still, this means that if you want to use both modes, you will need to install MySQL *and* Postgres.

Downloading the Application

The application we will use during the book is ready for you to get from GitHub.[2] You can download it directly, but we recommend you fetch it using Git, as you will eventually need it to move in between branches. If you don't have Git on your computer already, check the instructions at https://git-scm.com/book/en/v2/Getting-Started-Installing-Git and install it.

Once you have Git, clone the application by running the following on your terminal:

```
% git clone https://github.com/Gawyn/rails-performance-book
```

Now, you should have the application on your computer under the rails-performance-book folder.

SQLite

SQLite is a remarkable database. Lightweight, self-contained, and requiring zero configuration, it has been, for many years, the default choice in the Ruby on Rails stack. It was commonly used as the "go-to" database in development, but it was almost always replaced by a different database when the application hit production. In recent years, SQLite has made significant strides to become more viable for production usage, including in server-side applications, like Rails ones. Write-Ahead Logging (WAL) 2.0 improves concurrency, allowing for better performance. On the read side, the query planner has been optimized, reducing the number of unnecessary full table scans. Many Rails applications can bring their development mode SQLite setup to production with no issues whatsoever. And yet, in this book, we are targeting what we call "planetary scale." In this case, SQLite may not be there, at least not yet. SQLite still serializes writes, which will harm the system performance in a write-heavy use case. On top of that, PostgreSQL and MySQL still offer better indexing tools and query planning in massive datasets.

---

2.   https://github.com/Gawyn/rails-performance-book

Setting Up Ruby

Your next step is to set up Ruby. Central to any Ruby on Rails application is the version of Ruby in which we are running that application. The rails-performance-book application will use the latest Ruby 3.4.x version. Still, it's a good practice to use a Ruby version manager tool, and I encourage you to do that. Just as we have two popular SQL implementations, we have four popular version manager tools in the Ruby space: asdf,[3] chruby,[4] rbenv,[5] and rvm.[6] rvm is the original Ruby version manager (created in 2009, two years before rbenv), but nowadays, rbenv seems to be more popular. rvm is heavier, but also more versatile; rbenv is, in comparison, more lightweight and predictable. Neither of them is a wrong choice, and all of them are commonly found in professional environments; still, rbenv seems to have become the more dominant option in the last years. This is the one that I used when writing rails-performance-book, but you can also work with rvm, asdf, or chruby.

Thanks to its popularity, rbenv is easily available, and installing it is quite straightforward. On macOS and Linux, I recommend installing it using Homebrew:

```
% brew install rbenv ruby-build
```

ruby-build is a command-line tool that simplifies the installation of Ruby versions. We need it because rbenv doesn't manage the Ruby installation process itself, but it delegates it on ruby-build.

Next, you need to change your terminal configuration so it automatically loads rbenv on init. Executing rbenv init on your terminal will give you the instructions on what to do, which will typically imply changing the script that your shell runs every time it's initialized. For example, if you use zsh, this is what you will get:

```
% rbenv init
# Load rbenv automatically by appending
# the following to ~/.zshrc:

eval "$(rbenv init - zsh)"
```

Once you do that, just open a new terminal, and rbenv should already be up and ready to use. Now, it's time to install the Ruby version that we will use while playing with rails-performance-book. Just run the following on your terminal:

---

3.   https://github.com/asdf-vm/asdf
4.   https://github.com/postmodern/chruby
5.   https://github.com/rbenv/rbenv
6.   https://github.com/rvm/rvm

```
% rbenv install 3.4.1
```

Et voilà, you have Ruby 3.4.1 installed on your machine!

With this setup, switching Ruby versions is easy. You can check the Ruby versions currently available for rbenv in your machine by running rbenv versions. If you want to change the default version of Ruby, you can do so by executing rbenv global VERSION. The default version will be overridden if there is a local version defined in the folder; you can set a local version with rbenv local VERSION. This works by creating a .ruby-version text file containing the local Ruby version. You probably have noticed that the application rails-performance-book automatically loads the right Ruby version if you enter its folder. This is because there is a .ruby-version file that is setting it for you.

Installing the Database(s) and the Caching Stores

As mentioned, I wrote rails-performance-book to support two different relational databases as the primary data source: Postgres and MySQL. The process of installing these two databases can be a bit complicated, but you can find plenty of help online, specifically, in the official documentation of both Postgres[7] and MySQL.[8]

There is a third data storage system that you will use in the course of this book. You will eventually get to explore using faster, simpler key-value stores to speed up your data reads. While you can use many systems to perform the same function, in this book we comment on and use two: Redis and Memcached. This is not a random choice. We will get further into this in Chapter 3, Understanding All the Faces of Caching, on page 47, but Redis and Memcached are both very popular and significantly different, letting us explore very different use cases.

But to get access to all those sweet features, you will first need to install them. Getting Memcached in your machine if you run MacOS or Linux is quite simple thanks to Homebrew: brew install memcached will get it done. Redis is also very easy to install with Homebrew: brew install redis. Unfortunately, installing both Redis and Memcached on a Windows machine is a little bit more complicated. In general, developing Rails applications in a Windows environment can be a bit more challenging, but it can be done. In this case, I will refer you to documentation and the Internet.

---

7.   https://www.postgresql.org/download/

8.   https://dev.mysql.com/doc/mysql-installation-excerpt/5.7/en/

Finally, a novelty for Rails 8: Solid Cache. Solid Cache is a database-backed Active Support cache store, so cached objects will be written directly on the disk instead of going into memory. Your test application already comes with Solid Cache configured and ready to use with MySQL and PostgreSQL. Again, we will go into more detail about Solid Cache, caching, and the trade-offs involved into choosing it in Chapter 3, Understanding All the Faces of Caching, on page 47.

Setting Up Rails

In a book titled *Rails Scales!*, the most basic and essential block is, you guessed it, Ruby on Rails. It is important for you to use exactly the same version of Rails as the one we will use in the book. Of course, the general lessons of this book should be applicable to any Rails version (or even any web application!), but if you want to avoid the trouble of dealing with breaking changes in Rails, stay with the recommended version.

As was the case with Ruby, this book runs a fairly new version of Rails, which right now means the latest Rails 8.0.x. In any case, to manage the Rails—and all the other Ruby libraries—you have bundler. If you are a Ruby software engineer you totally know what I am talking about, but if not, here you have it: Bundler is by far the most popular package manager in the Ruby ecosystem, helping you to manage an application's dependencies and ensuring its compatibility. With it, you can define a list of dependencies in the Gemfile, declaring the library and the required version, so installing a compatible list of dependencies is a relatively simple endeavor. To install Bundler, just run gem install bundler on your terminal. Remember that if you are using a Ruby version manager like rbenv, each version of Ruby will require you to install its own version of bundler and all the dependencies of the application.

Once you have Bundler installed, you can proceed to install all the dependencies of rails-performance-book just by running bundle install on the terminal from the application root folder. Great! Before moving on, create the database required by the application:

```
% rails db:create; rails db:migrate
```

This will create the database and run the migrations on your default database (for example, MySQL). If you want to do it in the other (for example, Postgres), run this:

```
% DB_MODE=postgres rails db:create; DB_MODE=postgres rails db:schema:load
```

Loading the Example Dataset

We are almost ready to go! The final step before moving on is loading the example dataset into our data store(s). This is very important. The performance of an application is dramatically altered by the size of the dataset with which it operates. This is why you will be using a ready-to-use data set that, while significantly smaller than the one run on production by big companies, will hopefully be big enough to illustrate some of the real problems those huge corporations face when scaling their applications.

For that purpose, rails-performance-book provides a script to populate its own database. Following a Rails pattern, you will find the script at db/seeds.rb; the script loads into the relational database data that can be found in CSV format in the file db/data.csv. Executing the script is as easy as executing rails db:seed from your terminal. You will load quite a lot of data into the database, so don't get worried if the script takes some time to complete. This is the script if you want to take a look. You will understand better what the data means when we comment on database access in Chapter 2, Optimizing Data Access with ActiveRecord, on page 11.

```ruby
rails-performance-book/db/seeds.rb
require 'csv'

pp 'Destroying previous DB'
[Customer, Film, Inventory, Language, Rental, Store].each(&:delete_all)

pp 'Creating films'
data = CSV.read('lib/data.csv')
long_text = File.open('lib/assets/long_text.txt').read[0..64000]
n = data.count
language_i = 1
data.each_with_index do |content, i|
  title, language_name = content
  puts "Creating film #{i+1} of #{n}"
  language = Language.where(name: language_name).first
  unless language
    language = Language.new(id: language_i, name: language_name)
    language.save
    language_i += 1
  end
  Film.new(
    id: i + 1,
    title: title,
    language: language,
    big_text_column: long_text
  ).save
end

pp "Creating 10 stores"
```

```ruby
10.times do |i|
  pp "Creating store number #{i+1}"
  store = Store.new(id: i+1, name: "Store #{i+1}")
  store.save(validate: false)

  film_ids = Film.pluck(:id)

  attrs = film_ids.map { |film_id| {film_id: film_id, store_id: store.id} }

  Inventory.insert_all attrs
end

[
  'Yukihiro Matsumoto', 'Enthusiastic Rubyist', 'Experienced Rubyist',
  'Ruby Lover', 'Newbie Rubyist', 'DuckTyping Fan',
  'Rails Expert', 'Fullstack Developer', 'Hobbyist Programmer', 'MVC Guru'
].each_with_index do |name, i|
  customer = Customer.new(id: i+1, name: name)
  customer.save
  store = Store.find(i+1)

  100.times do |i|
    rental_date = (10 + (i * 7)).days.ago.beginning_of_day
    Rental.create(
      customer: customer,
      inventory: store.inventories.sample,
      rental_date: rental_date,
      returnal_date: rental_date + 3.days
    )
  end
end

max_customer_id = Customer.maximum(:id) || 0
1000.times do |i|
  Customer.create(id: max_customer_id + i + 1, name: "Dummy Customer")
end

# Matz follows everyone
Customer.where("id > 1").each do |customer|
  Following.create(follower_id: 1, followed_id: customer.id)
end
```

Remember that if you plan to use both MySQL and Postgres, you will need to load the dataset in both databases. You can do that by running rails db:seed twice, once without any extra parameter and again with whichever database is not the default. If you haven't edited database.yml, that will be Postgres, so you just need to execute DB_MODE=postgres rails db:seed.

Summing Up

All great trips start with a first step: this was your first step in the path of learning scalability in Rails applications. You downloaded the book application, installed a Ruby version manager and the right version of Ruby for this book, set up Ruby on Rails, and finally, installed all the data storages (including the relational database) and loaded the example dataset. You can make sure that everything is fine if you run rails server on the application root folder and get something like this:

```
> rails server
=> Booting Puma
=> Rails 8.0.1 application starting in development
=> Run `bin/rails server --help` for more startup options
Puma starting in single mode...
* Puma version: 6.5.0 ("Sky's Version")
* Ruby version: ruby 3.4.1 (2024-12-25 revision 48d4efcb85)
  +PRISM [arm64-darwin22]
*  Min threads: 5
*  Max threads: 5
*  Environment: development
*          PID: 9426
* Listening on http://127.0.0.1:3000
* Listening on http://[::1]:3000
Use Ctrl-C to stop
```

That's everything. Now your machine is ready to run rails-performance-book, and you and I are about to start our journey. Let's go!

## CHAPTER 2

Optimizing Data Access with ActiveRecord

You've heard the claim: "Rails doesn't scale." Like most generalizations, it's false, but that's small comfort when you're trying to figure out why this particular Rails application doesn't scale.

And in general, it's impossible to diagnose why a Rails application doesn't scale without performing a thorough investigation. If you allow me to paraphrase a famous quote from *Anna Karenina*, one could say that every poorly performing system fails in its own unique way, having gotten there following its own peculiar path to failure.

Still, some paths are more common than others, so you can usually make an educated guess as to why a system is performing poorly. Because *typically*, the performance bottleneck is going to be the database and, most commonly, certain data accesses executed by the Rails app.

This is completely normal. The vast majority of applications spend a lot of time moving data around—exposing information to end-users or to other applications via multiple interfaces or just moving it from one data cluster to another. Given this, you can see why the tool you use to interact with the data is crucial. It will affect performance, reliability, and developer experience.

Ruby on Rails has a specific philosophy on how to interact with data that affects the application as a whole, including its performance and scalability. In this chapter, we will explore what this philosophy entails while learning its quirks and the best way to use it to make our applications highly scalable.

Computer Science or Information Technology?

In 2017, *The Economist* published a story titled "The world's most valuable resource is no longer oil, but data." The article argued that by feeding the machine learning models that have disrupted countless industries, data has become a new kind of fuel that powers the whole global economy. That may very well be true, but we software engineers know that data—in particular, digitized data—has been a crucial component of the vast majority of businesses long before the dawn of the AI revolution. In the 80s and 90s, when the field that is now commonly referred to as "computer science" or "software engineering" started to rise as a force to be reckoned with, the most commonly used term to refer to this new area was "IT"—Information Technology. While the term in the United States has become associated with the least glamorous part of software engineering, to this day, in some languages a computer scientist is still referred to with a word that plainly links the discipline with information: "Informatik" in German or "Informático" in Spanish are only two examples.

Referring to the systems we build as "information technology" may sound very old-fashioned, but I do like the term. It reminds software engineers of the real focus of our work: to give access to information. A very small percentage of us work in parts of the field that don't involve the direct manipulation of data. The number of computer scientists who spend their days designing a new processor or even a new programming language is much smaller than those who work on extending or maintaining a set of APIs supported by an application written in Spring, Django, or Rails.

Managing Data the Rails Way

There are many different kinds of abstractions that can be used on the data layer; some have a lower level of abstraction and are "closer" to the way the database works, while others have a higher one. Ruby is a high-level object-oriented programming (OOP) language, and therefore, it makes sense that the most popular data-mapping abstractions would match its high-level, OOP-ish spirit. This type of data abstraction is called ORM—object-relational mapping. In essence, ORM maps runtime objects to a set of data. This is paired with a relational database management system (RDBMS), which stores data in a structured format using rows, columns, and tables. ORM maps each row to a different object, with a class corresponding to each table and an attribute for each column.

The most popular Ruby ORM, and the one used by Rails, is ActiveRecord. ActiveRecord is, in my opinion, one of the best—if not the best—tools in the whole Ruby ecosystem, managing to hit a sweet spot: capturing the magic that is commonly associated with Rails while being expressive enough to feel somewhat transparent. ActiveRecord offers a layer of abstraction on top of the database that significantly simplifies access to our data and it also solves many of the issues related to interacting directly with the database.

Nevertheless, the use of any ORM, even one as good as ActiveRecord, comes with its own drawbacks. So, let's look at the most typical problems that arise with the use of any ORM and see how to fix them. After that, we will move deeper into the data layer of our Rails application to see how it interacts with the database itself. We will learn how to analyze a given query to understand how the database is executing it and how to optimize queries to maximize performance.

Removing n+1s and Preloading Data

Of all the issues in database access, one is particularly notorious. Performance monitoring services give it special attention; it's even used as a common question in software engineering interviews. This problem is the n+1 query problem. It is particularly important if, as with Rails, we use an ORM. In this section, you'll learn what n+1s are and how to detect them, and you'll learn techniques to avoid them.

Meeting Your Enemy: the n+1

N+1s arise when trying to fetch an N amount of records in a specific and highly inefficient way: instead of fetching all of them in one query, you go about fetching them one by one, thereby ending up executing N queries. Running SELECT * FROM movies WHERE ID IN (1, 3, 4, 5, 6, 7, 8, 9, 10) performs significantly better than executing 10 separate queries for multiple reasons: one query produces way less overhead and allows the database engine to retrieve results more efficiently; it also makes more optimized use of the resources of both the network and the database itself. Despite being a very well-known issue to a lot of developers, it's still one of the most frequent sources of problems in Rails applications, to the point that some of the most popular performance monitoring platforms (like New Relic) have specific mechanisms to detect it.

If you were writing your own queries, it's unlikely that you would fall into this particular pitfall. Writing the same query over and over would be enough to suggest that something is wrong. The n+1 query problem is an issue in ORMs because of that abstraction layer between database and application. The abstraction layer hides the loop, making it seem like nothing unreasonable is happening.

The companion application for this book has an n+1 problem, and we are going to fix it in this section. Take a look at the app now. The issue is in the stores#show action. The n+1 is triggered by the following view, which you can find in app/views/stores/show.html.erb:

```
rails-performance-book/app/views/stores/show.html.erb
<table>
  <% @films.each do |film| %>
    <tr>
      <td><%= film.title %></td>
      <td><%= film.language.name %></td>
    </tr>
  <% end %>
</table>
```

Looks harmless, doesn't it? Unfortunately, it isn't. The last line of this view will run N queries, where N is the number of films owned by the store, each corresponding to one time through the loop. This means hundreds of unnecessary queries. Why didn't the previous line (film.title) trigger the same problem? Well, title is a column in the films table, and you already fetched the required row. film.language.name is calling the column name in the associated rows from the languages table. To access language.name, your application will have to first fetch film.language. There's a good chance that this problem won't be detected until the code hits production, as the datasets that are typically used in testing and staging environments tend to be smaller. In mature systems, production data can be big enough for an n+1 to cause serious trouble, including outages.

Next, you are going to find proof of the problem by calling that action in your own instance of the application. Access the URL of stores/1, so the view we have just seen gets rendered. Check the log, and you will find something similar to this:

```
Started GET "stores/1" for ::1 at 2024-08-15 23:58:35 -0400

Processing by StoresController#show as HTML
  Parameters: {"id"=>"1"}
  Store Load (0.3ms)  SELECT `stores`.* FROM `stores`
    WHERE `stores`.`id` = 1 LIMIT 1
  ↳ app/controllers/stores_controller.rb:3:in `show'
  Rendering layout layouts/application.html.erb
  Rendering stores/show.html.erb within layouts/application
  Film Load (1267.0ms)  SELECT `films`.* FROM `films`
    INNER JOIN `inventories` ON `films`.`id` = `inventories`.`film_id`
    WHERE `inventories`.`store_id` = 1
  ↳ app/views/stores/show.html.erb:2
  Language Load (0.3ms)  SELECT `languages`.* FROM `languages`
    WHERE `languages`.`id` = 1 LIMIT 1
```

```
↳ app/views/stores/show.html.erb:5
Language Load (0.2ms)  SELECT `languages`.* FROM `languages`
  WHERE `languages`.`id` = 2 LIMIT 1
↳ app/views/stores/show.html.erb:5
Language Load (0.2ms)  SELECT `languages`.* FROM `languages`
  WHERE `languages`.`id` = 3 LIMIT 1
↳ app/views/stores/show.html.erb:5
# Lots of very similar looking queries here...

  Rendered stores/show.html.erb within layouts/application
    (Duration: 5331.8ms | GC: 672.3ms)
  Rendered layout layouts/application.html.erb
    (Duration: 5347.0ms | GC: 672.3ms)
Completed 200 OK in 5355ms
  (Views: 4028.9ms | ActiveRecord: 1321.5ms (10397 queries, 10381 cached)
    | GC: 672.3ms)
```

Executing this extremely simple action took more than five seconds! Of that time, the majority was spent in the view. Moreover, the n+1 is also causing havoc in our memory usage. Check the garbage collection (GC) part. This is the amount of time our computer is spending managing the allocation and release of memory. Almost 700 milliseconds is an extremely high amount of time for such a simple operation! Moreover, if you are using any version of Rails earlier than 7.2, you will see the number of memory allocations instead of the time spent on GC.[1] When I tried this, my application allocated over 6.5 million objects. This is bananas!

The log presented us with a very bleak situation but also one that is fairly typical of an n+1 problem. The log showed how our Rails application is executing hundreds of different SELECT calls on the languages table, which is a waste. N+1 is a problem that leaves a very recognizable pattern in the logs, with a flood of extremely similar-looking SELECT statements, one after the other. While there are more sophisticated ways to catch n+1s, in most cases, a quick glance at the log of a slow request will reveal the guilty query. Unfortunately, complex applications can make n+1 detection difficult, but that's when we can use more sophisticated tools to catch them. The Bullet gem[2] has been around for more than 10 years, and not only detects n+1s but also unnecessary data fetches. On top of that, it suggests opportunities to use some performance improvement techniques, like counter-caching (storing the precomputed count of associated records) and others. Prosopite (https://github.com/charkost/prosopite) is a popular gem of very recent creation that is able to detect n+1 in some edge cases that are not currently supported by

---

1.   https://github.com/rails/rails/pull/51770
2.   https://github.com/flyerhzm/bullet

Bullet. Moreover, most APM systems (APM stands for application performance monitoring), like Scout or New Relic, feature n+1 autodetection.

As you see, there are plenty of options to catch those pesky n+1s. It's not surprising, because an n+1 is a bad problem to have in your application, one that can become even worse in certain situations, such as when the database is in a different host than the Rails application, something fairly typical in production environments. In this case, each query will imply another trip around the network, increasing the gravity of the problem.

Fortunately, fixing n+1s is extremely simple thanks to ActiveRecord.

Preloading Data with ActiveRecord

As we have just seen, the layer of abstraction added by ActiveRecord has its drawbacks. In the case of the n+1 problem, we may be inadvertently making inefficient and potentially very dangerous queries. With the ActiveRecord::QueryMethods.includes method, we can preload associated records in advance, avoiding the n+1 problem.

Let's see how the includes method works. In app/controllers/stores_controller.rb you will find the action that fetches the data from the database for it to be rendered in the view:

rails-performance-book/app/controllers/stores_controller.rb
```
def show
  @store = Store.find(params[:id])
  @films = @store.films
end
```

To fix the n+1, we will need to preload the associated row in the table languages for each film. Doing it is as easy as adding a call to the includes method at the end of the query and passing the name of the association as a parameter. This is how the new action should look:

rails-performance-book-completed/app/controllers/stores_controller.rb
```
def show
  @store = Store.find(params[:id])
  @films = @store.films.eager_load(:language)
end
```

Refresh the page and check the log. You will see that all those hundreds of SELECT statements on the languages table have been replaced by a single query, one that fetches all the languages by their ID in one go:

```
Started GET "/stores/1" for ::1 at 2024-12-14 21:09:47 +0100
Processing by StoresController#show as HTML
  Parameters: {"id"=>"1"}
```

```
  Store Load (0.3ms)  SELECT `stores`.* FROM `stores`
    WHERE `stores`.`id` = 1 LIMIT 1
  ↳ app/controllers/stores_controller.rb:3:in `show'
  Rendering layout layouts/application.html.erb
  Rendering stores/show.html.erb within layouts/application
  Film Load (929.6ms)  SELECT `films`.* FROM `films`
    INNER JOIN `inventories` ON `films`.`id` = `inventories`.`film_id`
    WHERE `inventories`.`store_id` = 1
  ↳ app/views/stores/show.html.erb:2
  Language Load (0.4ms)  SELECT `languages`.* FROM `languages`
    WHERE `languages`.`id` IN
      (1, 2, 3, 4, 5, 6, 7, 8, 9, 10, 11, 12, 13, 14)
  ↳ app/views/stores/show.html.erb:2
  Rendered stores/show.html.erb within layouts/application
    (Duration: 1579.8ms | GC: 269.3ms)
  Rendered layout layouts/application.html.erb
    (Duration: 1586.2ms | GC: 269.5ms)
Completed 200 OK in 1616ms
  (Views: 654.5ms | ActiveRecord: 951.6ms
    (3 queries, 0 cached) | GC: 269.5ms)
  Rendered stores/show.html.erb within layouts/application
    (Duration: 5331.8ms | GC: 672.3ms)
  Rendered layout layouts/application.html.erb
    (Duration: 5347.0ms | GC: 672.3ms)
Completed 200 OK in 5355ms
  (Views: 4028.9ms | ActiveRecord: 1321.5ms (10397 queries, 10381 cached)
    | GC: 672.3ms)
```

Significantly more efficient, isn't it? Executing the action took over five seconds before. Now, it takes a second and a half. We improved the performance by 70 percent! Moreover, the improvement could have been even higher. As we will see later, the films table holds some very heavy rows, which limits the speed at which ActiveRecord can operate. Still, you can see how includes made a heavy impact on the performance of the endpoint.

On top of this, the includes API allows us to do far more than preloading one association. We can preload multiple associations just by passing multiple parameters in the includes call. Calling Film.includes(:stores, :language) will result in the stores and languages associated with all films being preloaded:

```
Film Load (30.4ms)  SELECT `films`.* FROM `films` /* loading for pp */ LIMIT 11
Inventory Load (45.7ms)  SELECT `inventories`.* FROM `inventories`
  WHERE `inventories`.`film_id` IN (1, 2, 3, 4, 5, 6, 7, 8, 9, 10, 11)
Store Load (0.5ms)  SELECT `stores`.* FROM `stores`
  WHERE `stores`.`id` IN (1, 2, 3, 4, 5, 6, 7, 8, 9, 10)
Language Load (0.4ms)  SELECT `languages`.* FROM `languages`
  WHERE `languages`.`id` IN (1, 2, 3, 4, 5)
```

Another feature of the includes method is the ability to preload nested associations. For example, a call to Store.includes(films: :language).find(1) will fetch the store with ID=1 and preload the films associated with that store *and* the languages associated with those films. Neat!

Using the Solutions: includes, preload, eager_load

While the recommended way to fix n+1s in Rails is using includes, there are multiple ways to preload data; some of them are also implemented in the ActiveRecord API. Let's take a look at them.

Under the hood, includes calls preload, *at least in most cases*. You can change the controller to execute @films = @store.films.preload(:language), and it will work in the same way: making one query per association. We can find a departure from this behavior—a departure that will allow us to introduce the other canonical way of preloading data in ActiveRecord, eager_load. With eager_load, we are fetching all the associated objects in the same query using a LEFT OUTER JOIN, instead of a different query for each association.

Change the controller, so it loads the films using @films = @store.films.eager_load(:language) and check the change in the logs:

```
SQL (2128.9ms)  SELECT `films`.`id` AS t0_r0, `films`.`title` AS t0_r1,
`films`.`created_at` AS t0_r2, `films`.`updated_at` AS t0_r3,
`films`.`language_id` AS t0_r4, `films`.`big_text_column` AS t0_r5,
`languages`.`id` AS t1_r0, `languages`.`name` AS t1_r1,
`languages`.`created_at` AS t1_r2, `languages`.`updated_at`
AS t1_r3 FROM `films`
INNER JOIN `inventories` ON `films`.`id` = `inventories`.`film_id`
LEFT OUTER JOIN `languages` ON `languages`.`id` = `films`.`language_id`
WHERE `inventories`.`store_id` = 1
```

Using preload generated two queries. eager_load generated only one, albeit, a more complex, slow, and resource-expensive one. preload just fetched the data from each table in a completely isolated way; eager_load merges the data in the process of fetching it executing multiple JOIN statements. A JOIN statement in a SQL query combines rows from two or more tables based on a shared association.

Talking about JOIN SQL statements, there is a third method that is sometimes used to access associations in Rails: the method is joins. It looks similar to eager_load since it also executes a JOIN query—this time an INNER JOIN and not a LEFT OUTER JOIN. However, there is a crucial difference that makes it a no-go to fix n+1s: it doesn't load the associated records in memory. This means that accessing the languages associated with a movie will end up causing an n+1. joins is not designed for preloading purposes.

Most-Used Types of JOINs

There are different kinds of JOINs you can use to fetch data from multiple tables. The most common ones are:

- INNER JOIN: Selects records that have matching values in both tables

- LEFT JOIN (or LEFT OUTER JOIN): Selects all records from the "left" table (the first one in the query) and the matched records from the "right" table (the other one). If there is no match, the record will still be returned, but the result will be NULL for the values coming from the "right" table.

- FULL JOIN (or FULL OUTER JOIN): Selects all records from both the "left" and the "right" table. If there is no match, the record will still be returned, but the result will be NULL for the values coming from the missing table.

So, what to do with all this information? As a rule of thumb, it is better to let includes decide which method to use. It will dynamically pick eager_load when fetching the data in one query is needed, like in cases in which we are filtering by the associated table. For example, Film.includes(:language).where(language: {name: 'english'}) will use eager_load instead of preload so it can filter out the films that are not in English.

includes defaults to preload for a good reason: eager_load can get very expensive, memory-wise, and this can have a very significant impact when working with large datasets. While traditionally, the preferred approach to managing databases was to do as much as possible in one command, from an application perspective, many times it makes sense to have as few JOINs as possible. This is called "join decomposition." It is true that decomposing a query that has multiple JOINs into different queries adds overhead (for example, the trips around the network or the time spent in parsing each query); however, using more granular queries can be a trade-off since it facilitates the use of caches (you may have already performed one of the queries before), and it may reduce the amount of data that is accessed to complete the query; this can make this approach more performant.

After working so much on the theory, now let's test all this by running some code and benchmarking it.

Benchmarking Our Optimizations

Before closing this section on preloading data, let's use some benchmarking so we can directly compare the methods that we have just explored. You can run the following exercises using the rails-performance-book application; they are implemented as rake tasks.

The first benchmarked exercise performs a relatively simple task: to retrieve the titles of all the films in the database. You can run it from your own computer by executing `rake benchmark_preload_simple` from the root folder of the Rails application. These are the results that I got in my machine:

Query Type	Real Time	User Time	CPU Time	Improvement in User Time
n + 1	9.545s	4.873s	6.296s	-
Preload	1.34s	0.195s	0.574s	25x
Eager Load	0.99s	0.238s	0.536s	20x

The task also offers some information on the memory usage of each of our algorithms. In a previous section of the book, we have already introduced the importance of efficient memory usage, so we won't repeat ourselves here. This is how our three options behaved, memory-wise:

Query Type	Allocated Objects	Allocated Memory
n + 1	5,301,574	1564.23 MB
preload	148,827	682.34 MB
eager_load	250,610	697.21 MB

Of course, n+1 needs to allocate much more memory to work: double the size and between 20 and 35 times more than eager_load and preload. Moreover, this table also suggests a possible explanation for why eager_load is somewhat slower than preload. Check the amount of temporarily allocated objects that eager_load is using compared to preload.

The second exercise is slightly more complex. It can easily take a few minutes, so be ready to wait for a bit. For each store, it retrieves the language of each and every film owned by that store. You can run this from your own computer by running `rake benchmark_preload_complex`. These are the results I got on my machine:

Query Type	Real Time	User Time	CPU Time	Improvement in User Time
n + 1	73.191s	36.136s	43.524s	-
Preload	17.468s	8.876s	12.319s	23x
Eager Load	16.898s	9.176s	12.137s	16x

I haven't added memory profiling to this exercise, as it made it very slow, but in similar examples, it was possible to appreciate the same pattern as in the first example: n+1 using way more memory than the other two.

In general, the results show the same pattern as in the "simple" example. Both eager_load and preload fix the n+1 problem. And in between those two, preload gets a slight edge. Still, my suggestion would be to use includes if there is no specific reason to do otherwise. The basic idea when using a library or a framework is that you are able to stand on the shoulders of someone who has spent a significant amount of time on an issue *so you don't have to.* This is incredibly empowering, not only for entry-level engineers but even for experienced engineers entering a new area of the field. Rails and ActiveRecord are very mature, battle-tested technologies. The Rails way will usually be the best way.

Let's dig deeper into how to leverage the benefits that ActiveRecord provides us with.

Discovering Wide Fetching and Narrow Fetching

A common pattern in this book will be to describe the default behavior of ActiveRecord (and more generally, Rails), explain why it was chosen as the default, and finally, describe the cases in which taking a custom path makes sense. This is certainly the case for the position ActiveRecord takes by default when fetching from the database. I call this, "wide fetches."

Fetching Everything by Default

What is a "wide fetch," you ask? Demonstrating this is as simple as doing any query using ActiveRecord. For example, let's use the Rails console to fetch one film:

```
moviestore(main):001:0> Film.limit(1)
Film Load (7.3ms)  SELECT `films`.* FROM `films` /* loading for pp */ LIMIT 1
```

Notice the "films".* in the second line? That * can be really dangerous. It means that we are fetching the whole of the row, including each and every column. We are picking as much data from the selected rows as possible, therefore making the fetch "wide." Of course, this makes a lot of sense from the point of view of ActiveRecord. The library has no way to know which columns are going to be used. If your database design is solid, the table is supposed to be a fairly consistent unit of meaning for OOP purposes. This is also philosophically consistent with Rails: convention over configuration.

Moreover, the example we have just executed was fairly harmless. We are only retrieving one record in what looks like a relatively small table. However, as applications mature, this can become problematic. Let me tell you a story about that.

Escaping the Curse of the *: a Real-Life Experience

Years ago, I was asked to fix a performance issue that was heavily impacting a very important customer. A quick glance at our logs revealed that a typically innocuous endpoint in our API, one that was necessary to render some of our main pages, had unusually high latency. Moreover, the issue only affected this particular customer. Everyone else was able to use this endpoint with a latency of single unit milliseconds, but this client was getting double-digit *seconds* pretty often.

This endpoint, which was typically really fast, had a peculiarity: it wasn't paginated. If you don't know what "pagination" means, don't worry; we will get deep into pagination later in the book, in Chapter 7, Designing Product for Performance, on page 161. For the time being, you just need to know that pagination is the process of dividing a set of data into smaller pieces, so one does not need to fetch it all in one go. This endpoint was not paginated by design. It returned a very small amount of data (id and name) for the totality of a particular collection. We had a different endpoint for the same collection that behaved more traditionally, returning a bigger payload with pages. The most obvious possible issues had already been discarded:

- There was a significant amount of data associated with that account, but far from something that should cause a problem.

- The total size of the response was well under 100 KB.

Further investigation of some of the slowest traces showed that the problem was with a SQL query—a query so slow that sometimes it timed out. In many cases, when working with performance issues, finding the root cause is a huge step toward fixing the problem. However, the mystery in this case was that the query was extremely straightforward, something akin to:

```
Film Load (7.3ms)  SELECT `films`.* FROM `films` /* loading for pp */ LIMIT 1
```

At this point, I was at a loss. However, years of experience have taught me that applying best practices for performance sometimes brings unexpectedly positive results. We modified the code to limit the amount of data that was being fetched from the database...*et voilà*, the query became incredibly fast.

Solving the problem was not enough. Before closing the matter, a thorough post-mortem had to be performed. Checking the data model explained why using a "narrow fetch" had such a dramatic effect: the table had over 30 columns. In a "wide fetch," all of them were being pulled from the database, even if only two were used by the business logic. However, the number of columns *per se* is rarely a cause for trouble. It's less dangerous to fetch tens of integer columns than one TEXT column.

Let's illustrate this. Imagine a table with 50 integer columns. Fetching a row means just 200 bytes (50 * 4 bytes); fetch ten thousand records from that table and you are getting 2 MB worth of data. Fetch only one TEXT column and you are into—literally—unknown territory. The TEXT data type is not part of the SQL standard, but many databases implement it with slightly different specifications; one of those differences was the max size. In MySQL, TEXT has a maximum size of 65,536 bytes or 64KB. In the worst case, fetching 10,000 records with one TEXT column implies pulling 640MB out of the database. That hurts.

Alas, it can get worse. Our company was using PostgreSQL. According to the PostgreSQL manual, the TEXT data type has "variable *unlimited* length" (emphasis mine). In my experience, any feature that allows anything to be unlimited suggests pain in the future. In reality, PostgreSQL implementation of the TEXT data type is not really unlimited, and has a few quirks:

> Long strings are compressed by the system automatically, so the physical requirement on disk might be less. Very long values are also stored in background tables so they do not interfere with rapid access to shorter column values. In any case, the longest possible character string that can be stored is about 1 GB.

So, the max size is 1GB. In the worst case, when fetching 10,000 records, you are downloading a whopping 10TB of data. This can cause problems on many different levels, which we'll explore now.

Before commenting on the issues caused by manipulating unnecessary big chunks of data, I would like to dispel a possible concern you may be having. It's reasonable to think that, while it may be theoretically possible to have 1 GB TEXT fields, it will not happen. In my experience, while rare, it does happen. There are two situations in which surprisingly large objects tend to appear:

- Fields open for free users. If your application is open for anyone on the Internet to freely manipulate it, you need to assume that someone will eventually do their worst. It's a bit like the "chaos monkey" concept but with really mean and ill-intentioned chaos monkeys. On one occasion, we found a user who was storing the whole U.S. Constitution (including all its amendments) in our database. This was causing errors down our data pipelines. Moreover, given that these malevolent users share a database cluster with your regular customers, they can cause a database meltdown that will affect everyone, not only them.

- Storing serialized objects. It's a common pattern to save complex data as a serialized object in the database. ActiveRecord supports the serialization of model attributes out of the box,[3] using YAML or JSON. The complexities of serialization are out of the scope of the book, but I would like to point out why serialized objects can become an issue. First, the serialization itself already implies a certain overhead that eventually piles up. Second, and more importantly, serialization is almost always applied to complex attributes that tend to be bigger.

Chaos Monkeys

In the early 2010s, Netflix pioneered the discipline of Chaos Engineering. It emerged from the need to ensure the reliability of the new software architectures that were appearing at that time, many including hundreds of cloud-based systems that were constantly interacting with each other. The Chaos Monkey was one of the tools created for Chaos Engineering. In essence, the Chaos Monkey randomly shuts down parts of the infrastructure to test its resilience and fault tolerance.

Going back to our story, we found that the data our customer was storing included pretty complex serialized objects. The columns that held the serialized data were discarded during the rendering process as they were not part of the response, but that didn't matter; we were still fetching multiple GBs of data just to render a few KBs. This was slow for two reasons. The obvious one was the fact that our database cluster was on a different host, and those GBs needed to be sent through the network. The less obvious and more fascinating one was that the database was not able to store the whole response in memory and needed to write to disk in the middle of the response. Combined, they made for an extremely slow query and a very bad experience for our customer.

As we said before, the problem was expeditiously solved by using a "narrow fetch." This is how optimizing that endpoint with "narrow fetches" looked on our dashboards in the figure on page 25.

Impressive, isn't it? The change was as simple as a one-liner. In fact, ActiveRecord offers us more than one method to limit the scope of a query. So, let's learn about those methods.

---

3. https://api.rubyonrails.org/v8.0.1/classes/ActiveRecord/AttributeMethods/Serialization/ClassMethods.html

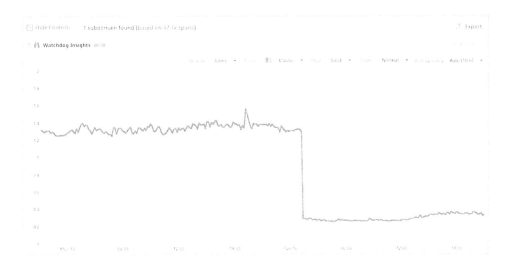

Fetching Lean with ActiveRecord: pluck and select

There are two ways of limiting the scope of that pesky * in ActiveRecord: pluck and select. They are very different. If preload and eager_load returned very similar results but executed very different SQL queries, pluck and select are the opposite: they both trigger exactly the same SQL query, but the returned objects are completely different. You can check it out using the Rails console:

```
moviestore(main):001:0> Film.pluck(:id, :title).class
  Film Pluck (15.3ms)  SELECT `films`.`id`, `films`.`title` FROM `films`
=> Array
moviestore(main):002:0> Film.select(:id, :title).reload.class
  Film Load (18.9ms)  SELECT `films`.`id`, `films`.`title` FROM `films`
=> Film::ActiveRecord_Relation
```

Same query, different results. In both cases, the response has been limited to the id and title columns, and you cannot see the * any longer. However, while select still returns an ActiveRecord_Relation object (the same as a query that uses a "wide fetch"), pluck returns a humble array. The structure of the said array is extremely simple, returning the requested attributes in exactly the same order they were put in the method call:

```
moviestore(main):003:0> Film.pluck(:id, :title)
  Film Pluck (11.1ms)  SELECT `films`.`id`, `films`.`title` FROM `films`
=>
[[86433, "Endless Poetry"],
 [86434, "The Dance of Reality"],
 [86435, "Mad Max: Fury Road"],
 [86436, "Parasite"],
 [86437, "Drive my Car"],
 ...
```

The power of pluck dwells in its simplicity: arrays are significantly cheaper to instantiate than ActiveRecord models. Moreover, the response of select can be dangerously deceptive. The returned object looks like the regular response from a "wide fetch," including all its methods; nevertheless, it is different in a key way: any attribute that has not been explicitly pulled will return nil. For example, trying to get the language of a film will return an error if language_id has not been included as a parameter in the select call:

```
moviestore(main):030:0> Film.where(title: 'Yojimbo').last.language.name
  Film Load (2.1ms)  SELECT `films`.* FROM `films`
    WHERE `films`.`title` = 'Yojimbo' ORDER BY `films`.`id` DESC LIMIT 1
  Language Load (0.3ms)  SELECT `languages`.* FROM `languages`
    WHERE `languages`.`id` = 4 LIMIT 1
=> "japanese"

moviestore(main):031:0> Film.where(title: 'Yojimbo')
  .select(:id, :title).last.language.name

  Film Load (1.7ms)  SELECT `films`.`id`, `films`.`title` FROM `films`
    WHERE `films`.`title` = 'Yojimbo' ORDER BY `films`.`id` DESC LIMIT 1

  Film Load (0.4ms)  SELECT "films"."id", "films"."title" FROM "films"
    WHERE "films"."title" = $1 ORDER BY "films"."id" DESC
    LIMIT $2  [["title", "Yojimbo"], ["LIMIT", 1]]

  (moviestore):9:in `<main>': missing attribute 'language_id'
    for Film (ActiveModel::MissingAttributeError)
```

As a rule of thumb, pluck is preferable to select. The fact that it does not return an ActiveRecord_Relation makes it more explicit to anyone manipulating the object that this is not a regular object. Ruby is a duck-typed language, and we, as developers, need to be careful to write readable, clear-cut code. Nevertheless, select still has a place when the use of some of the model methods is necessary.

Applying Narrow Fetches

Let's bring what we just learned into practice. There is an endpoint ready for you to optimize: it's /api/v1/films/lean.json. As in the story, it's an endpoint that returns a very limited amount of information (id and title) for all films. This is what you will get if you call that endpoint:

```
Started GET "/api/v1/films/lean" for ::1 at 2024-12-15 02:35:16 +0100
Processing by Api::V1::FilmsController#lean as HTML
  Film Load (741.9ms)  SELECT `films`.* FROM `films`
  ↳ app/controllers/api/v1/films_controller.rb:20:in `map'
Completed 200 OK in 1101ms
  (Views: 0.1ms | ActiveRecord: 742.3ms (1 query, 0 cached) | GC: 154.1ms)
```

Over one second! That's pretty bad, particularly for an endpoint that has only one query, and a very simple one at that. And yet, more than 75 percent of the latency comes from that particular database query.

rails-performance-book/app/controllers/api/v1/films_controller.rb
```ruby
def lean
  render json: json_response
end

private

def json_response
  Film.all.map { |m| {id: m.id, title: m.title} }.to_json
end
```

Why is this query so bad? Could it be that we are fetching some big, unlimited text column that is slowing us down? Well, that's exactly the case. If you check the database schema (in db/schema.rb), you will find that the films table includes this:

```ruby
create_table "films", force: :cascade do |t|
  [...]
  t.text "big_text_column"
  [...]
end
```

Yes, that's exactly it. Each and every film in our database is loaded with a long "Lorem Ipsum" text occupying a total of ~75 KB. Multiply by the number of films in the database, and you are manipulating 750 MB of extra data that you absolutely do not need.

Fixing this is very easy. Go back to the controller and replace the "wide fetch" with a pluck. You will also need to modify the block a bit:

```ruby
# app/controllers/api/v1/films_controller.rb

def json_response
  Film.pluck(:id, :title).map { |m| {id: m.first, title: m.last} }.to_json
end
```

Now, test your changes by calling /api/v1/films/lean.json once again:

```
Started GET "/api/v1/films/lean" for ::1 at 2024-12-15 02:38:08 +0100
Processing by Api::V1::FilmsController#lean as HTML
  Film Pluck (11.7ms)  SELECT `films`.`id`, `films`.`title` FROM `films`
  ↳ app/controllers/api/v1/films_controller.rb:20:in `json_response'
Completed 200 OK in 76ms
  (Views: 0.1ms | ActiveRecord: 16.1ms (1 query, 0 cached) | GC: 36.1ms)
```

The request took only 76 ms to complete. Moving from a "wide fetch" to using pluck has reduced latency by 14 times!

Avoiding Other Kinds of Wide Fetching

Before moving on to benchmarking, let's briefly look at a different type of "wide fetching." In the case we just talked about, the issue was caused by a combination of having a lot of rows and those rows containing a lot of data. Our solution was to reduce the amount of data we fetch for each row without diminishing the number of rows we obtained from the database; this worked well enough. However, in some cases, it will be mandatory to reduce the number of rows instead. When this is done for returning data, it is done by adding pagination, which is something we will discuss extensively later in this book.

However, in other use cases, you may need to apply the same principle as in pagination: to fetch that huge number of records in batches, not all at the same time. This is common when running a backfill on a very big dataset. For example, deleting all the records of a churning customer may seem like a trivial task, and it is if the customer doesn't have billions of records. In that case, though, removing all that data in one go may prove itself painfully slow or even impossible.

Fortunately, ActiveRecord provides us with a method to fetch data in batches. It is very appropriately named .find_in_batches. In essence, it will retrieve a group of ActiveRecord objects in smaller, more manageable "chunks" instead of fetching all of them from the database and loading them into memory at once. This is an example of how it works:

```
ms(main):001:1* Film.where(language_id: 1).find_in_batches.each do |batch|
ms(main):002:1*   p batch.count
ms(main):003:0> end
  Film Load (90.8ms)  SELECT `films`.* FROM `films`
    WHERE `films`.`language_id` = 1 ORDER BY `films`.`id` ASC LIMIT 1000
1000
  Film Load (76.8ms)  SELECT `films`.* FROM `films`
    WHERE `films`.`language_id` = 1 AND `films`.`id` > 1791
    ORDER BY `films`.`id` ASC LIMIT 1000
1000
  Film Load (72.6ms)  SELECT `films`.* FROM `films`
    WHERE `films`.`language_id` = 1 AND `films`.`id` > 3584
    ORDER BY `films`.`id` ASC LIMIT 1000
1000
  Film Load (78.0ms)  SELECT `films`.* FROM `films`
    WHERE `films`.`language_id` = 1 AND `films`.`id` > 5372
    ORDER BY `films`.`id` ASC LIMIT 1000
1000
  Film Load (91.5ms)  SELECT `films`.* FROM `films`
    WHERE `films`.`language_id` = 1 AND `films`.`id` > 7159
    ORDER BY `films`.`id` ASC LIMIT 1000
```

```
1000
  Film Load (63.3ms)  SELECT `films`.* FROM `films`
    WHERE `films`.`language_id` = 1 AND `films`.`id` > 8953
    ORDER BY `films`.`id` ASC LIMIT 1000
806
=> nil
```

.find_in_batches allows you to tune it with a few options. The most relevant for us is batch_size, which lets you configure—you guessed it—the size of the batches. Feel free to check the other options in the Rails documentation.[4]

Benchmarking Our Optimizations

In this case, it's also easy to prove through benchmarking how much better using narrow fetches is. Again, you will find the following exercise in the rails-performance-book application implemented as a rake task.

This benchmarked exercise accomplishes a pretty straightforward task: to retrieve the id and the title of each and every film in our database. You can run it from your own computer by executing rake benchmark_narrow_fetches from the root folder of the Rails application. These are the results:

Query Type	Real Time	User Time	CPU Time	Improvement in User Time
Wide fetch	1,995.72ms	212.98ms	766.96ms	-
Select fetch	53.45ms	53.45ms	55.77ms	4x
Pluck fetch	26.23ms	18.31ms	19.41ms	12x

And here you have the results for memory usage:

Query Type	Allocated Objects	Allocated Memory	Retained Objects	Retained Memory
Wide fetch	149,150	681 MB	2,986	385.67 KB
Select fetch	107,357	12.1 MB	4	0.66 KB
Pluck fetch	44,925	2.35 MB	2	0.58 KB

Both narrow fetching methods show a very clear improvement over "wide fetching." Still, pluck is clearly superior to select both for performance and memory purposes.

So far, we have tackled two of the most common issues with data access in Rails applications: n+1 and wide fetches. In both cases, we were optimizing the access pattern, not the queries themselves. In the rest of the chapter, our main focus will be to improve how the database accesses the data and how they use indexes to do it efficiently. Indexes are data structures that, in a

---

4.   https://apidock.com/rails/ActiveRecord/Batches/find_in_batches

similar fashion to a book index, help us find data faster. Before getting deeper into all this, we need to understand just what happens when we execute a query.

Explaining EXPLAIN

Fortunately, most SQL implementations provideFortunately, most SQL implementations provide a tool that describes how a query will be executed by the database engine: the keyword EXPLAIN. Note that the response of EXPLAIN will differ between SQL implementations or even between different versions of the same database. The following examples are from MySQL 8.0.31. At the end of this section, we will look at some examples of the response returned by the other major implementation of SQL, Postgres.

ActiveRecord offers us an easy way to access the keyword while still using its API: just call .explain when executing a query, and you'll get the analysis instead. Let's take an extremely simple query, fetching an object by one of its columns:

```
moviestore(main):001:0> Film.where(title: "Breathless").explain
  Film Load (4282.6ms)
  SELECT `films`.* FROM `films`
  WHERE `films`.`title` = 'Breathless'
=>
EXPLAIN for: SELECT `films`.* FROM `films`
  WHERE `films`.`title` = 'Breathless'

+----+-------------+-------+------------+------+---------------+
| id | select_type | table | partitions | type | possible_keys |
+----+-------------+-------+------------+------+---------------+
|  1 | SIMPLE      | films | NULL       | ALL  | NULL          |
+----+-------------+-------+------------+------+---------------+

+------+---------+------+-------+----------+-------------+
| key  | key_len | ref  | rows  | filtered | Extra       |
+------+---------+------+-------+----------+-------------+
| NULL | NULL    | NULL | 10168 |     10.0 | Using where |
+------+---------+------+-------+----------+-------------+

1 row in set (0.01 sec)
```

This may seem a lot to take in. Let's break down that table. The terms in italics are the ones that will be most useful:

- id: The sequential number of the SELECT in the query. This makes sense if, for example, you have multiple nested SELECT statements (as in subselects). Here, we only have one. This is the most common case, by far.

- select_type: The type of SELECT. It will typically be SIMPLE as long as the query doesn't use UNION or subqueries.

- table: The name of the table that is referred to by the query

- partitions: The partition from which the query results were fetched. In the case of non-partitioned tables, it returns NULL.

- type: The join type performed by the query. You can check all the join types in the MySQL documentation (https://dev.mysql.com/doc/refman/8.0/en/explain-output.html#explain-join-types).

- *possible_keys*: The indexes that the database engine considered using to execute the query.

- *key*: The index that the database engine ended up using to execute the query

- key_len: The length of the chosen key

- ref: It shows what is being compared or checked against the index when making the query. If, as in the example, we are not using any index, it will return NULL. If there was an index on the title column, given that we are comparing the column with a constant (the string "Breathless"), this field would return const.

- *rows*: An estimation of the number of rows that the database engine will need to scan to get the result. It's the closest thing to the "cost" of the query time-wise.

- *filtered*: The percentage of table rows that get filtered by the query condition

- *Extra*: Other information about the query that doesn't fit neatly in any of the previous fields. You can find all the possible options for the field in the MySQL documentation.

You'll have noticed that I've repeated the word "index" multiple times. Some of these fields only make sense if we are hitting an index: these fields are possible_keys, key, key_len, and ref. This is not surprising. Typically, one of the most common uses of EXPLAIN is to check that the database engine is using the right indexes. We will discuss this in our next section.

This first example has served us well in illustrating the basics of EXPLAIN, but what happens if we use it with a more complex query? Let's try something we talked about earlier in this chapter—a query that uses JOIN. The following query gets all the films in French and orders them by the title:

```
ms(main):110:0> Film.joins(:language)
.where("languages.name = 'french'").order("title").explain
  Film Load (9834.2ms)  SELECT `films`.* FROM `films` INNER JOIN `languages`
  ON `languages`.`id` = `films`.`language_id`
  WHERE (languages.name = 'french') ORDER BY title
=>
EXPLAIN for: SELECT `films`.* FROM `films` INNER JOIN `languages`
ON `languages`.`id` = `films`.`language_id`
WHERE (languages.name = 'french') ORDER BY title
+----+-------------+-----------+------------+------+---------------+
| id | select_type | table     | partitions | type | possible_keys |
+----+-------------+-----------+------------+------+---------------+
|  1 | SIMPLE      | languages | NULL       | ALL  | PRIMARY       |
|  1 | SIMPLE      | films     | NULL       | ALL  | NULL          |
+----+-------------+-----------+------------+------+---------------+

+------+---------+------+-------+----------+
| key  | key_len | ref  | rows  | filtered |
+------+---------+------+-------+----------+
| NULL | NULL    | NULL |    14 |     10.0 |
| NULL | NULL    | NULL | 10060 |     10.0 |
+------+---------+------+-------+----------+

+----------------------------------------------+
| Extra                                        |
+----------------------------------------------+
| Using where; Using temporary; Using filesort |
| Using where; Using join buffer (hash join)   |
+----------------------------------------------+

2 rows in set (0.00 sec)
```

Let's analyze the result of EXPLAIN. The first peculiarity you will notice is that the table includes two rows, not one. This is because our query is, actually, two: one filtering the table languages to get French (name = 'french') and another joining with the films table and ordering the result by title. In the analysis itself, one of the main differences is in the Extra field. You can see that there is new information: on the first query, we have Using temporary and Using filesort. This is an infamous duo to look for when trying to optimize an application. Don't take my word for it; this is from the official MySQL documentation:

If you want to make your queries as fast as possible, look out for Extra column values of Using filesort and Using temporary

Using temporary means that the database needed to create a temporary table to hold the results. This will typically be very expensive, performance-wise. Using filesort means that the database wasn't able to get the results already ordered (meaning, there was no index supporting that type of sort), and therefore, the database had to make another pass through all the records to put them in order. That can also be expensive. Finally, Using join buffer (hash join) means that MySQL had to use a buffer to perform the join, and in this case, it was done using a hash join; the other join buffer types are Block Nested Loop and Batched Key Access.

These are the basics of EXPLAIN. As I said before, it is typically used with indexes to analyze how the database is using them. In the next section, we will add indexes to our application. However, before advancing, there are a few peculiarities of EXPLAIN that need to be talked through.

Getting Deeper into Your Query: EXPLAIN ANALYZE

Some SQL implementations give us an extra tool to dive deep into the execution of our queries by allowing us to extend the functionality of EXPLAIN. The most commonly used is ANALYZE.

Unfortunately, ActiveRecord doesn't provide a way to execute EXPLAIN ANALYZE out of the box. However, we Rubyists are lucky to be part of an incredibly helpful and collaborative community, and of course, we do have gems[5] that add EXPLAIN ANALYZE to ActiveRecord. Still, if you want to run EXPLAIN ANALYZE from your Rails console without adding any new dependencies, you can always execute raw SQL from it. The way to run pure SQL from ActiveRecord is ActiveRecord::Base.connection.execute. Moreover, remember that you can use the method to_sql to transform any ActiveRecord query to a SQL-formatted string. In summary, if you want to analyze a query, you can do something like this:

```
moviestore(main):001:0> sql = Film.where(title: 'Breathless').to_sql
=> "SELECT `films`.* FROM `films`
WHERE `films`.`title` = 'Breathless'"
moviestore(main):002:0> puts ActiveRecord::Base.connection
.execute("EXPLAIN ANALYZE #{sql}").first.first
   (3219.9ms)  EXPLAIN ANALYZE SELECT `films`.* FROM `films`
   WHERE `films`.`title` = 'Breathless'
-> Filter: (films.title = 'Breathless')
(cost=42178.74 rows=1006)
(actual time=9.467..3156.646 rows=135 loops=1)
   -> Table scan on films
   (cost=42178.74 rows=10060)
   (actual time=9.460..3151.948 rows=10395 loops=1)
```

EXPLAIN ANALYZE returns to us how the query was executed, step by step. The order is from the bottom to the top, so "Table scan" happened before "Filter." Each of the steps has a few attributes, divided into two groups. In the first

---

5. https://github.com/pawurb/activerecord-analyze

group—in between the first parentheses—you will find two estimations: one for the cost of executing that particular step (as in the amount of time spent on it) and one for the number of rows that it will return. For example, the "Table scan on films" has a cost of 42178.4 (it's a unitless measure), and it returns 10060 rows. In the second parentheses, you first find the actual time that the database engine has spent executing the query. The field actual_time is an interval, with the first expressing the number of milliseconds it took to find the first row that matched the query and the second expressing the time it took to find the last one. The rows attribute returns the actual number of rows returned by that step of the query. Finally, there is the number of loops performed by that step.

The previous query was a very straightforward example. What if we run EXPLAIN ANALYZE on a more complex instruction? Let's check what happens if we analyze the same query we used in the previous section—the one fetching all the films in French and ordering them by title:

```
moviestore(main):001:0> sql = Film.joins(:language)
.where("languages.name = 'french'").order("title").to_sql
=> "SELECT `films`.* FROM `films` INNER JOIN `languages`
ON `languages`.`id` = `films`.`language_id`
WHERE (languages.name = 'french') ORDER BY title

moviestore(main):014:0> puts ActiveRecord::Base.connection
.execute("EXPLAIN ANALYZE #{sql}").first.first
   (2147.1ms)  EXPLAIN ANALYZE SELECT `films`.* FROM `films`
   INNER JOIN `languages` ON `languages`.`id` = `films`.`language_id`
   WHERE (languages.name = 'french') ORDER BY title
-> Sort: films.title  (actual time=1967.059..2026.097 rows=1215 loops=1)
   -> Stream results
   (cost=42753.42 rows=1408)
   (actual time=12.656..1743.883 rows=1215 loops=1)
       -> Inner hash join (languages.id = films.language_id)
       (cost=42753.42 rows=1408)
       (actual time=12.538..1733.674 rows=1215 loops=1)
           -> Table scan on films
           (cost=29602.84 rows=10060)
           (actual time=2.401..1720.335 rows=10395 loops=1)
           -> Hash
               -> Filter: (languages.`name` = 'french')
               (cost=1.65 rows=1) (actual time=9.558..9.575 rows=1 loops=1)
                   -> Table scan on languages
                   (cost=1.65 rows=14)
                   (actual time=9.552..9.564 rows=14 loops=1)
```

This is a much better example of how powerful EXPLAIN ANALYZE can be. Thanks to the step-by-step analysis, we can see where our database is spending most of the time in this very slow query: it's in performing the JOIN, not in the filters. You can see that in the actual_time attribute. The reason is that the JOIN has to manipulate the full films table, which is very heavy. This problem is a subset of the "wide fetching" issues that we discussed before. As a performance engineer, you have multiple ways to get around this; the easiest one is to use pluck.

All these examples were executed on MySQL 8.0.31. This is important, as different implementations of SQL will have different implementations of EXPLAIN, with completely different outputs. This book was not written with one particular SQL flavor in mind, but in this particular case, it's impossible not to be specific. That's why I decided to cover EXPLAIN for both MySQL and Postgres. So, let's see what we get when these operations are executed on PostgreSQL 14.5.

Using EXPLAIN in PostgreSQL

We're going to run the same queries we used in the previous section, but this time on a Postgres database. Remember that you can use Postgres instead of MySQL on the Rails application by setting the ENV variable DB_MODE. This will get you a Rails console connected to your Postgres instance: DB_MODE=postgres rails c.

Let's try our first query, the one filtering the films table by the title column:

```
moviestore(main):019:0> Film.where(title: "Breathless").explain
  Film Load (67.7ms)  SELECT "films".* FROM "films"
  WHERE "films"."title" = $1  [["title", "Breathless"]]
=>
EXPLAIN for: SELECT "films".* FROM "films"
WHERE "films"."title" = $1 [["title", "Breathless"]]
                      QUERY PLAN
---------------------------------------------------------
 Seq Scan on films  (cost=0.00..279.94 rows=135 width=60)
   Filter: ((title)::text = 'Breathless'::text)
(2 rows)
```

As you can see, Postgres doesn't offer the same table as the MySQL version of EXPLAIN. This output is more similar to EXPLAIN ANALYZE in MySQL than to EXPLAIN. The attribute cost is an interval, similar to what actual_time expresses on MySQL, but here, the unit used is artificial, with 1 signifying the cost of reading an 8KB page. The start-up number is first: this is the time spent before the output phase. The second value is the total cost of the query. As in MySQL, rows is the estimated number of rows that the query will return. Finally, width is the estimated size in bytes of the returned rows.

Let's check what we get with a more complex query:

```
moviestore(main):010:0> Film.joins(:language).where("languages.name = 'french'")
.order("title").explain
  Film Load (262.8ms)  SELECT "films".* FROM "films"
  INNER JOIN "languages" ON "languages"."id" = "films"."language_id"
  WHERE (languages.name = 'french') ORDER BY title
=>
EXPLAIN for: SELECT "films".* FROM "films"
INNER JOIN "languages" ON "languages"."id" = "films"."language_id"
WHERE (languages.name = 'french') ORDER BY title
                              QUERY PLAN
-------------------------------------------------------------------------
 Sort  (cost=322.84..324.58 rows=693 width=60)
   Sort Key: films.title
   -> Hash Join  (cost=1.20..290.15 rows=693 width=60)
         Hash Cond: (films.language_id = languages.id)
         -> Seq Scan on films  (cost=0.00..253.95 rows=10395 width=60)
         -> Hash  (cost=1.19..1.19 rows=1 width=8)
             -> Seq Scan on languages  (cost=0.00..1.19 rows=1 width=8)
                 Filter: ((name)::text = 'french'::text)
(8 rows)
```

This result is very similar to what EXPLAIN ANALYZE returned on MySQL.

PostgreSQL also allows you to use EXPLAIN ANALYZE. Moreover, there is an extra option you can use with ANALYZE: BUFFERS. Calling EXPLAIN (ANALYZE, BUFFERS) will give you extra information on the amount of IO work the query implies. This is what we get in our simple query:

```
moviestore(main):035:0> sql = Film.where(title: "Breathless").to_sql
=> "SELECT \"films\".* FROM \"films\"
  WHERE \"films\".\"title\" = 'Breathless'"
moviestore(main):036:0> puts ActiveRecord::Base.connection
.execute("EXPLAIN (ANALYZE, BUFFERS) #{sql}").values
  (277.7ms)  EXPLAIN (ANALYZE, BUFFERS) SELECT "films".* FROM "films"
  WHERE "films"."title" = 'Breathless'
Seq Scan on films  (cost=0.00..279.94 rows=135 width=60)
(actual time=0.082..181.552 rows=135 loops=1)
  Filter: ((title)::text = 'Breathless'::text)
  Rows Removed by Filter: 10260
  Buffers: shared hit=150
Planning Time: 0.159 ms
Execution Time: 181.643 ms
```

Let me add a note before moving further. I want to bring to your attention the fact that when executing raw SQL queries, we don't get the layer of abstraction provided by ActiveRecord. This means that the same query will return objects of different classes depending on the database and the library you are using to connect to them. In our example, running a query on

Postgres will get you a PG::Result object; doing so on MySQL will return a Mysql2::Result. Those classes are roughly conceptually equivalent, but they do have different APIs. If you check the examples, to access the result on a Mysql2::Result, we used .first.first; when querying Postgres, we had the more succinct .values.

OK, let's move ahead with our examples. This is what we get for our more complex one:

```
moviestore(main):001> sql = Film.joins(:language)
  .where("languages.name = 'french'").to_sql
=> "SELECT `films`.* FROM `films`
  INNER JOIN `languages` ON `languages`.`id` = `films`.`language_id`
  WHERE (languages.name = 'french')"

moviestore(main):002:0> puts ActiveRecord::Base.connection
.execute("EXPLAIN (ANALYZE, BUFFERS) #{sql}").values
Sort  (cost=322.84..324.58 rows=693 width=60)
(actual time=8.629..8.751 rows=1215 loops=1)
  Sort Key: films.title
  Sort Method: quicksort  Memory: 219kB
  Buffers: shared hit=151
  ->  Hash Join  (cost=1.20..290.15 rows=693 width=60)
  (actual time=0.272..6.763 rows=1215 loops=1)
        Hash Cond: (films.language_id = languages.id)
        Buffers: shared hit=151
        ->  Seq Scan on films  (cost=0.00..253.95 rows=10395 width=60)
        (actual time=0.123..1.808 rows=10395 loops=1)
            Buffers: shared hit=150
        ->  Hash  (cost=1.19..1.19 rows=1 width=8)
        (actual time=0.058..0.059 rows=1 loops=1)
            Buckets: 1024  Batches: 1  Memory Usage: 9kB
            Buffers: shared hit=1
            ->  Seq Scan on languages  (cost=0.00..1.19 rows=1 width=8)
            (actual time=0.021..0.027 rows=1 loops=1)
                Filter: ((name)::text = 'french'::text)
                Rows Removed by Filter: 14
                Buffers: shared hit=1
Planning:
  Buffers: shared hit=6
Planning Time: 1.837 ms
Execution Time: 23.451 ms
```

As you can see, The ANALYZE and BUFFERS options add some significant information. We don't only get the cost but also the actual_time. You can even see the algorithm used by Postgres to sort the rows (quicksort).

And we are done! This was a pretty short and kind of shallow introduction to EXPLAIN. Still, what you have learned here should be more than enough for you to start analyzing your problematic queries. Most of the time, you won't need to go deep into the output of EXPLAIN; checking the basics, like which steps are the most expensive, will suffice. Moreover, the power of EXPLAIN will be even more clear once we delve into our next topic: indexing.

Indexing

We've mentioned the well-known stereotype that "Rails doesn't scale." The reality is that, in many cases, those terrible, unfixable "Rails" issues are not due to Rails at all. Sometimes, they are the result of very junior engineers being able to bring businesses to life thanks to Rails' simplicity: small, inexperienced teams can go from "zero to one"[6] empowered by Ruby on Rails. The catch is that despite all the power that Rails gives you, one can still make big mistakes when setting up the database. This will lead to performance issues; most of the time, the problem will be slow queries. If you find a slow query, the first step is to check the indexes that this query is hitting…or not hitting.

Understanding Indexes

Let's start by defining what an index is. Imagine the following situation: you are asked to find all the words starting with the letters "rub". Imagine you have a dictionary. Easy enough, isn't it? What if, instead, you are asked to get all the worlds that *end* in "uby"? The problem becomes orders of magnitude harder because the dictionary is basically worthless to do something like that. To do it, we would need a reverse dictionary, with the entries alphabetized by their reversal (this is actually a thing; you can even find an online version).[7]

The issue here is that dictionaries work based on an index; all the words are ordered based on the first character (a-z). If the first character is the same, then they are ordered by the second, and so on. Database indexes work in a similar way. They establish different paths (implemented in data structures like hash tables or balanced trees) based on different columns (or groups of columns) so the database engine is able to guide itself to complete a query in a faster way. Imagine you are doing the database engine work and need to find all the rentals with customer_id 5. In this dataset, there are 1000 rentals, belonging to 100 customers. Without an index, you will need to check on all 1000 rentals because a rental with customer_id 5 could be stored first and/or last. If you have an index on customer_id, all the rentals by the same customer

---

6. https://en.wikipedia.org/wiki/Zero_to_One
7. https://closedtags.com/reverse-english-dictionary/

are grouped together; moreover, the data structure in which the index is stored is designed to help the database engine to get to the desired group as fast as possible.

However, indexes do imply a trade-off: they are an overhead on the write. Every time you insert a new row in your table, you will also need to modify the index. Moreover, indexes use storage—an amount of space that, in some cases, can be significant. For example, if you have a heavily indexed table that has relatively small rows, you may find that the indexes are larger than the data itself. Still, a well-thought-out index is almost always a worthy trade-off.

In the ActiveRecord convention, all tables come with a primary key named id. This means a few things: id is unique and it's indexed. Right now, those are the only indexes that exist on our application tables. So, what happens if you query a table filtering by an indexed key? The performance is much different—in fact, much better.

```
moviestore(main):001:0> Film.where(id: 1).explain
  Film Load (1.6ms)  SELECT `films`.* FROM `films` WHERE `films`.`id` = 1
=>
EXPLAIN for: SELECT `films`.* FROM `films` WHERE `films`.`id` = 1
+----+-------------+-------+------------+-------+---------------+
| id | select_type | table | partitions | type  | possible_keys |
+----+-------------+-------+------------+-------+---------------+
|  1 | SIMPLE      | films | NULL       | const | PRIMARY       |
+----+-------------+-------+------------+-------+---------------+

+---------+---------+-------+------+----------+-------+
| key     | key_len | ref   | rows | filtered | Extra |
+---------+---------+-------+------+----------+-------+
| PRIMARY | 8       | const |    1 |    100.0 | NULL  |
+---------+---------+-------+------+----------+-------+

1 row in set (0.00 sec)
```

As you can see, the query was incredibly fast, taking only 1.6 ms. You can also observe that some values in the EXPLAIN that were empty before now are populated: PRIMARY is both in possible_keys and key. key_len returns the length of the id column, and ref returns const because we are comparing the id column with a constant, the number 1.

What happens if we make a query on the same table, filtering by a column that is not indexed? The results are wildly different:

```
moviestore(main):012:0> Film.where(language_id: 1).explain
  Film Load (232.6ms)  SELECT `films`.* FROM `films`
  WHERE `films`.`language_id` = 1
=>
```

```
EXPLAIN for: SELECT `films`.* FROM `films` WHERE `films`.`language_id` = 1
+----+-------------+-------+------------+------+---------------+
| id | select_type | table | partitions | type | possible_keys |
+----+-------------+-------+------------+------+---------------+
|  1 | SIMPLE      | films | NULL       | ALL  | NULL          |
+----+-------------+-------+------------+------+---------------+

+------+---------+------+-------+----------+-------------+
| key  | key_len | ref  | rows  | filtered | Extra       |
+------+---------+------+-------+----------+-------------+
| NULL | NULL    | NULL | 10603 |     10.0 | Using where |
+------+---------+------+-------+----------+-------------+

1 row in set (0.00 sec)
```

It's much, much slower. As you can see in the rows column, the query had to scan the whole dataset to get the result. No wonder it's so inefficient!

Adding Indexes

This lack of indexes has a very real impact on our application. In one of our endpoints, we list the films we have by language. You can try this endpoint by hitting /api/v1/films?language=french. It isn't terribly slow, with the response returning in double-digit milliseconds. This is because the dataset doesn't include enough films for that to be a problem. However, we could certainly make it better.

A quick check on the code (you can find it at app/controllers/api/v1/films_controllers won't reveal anything particularly smelly. The query scope is clearly defined:

rails-performance-book/app/controllers/api/v1/films_controller.rb
```
    query = Film.where(language_id: language.id).order("title asc")
  end

  query.select(:id, :title, :updated_at)
  end
end
```

As you can see, the query includes a filter on the language_id column and an ordering instruction on the title column. If you run that query on the Rails console using .explain (using MySQL as the database, not Postgres), you will see the feared Using filesort on the Extra field; we only avoided the Using temporary because the dataset isn't big enough, but believe me, this query will not scale much further than this.

To fix this, we need an index. Our index will need to include both columns and in that particular order: language_id first, then title. This is because the query first picks the films with a specific language, and then orders all the films picked in the first step by the language.

You can do this directly by interacting with the database, but it's a good practice to use a Rails migration. Migrations are easier to write (and use), maintain schema versioning, are database agnostic, and also bring to the table simple rollback capability. You can create one with the command `rails g migration AddLanguageIdAndTitleIndexToFilms`. The migration needs to look like this:

rails-performance-book-completed/db/migrate/202...4441_add_language_id_and_title_index_to_films.rb
```
class AddLanguageIdAndTitleIndexToFilms < ActiveRecord::Migration[8.0]
  def change
    add_index(:films, [:language_id, :title])
  end
end
```

Run the migration (`rails db:migrate`), and you have added a new index to the database! Use `EXPLAIN` to check the query in the controller and you will see that now it's using the right indexes:

```
moviestore(main):004:0> Film.where(language_id: 1).order("title asc")
.select(:id).explain
  Film Load (8.6ms)  SELECT `films`.`id` FROM `films`
  WHERE `films`.`language_id` = 1 ORDER BY title asc
=>
EXPLAIN for: SELECT `films`.`id` FROM `films`
WHERE `films`.`language_id` = 1 ORDER BY title asc
+----+-------------+-------+------------+------+
| id | select_type | table | partitions | type |
+----+-------------+-------+------------+------+
|  1 | SIMPLE      | films | NULL       | ref  |
+----+-------------+-------+------------+------+

+------------------------------------+
| possible_keys                      |
+------------------------------------+
| index_films_on_language_id_and_title |
+------------------------------------+

+------------------------------------+
| key                                |
+------------------------------------+
| index_films_on_language_id_and_title |
+------------------------------------+

+---------+-------+------+----------+-------------+
| key_len | ref   | rows | filtered | Extra       |
+---------+-------+------+----------+-------------+
| 5       | const | 1215 |    100.0 | Using index |
+---------+-------+------+----------+-------------+

1 row in set (0.00 sec)
```

The migration worked: you can see our new index on both `possible_keys` and `keys`. Moreover, the query is way faster now. This is because indexes help the database in multiple ways: they reduce the amount of data that the database needs to examine, avoiding a sequential scan to replace it with just running on the index; they also help the server to avoid the usage of temporary tables and sorting on the database engine level, as the results are already pre-sorted.

A few things to note: the order of the keys in the index is *extremely* important. Think again about the dictionary example: in a dictionary, words are ordered alphabetically by the first letter, then by the second letter, and so on. Despite that, a traditional dictionary is *almost* useless if you want to get all the words that have "u" as their second letter. The same applies here. The *almost* is important. If you run a query ordering all the films by title `Film.order(:title).select(:title)`, you'll notice it's not particularly fast. However, if you analyze it using `EXPLAIN`, you will see something unexpected: the query optimizer doesn't find any candidate key to be used to perform the query (`possible_keys` is `NULL`), but it actually ends up using the index we just created (`key` is `index_films_on_language_id_and_title`). The reason for this is that, although it cannot be fully relied on to determine which rows to retrieve, it still can be used to make the query more efficient.

Finding the Right Opportunity to Add an Index

Earlier in this section, I told you that "a well-thought-out index is almost always a worthy trade-off," and I stand by it. However, what this means is debatable. The right way of thinking about it is that indexes are not something that emanates from the dataset itself but from the access patterns. Ordering by film title sounds like a reasonable proposition in the abstract, but you may not want that feature on your application and, therefore, not need it. Nevertheless, in some cases, an index is almost guaranteed to be useful, or even necessary to have a functioning system: for example, foreign keys (the column that establishes an association between two tables). You don't want to be running full table scans every time you try to access an association.

Picking the right order of a multicolumn index can also be problematic. Typically, the first columns on an index will have a larger number of different items, which is referred to as "cardinality". Still, a multicolumn index can sometimes be used for different access patterns; this is a trade-off in which you need to decide what works best.

Forcing an Index

In most cases, your database query optimizer will pick the best possible index for your particular query. On occasion, though, particularly when the dataset has an abnormal distribution (like an index on a column in which the majority of the elements have the same value), the database will choose an inefficient index. In this case, you can force the database to use an index. Unfortunately, ActiveRecord doesn't allow us to force the index out of the box, but...one of the beauties of Ruby is that it's very easy to monkey-patch things to overwrite existing code at runtime. One common way to do this in Rails is to write a method in a file that will be loaded after the original one. This method needs to have exactly the same namespacing as the original one. To put this into practice, just add the following code to an initializer:

rails-performance-book-completed/config/initializers/ar_force_index_extension.rb

```
class ActiveRecord::Base
  def use_index(index)
    from("#{table_name} USE INDEX(#{index})")
  end

  def force_index(index)
    from("#{table_name} FORCE INDEX(#{index})")
  end
end
```

Now, you have a new method available on all the ActiveRecord queries: force_index. Let's test it out against our new index on language_id:

```
ms(main):001:0> Film.where(language_id: 1).count
  Film Count (0.9ms)  SELECT COUNT(*) FROM `films`
  WHERE `films`.`language_id` = 1
=> 1215
ms(main):002:0> Film.where(language_id: 1).force_index("PRIMARY").count
  Film Count (10.2ms)  SELECT COUNT(*) FROM films
  FORCE INDEX(PRIMARY) WHERE `films`.`language_id` = 1
=> 1215
```

As you can see, forcing the wrong index on the query makes it significantly slower; in this particular case, 11x. This is an important lesson that I want you to take away from this: only force an index if you are *really* sure of what you are doing. 99.9% of the time, the query optimizer will pick the right one.

Benchmarking Our Optimizations

At this point, you should have a good grasp of why indexes make queries faster. Still, we should prove this with some good old benchmarking. This could be hard, as the query optimizer automatically chooses the best index for us, and adding and removing indexes before each test would be way too much work. Fortunately, we can use the force_index method we just demonstrated.

The two tasks are going to be very simple. In the first one, we will get all the titles in the database ordered alphabetically. In the second, we will get all the titles of a particular language, which are also ordered alphabetically. We will run each task in three different ways:

- With no index. While we cannot directly force the database to use no index, we can force a useless index for the query (like PRIMARY). In this case, the optimizer will just discard the index.

- With the index_films_on_language_id_and_title we created before.

- With a new index exclusively on the title column of the films table. You can create it yourself, or copy the one you will find in the completed branch of the application:

rails-performance-book-completed/db/migrate/20250208214759_add_title_index_to_films.rb
```ruby
class AddTitleIndexToFilms < ActiveRecord::Migration[8.0]
  def change
    add_index(:films, :title)
  end
end
```

The reason for having two kinds of indexes is to show that even indexes that are not ideal for a given query, like the "language and title" one for the query that only orders by title, can significantly help performance. Remember this when your table starts having too many indexes.

Now, it's time to run the benchmarks. You can do so by executing rake benchmark_indexes. These are the performance results that I obtained for the first task on my machine:

Query Type	Real Time	User Time	CPU Time	Improvement in User Time
no index	129.53ms	33.03ms	5.94ms	-
language + title index	54.27ms	15.36ms	0.96ms	~ 2x
title index	20.13ms	12.39ms	0.87ms	~ 3x

And this is how it used memory:

Query Type	Allocated Objects	Allocated Memory	Retained Objects	Retained Memory
no index	42,486	3.22 MB	2,424	0.33 MB

Query Type	Allocated Objects	Allocated Memory	Retained Objects	Retained Memory
language + title index	34,555	1.94 MB	2	0.58 KB
title index	34,536	1.93 MB	2	0.58 KB

Note that using any of the two indexes, including title, is better than using no index. Part of this may be explained by the very different amount of retained memory.

Now, for the second task, the one that returns the titles ordered alphabetically for one particular language (language_id = 3).

Query Type	Real Time	User Time	CPU Time	Improvement in User Time
no index	28.59ms	9.16ms	0.79ms	-
language + title index	11.25ms	7.37ms	0.46ms	~ 1.5x
title index	67.73ms	8.1ms	0.72ms	-

And this is how it used memory:

Query Type	Allocated Objects	Allocated Memory	Retained Objects	Retained Memory
no index	1,115	135 KB	50	7.87 KB
language + title index	806	97 KB	2	0.58 KB
title index	827	99 KB	2	0.58 KB

This second task is a little bit more naughty, as we are forcing one index (the title one) that doesn't seem to make a lot of sense. Observe, while forcing the "wrong" index had no effect on User Time, it did have a significant effect on Real Time. Still, the advantage of using an index for memory purposes remains in any case.

Summing Up

In this chapter, we explored some of the most common issues you'll run into when trying to optimize the way a Rails application accesses the database. Taking a more holistic approach, I recommend you get an understanding of what the database is really doing when you use that sweet, sweet ActiveRecord API to fetch and manipulate data. When using the database, less is always better. Less can mean four things:

- Fewer rows need to be examined to get the result. This typically means using indexing, so your database engine doesn't need to scan huge chunks of your table to complete the query.

- Less data being returned from the database to the clients. This means being careful with the amount of data that you are fetching from the database and trying to limit yourself to the data you need.

- Fewer database accesses. This means getting all the data that you need in as few queries as possible.

- Less complexity in the operations needed to obtain the result. This can involve doing things like join decomposition or avoiding subselects. Fortunately, most ORMs, including ActiveRecord, heavily facilitate this.

Those general principles apply in practice to some typical, specific problems:

- n+1s are a common issue with ORMs, in which a list of n associated objects is being retrieved with n queries instead of 1.

- "Wide fetches" are another common unintended consequence of using ORMs. A "wide fetch" is when the application retrieves a huge chunk of unneeded data to the point that performance is affected.

- Adding indexes is the most crucial tool to make your application faster. A well-thought-out index is always worth having.

Finally, we have also learned to analyze queries using EXPLAIN in both MySQL and PostgreSQL. This allows us to understand how a specific query is executed and, therefore, improve on it.

OK, you now understand how important optimizing database access is. But what if I told you there is a way to reduce the cost of that access to basically zero? That's where we're going in the next chapter.

## CHAPTER 3

Understanding All the Faces of Caching

Next to database access, caching is the most important technique for performance optimization. In this chapter, you are going to explore different ways of using caching in our Rails application.

Caching and Denormalizing

The importance of caching for improving system performance is best understood if it is explored hand-in-hand with the topic of denormalization. What are both techniques, how are they related, and how do they help us with performance optimization? This chapter will answer those questions and show you how best to implement caching and denormalization in your own application.

Let's start by defining those two terms.

Caching is the process by which a system stores frequently accessed data in smaller, faster storage so it can be served quicker. The most common algorithm used in caching is the following:

1. Check if the data is in the cache
2. If the data is in the cache (cache hit), just return it.
3. If the data is not in the cache (cache miss), retrieve it from the main data storage (typically the database), write it to the cache, and return it.

The diagram on page 48 illustrates the process.

The success of this caching mechanism depends on the hit ratio: this is the percentage of times that the system finds the data that it is searching for in the cache. For example, a cache with a 0 percent hit ratio is worse than useless. To the normal process, you would be adding one extra access to the cache, plus writing data to that cache, just to never access it again. This is rare but can theoretically happen. Imagine a system in which data is read only once: the algorithm will be only running the "bad path" of reading from

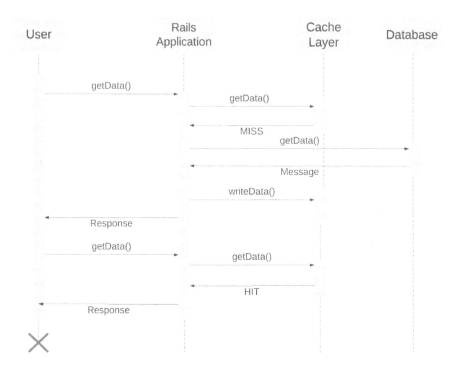

cache *and* having to fetch from the database *and* writing to the cache without ever getting the benefit of the good path. On the other hand, an ideal caching situation is when the data is *always* present in the cache. With the algorithm you just read about, this is not possible, because the first time the data is accessed, you will get a miss; that said, it's possible with other caching algorithms (like write-through caching, which you will read about later in this chapter).

While a hit ratio of 100 percent may be only achievable in certain specific cases, you would be surprised how high of a hit ratio one can get with a pretty simple caching system. The reason for this is that data access patterns don't follow an even distribution. Think, for example, about the X (formerly Twitter) use case: obviously, a tweet of a popular athlete announcing she is changing teams will be accessed more frequently than a tweet posted by a bot account with no followers. This is not something peculiar to X: you will find that the access frequency for data in most databases is far from uniform. One example is that more recent data is accessed more often than data from years ago. By leveraging this asymmetry in data access, caching can make our systems much faster.

For a more theoretical definition, here's Wikipedia's definition of *cache*:[1]

> In computing, a cache is a hardware or software component that stores data so that future requests for that data can be served faster; the data stored in a cache might be the result of an earlier computation or a copy of data stored elsewhere. A cache hit occurs when the requested data can be found in a cache, while a cache miss occurs when it cannot. Cache hits are served by reading data from the cache, which is faster than recomputing a result or reading from a slower data store; thus, the more requests that can be served from the cache, the faster the system performs. [...] To be cost-effective and to enable efficient use of data, caches must be relatively small.

And what about *denormalization*? To understand that, we first need to know what "normalization" is. Database normalization is a process for structuring a relational database to reduce data redundancy. Denormalization is the process of breaking that normalized state by duplicating data for multiple reasons, most commonly to improve performance. Let's check an example. These are three tables, films, rentals, and users. Note the structure of the table isn't the same one as our example; this one is simplified to make the example easier to follow:

id	name
1	Breathless
2	In the mood for love

id	name
1	Cristian Planas
2	Joe Doe

id	film_id	customer_id	rental_date	returnal_date
1	1	1	17/04/24	22/04/24
1	1	2	25/05/24	27/05/24
1	2	1	30/07/24	05/08/24

Now, if you want to check which movie was rented by whom on a specific date, you need to fetch from all three tables. It would be faster to do so if everything was in one table, and that's what denormalization does. The following is a denormalized rentals table.

film_name	customer_name	rental_date	returnal_date
Breathless	Cristian	17/04/24	22/04/24
Breathless	Joe	25/05/24	27/05/24
In the mood for love	Cristian	30/07/24	05/08/24

---

1. https://en.wikipedia.org/wiki/Cache_(computing)

By denormalizing our database, we can access our data faster, but the price to pay is introducing data redundancy. The problem with this is not only that the "rules" are being broken; normalization is the default for a reason. Duplicated data introduces a risk of data inconsistency. Given that the same data is located in two different spaces, every time it changes, we'll need to update it at the same time. For example, let's assume we decide to store the original names of the films instead of the English translation. If the backfill writing the translated name to the database breaks in the middle, we would have the same film with two different names, making it very hard to use.

Like in F1 racing, going faster increases risks. Our challenge is to gain speed (performance) while keeping the risks low.

So now, armed with the basic theoretical knowledge of caching and denormalization, it's time to see how to safely apply those techniques to make our application faster.

Using counter_cache in Rails

Let's start with one of the easiest and cleanest Rails tricks you have at your disposal: counter_cache. This feature has been in Ruby on Rails since Rails 0.9.0 (!) in 2004. The use case is simple in the context of a web application; often, the number of objects associated with a particular model needs to be counted. For example, in the API customers#index endpoint, the application renders the number of rentals each customer has done in the past. Try it out by calling /api/v1/customers from your browser and checking the log. You would get the same by running on the Rails console: Customer.all.map { |c| c.rentals.count }.

```
Started GET "/api/v1/customers" for ::1 at 2025-02-17 15:58:57 -0500
Processing by Api::V1::CustomersController#index as HTML
  Customer Load (0.6ms)  SELECT `customers`.* FROM `customers`
  ↳ app/controllers/api/v1/customers_controller.rb:3:in `map'
  Rental Count (4.5ms)  SELECT COUNT(*) FROM `rentals`
  WHERE `rentals`.`customer_id` = 1
  ↳ app/presenters/api/v1/customer_presenter.rb:12:in `to_json'
  Rental Count (0.2ms)  SELECT COUNT(*) FROM `rentals`
  WHERE `rentals`.`customer_id` = 2
  ↳ app/presenters/api/v1/customer_presenter.rb:12:in `to_json'
  Rental Count (0.2ms)  SELECT COUNT(*) FROM `rentals`
  WHERE `rentals`.`customer_id` = 3
  ↳ app/presenters/api/v1/customer_presenter.rb:12:in `to_json'
  Rental Count (0.2ms)  SELECT COUNT(*) FROM `rentals`
  WHERE `rentals`.`customer_id` = 4
  ↳ app/presenters/api/v1/customer_presenter.rb:12:in `to_json'
  Rental Count (0.2ms)  SELECT COUNT(*) FROM `rentals`
  WHERE `rentals`.`customer_id` = 5
```

```
↳ app/presenters/api/v1/customer_presenter.rb:12:in `to_json'
Rental Count (0.2ms)  SELECT COUNT(*) FROM `rentals`
WHERE `rentals`.`customer_id` = 6
↳ app/presenters/api/v1/customer_presenter.rb:12:in `to_json'
Rental Count (1.0ms)  SELECT COUNT(*) FROM `rentals`
WHERE `rentals`.`customer_id` = 7
↳ app/presenters/api/v1/customer_presenter.rb:12:in `to_json'
Rental Count (0.2ms)  SELECT COUNT(*) FROM `rentals`
WHERE `rentals`.`customer_id` = 8
↳ app/presenters/api/v1/customer_presenter.rb:12:in `to_json'
Rental Count (0.4ms)  SELECT COUNT(*) FROM `rentals`
WHERE `rentals`.`customer_id` = 9
↳ app/presenters/api/v1/customer_presenter.rb:12:in `to_json'
Rental Count (0.4ms)  SELECT COUNT(*) FROM `rentals`
WHERE `rentals`.`customer_id` = 10
↳ app/presenters/api/v1/customer_presenter.rb:12:in `to_json'

[...]
Completed 200 OK in 1551ms
 (Views: 2.1ms | ActiveRecord: 878.5ms
  (1011 queries, 0 cached) | GC: 93.1ms)
```

If you have arrived here after reading the previous chapter, I know what you are thinking: this looks like an n+1! Well, kinda. You can get the number of rentals per customer in one query so you solve the n+1:

```
moviestore(dev):001:0> Rental.group(:customer_id).count
  Rental Count (3.2ms)
  SELECT COUNT(*) AS `count_all`, `rentals`.`customer_id`
  AS `rentals_customer_id` FROM `rentals` GROUP BY `rentals`.`customer_id`
=> {1=>100, 2=>100, 3=>100, 4=>100, 5=>100,
  6=>100, 7=>100, 8=>100, 9=>100, 10=>100}
```

Still, that SELECT COUNT(*) … GROUP BY query can get pretty heavy. Moreover, it's a common use case to present different kinds of counter data in different interfaces: APIs or views. Those COUNTs can eventually get expensive: first, because they are so common; second, because they can get very slow as the table in which they are counting gets big enough.

But try looking at it this way: the number of associated records to an object should be an attribute of the object, something to be persisted and stored, maybe even in the same row of the object in our relational database. Aha, you are thinking, "This is kind of a *denormalization*." And you're right—you would be adding to the data model the materialization of data that is derived from what you already have. And there is no reason for you to add that counter to the data model—other than performance. But that's reason enough.

Let's do it. Adding the logic that counts the number of associated records of a specific class would be simple enough, and you could write that. But Rails, focused on improving the quality of life of us developers, already comes with that logic right out of the box. It's called counter_cache and implementing it is as easy as the following steps:

1. Add a column named rentals_count to the parent model of the association (in our use case, this is Customer). You can generate the migration executing this in the terminal:

```
% rails g migration AddRentalsCountToCustomers rentals_count:integer
```

This command will generate a migration file with this content:

rails-performance-book-completed/db/migrate/20250209164931_add_rentals_count_to_customers.rb
```
class AddRentalsCountToCustomers < ActiveRecord::Migration[8.0]
  def change
    add_column :customers, :rentals_count, :integer
  end
end
```

2. Add the counter_cache option to the belongs_to call in the child model. In this case, it will look something like this:

rails-performance-book-completed/app/models/rental.rb
```
belongs_to :customer, counter_cache: true
```

3. If the association is not new, you will need to backfill the values for our new rentals_count column. If you don't do this, it will only count the new associated objects. Rails provides us with the class method reset_counters. There are multiple ways to run backfills; if you already have an established procedure, follow it. In this case, maybe the most straightforward way is to create a new Rake task:

rails-performance-book-completed/lib/tasks/reset_customer_counters.rake
```
task reset_customer_counters: :environment do
  Customer.all.each do |customer|
    Customer.reset_counters(customer.id, :rentals)
  end
end
```

4. Finally, you need to replace the calls to .count with accesses to our new attribute that already holds that data. Modify the presenter file in app/presenters/api/v1/customer_presenter.rb so instead of having a customer.rentals.count call, the application does customer.rentals_count. You should have something like this:

rails-performance-book-completed/app/presenters/api/v1/customer_presenter.rb
```
class Api::V1::CustomerPresenter
  attr_reader :resource

  def initialize(customer)
    @resource = customer
  end
```

```
  def to_json
    {
      id: resource.id,
      name: resource.name,
      rental_counter: resource.rentals_count
    }
  end
end
```

And you are done! Now, feel free to try your changes and call api/v1/customers again using your browser. The difference is dramatic:

```
Started GET "/api/v1/customers" for ::1 at 2025-02-17 11:41:55 +0100
Processing by Api::V1::CustomersController#index as HTML
  Customer Load (2.6ms)  SELECT `customers`.* FROM `customers`
  ↳ app/controllers/api/v1/customers_controller.rb:3:in 'Enumerable#map'
Completed 200 OK in 27ms
  (Views: 1.7ms | ActiveRecord: 2.6ms (1 query, 0 cached) | GC: 13.4ms)
```

Check the last line of the log. It's not only faster, but it uses significantly less memory, too. Great success!

Counter-caching seems like an ideal feature to use. It comes out of the box with Rails and transforms a theoretically expensive calculation into an immediate response. Still, when adding new logic to improve performance, you should always consider the trade-offs. Are there any issues with using counter-caching?

Yes. First of all, counter_cache has the same risk as denormalization: this duplicating of the data, making our API read not from the source of truth (that would still be running a SELECT COUNT), but from a cached value. It isn't guaranteed that this cached value won't diverge at some point from the source of truth. In practice, this is rare (as long as only one application is writing to that table), since the counter_cache mechanism implemented by Rails runs the update of the cache in the same transaction as the creation of the record. But there is still no internal database mechanism guaranteeing that the value is right; there are options that do something similar (like materialized views),[2] but this does not. For example, someone could have run a backfill setting all the counter caches to zero.

Another issue you need to consider is that adding a counter cache is not free. You have just improved the performance of the *read*, by imposing the work on the write: that extra instruction to increase the counter cache every time

---

2.   https://www.postgresql.org/docs/current/rules-materializedviews.html

that a new Rental is created has a performance cost. You can see that by creating a new Rental from the Rails Console and checking what happens:

```
irb(main):001:0> Rental.create
  (customer: Customer.first, inventory: Inventory.first,
  rental_date: Time.now.beginning_of_day)
  Customer Load (0.7ms)  SELECT `customers`.* FROM `customers`
    ORDER BY `customers`.`id` ASC LIMIT 1
  Inventory Load (0.1ms)  SELECT `inventories`.* FROM `inventories`
    ORDER BY `inventories`.`id` ASC LIMIT 1
  TRANSACTION (0.2ms)  BEGIN
  Rental Create (4.9ms)  INSERT INTO `rentals`
    (`inventory_id`, `customer_id`, `rental_date`,
    `returnal_date`, `created_at`, `updated_at`)
    VALUES (623701, 1, '2024-12-07 17:00:00', NULL,
    '2024-12-08 08:14:33.304225', '2024-12-08 08:14:33.304225')
  Customer Update All (5.8ms)  UPDATE `customers`
  SET `customers`.`rentals_count` =
    COALESCE(`customers`.`rentals_count`, 0) + 1
    WHERE `customers`.`id` = 1
  TRANSACTION (3.3ms)  COMMIT
=>
```

See that line with the Customer Update All? Those few *ms* are our penalty in the write for optimizing for the read.

Finally, the most pressing issue when dealing with Rails on scale is the sheer number of updates that having a counter-cache can imply makes it prone to locking issues. Locking is when multiple database connections compete for the same data, causing performance issues or even deadlocks.

Imagine the following example: you are building a microblogging social network that needs to perform at a planetary scale (one of the most popular ones in the world was famously written in Rails originally). You decide to implement the followers' count with a counter cache. This will work just fine for the vast majority of users. Now, think about what happens with a very popular user. Every time that someone clicks on the "Follow" button next to his profile, you not only need to create a new record, but you will also need to update the same column on the same record. You can have hundreds or even thousands of Rails instances trying to update the same spot.

There are a few ways around this problem (like updating the counter asynchronously), but all of them require you to stop using the counter_cache feature.

And that's OK. Rails gives you a lot of tools that don't always work. They *do* work very often, and that's the power of Rails, which is the reason why it has become so popular and is still relevant today. However, they do not always serve your needs. This is the moment in which an experienced engineer shows her worth and moves beyond the comforting conventions of Rails to a tailor-made system that fits the needs of the business. So, let's dig deeper.

Setting Up Your Caching

While counter_cache is really useful, the most common technique that comes to mind when talking about caching in Rails is using it directly on the body of the response—typically the view or the body of a JSON API. This is something different from what you have been doing so far. We are not caching database queries anymore; we are caching actual responses. Next, you will explore how to use this kind of caching.

This time, the endpoint that you will work on is /films. In the controller, you will find a quite straightforward logic:

rails-performance-book/app/controllers/films_controller.rb
```ruby
def index
  @films = Film.includes(:language, :stores)
end
```

So far, so good: there is nothing that looks obviously wrong here, and you know that you are avoiding n+1s because the controller action uses includes. What about the view?

rails-performance-book/app/views/films/index.html.erb
```erb
<% @films.each do |film| %>
  <div class="film">
    <h2><%= film.title %></h2>
    <p>
      <%= "Language: #{film.language.name}" %>
    </p>
    <p>
      <%= "Available at #{film.stores.pluck(:name).join(', ')}" %>
    </p>
  </div>
<% end %>
```

It looks fine, too. The associations being accessed in the view are the same ones that the controller is preloading, so everything is fine in that regard. Accessing the endpoint in /films will show that, in fact, there are no n+1 issues:

```
Started GET "/films" for ::1 at 2024-12-17 11:59:37 -0500
Processing by FilmsController#index as HTML
  Rendering layout layouts/application.html.erb
  Rendering films/index.html.erb within layouts/application

  Film Load (4068.6ms)  SELECT `films`.* FROM `films`
  ↳ app/views/films/index.html.erb:1
```

```
Language Load (12.7ms)  SELECT `languages`.* FROM `languages`
WHERE `languages`.`id` IN (1, 2, 3, 4, 5, 6, 7, 8, 9, 10, 11, 12, 13, 14)
↳ app/views/films/index.html.erb:1

Inventory Load (283.2ms)  SELECT `inventories`.* FROM `inventories`
WHERE `inventories`.`film_id` IN (1, 2, 3, 4, 5, 6, 7, 8, 9, 10, 11, ...)
↳ app/views/films/index.html.erb:1

Store Load (3.7ms)  SELECT `stores`.* FROM `stores`
WHERE `stores`.`id` IN (1, 2, 3, 4, 5, 6, 7, 8, 9, 10)
↳ app/views/films/index.html.erb:1

Rendered films/index.html.erb within layouts/application
  (Duration: 3851.4ms | GC: 607.6ms)
Rendered layout layouts/application.html.erb
  (Duration: 3876.0ms | GC: 607.6ms)
Completed 200 OK in 3889ms
  (Views: 2836.8ms | ActiveRecord: 1041.3ms (4 queries, 0 cached)
    | GC: 607.6ms)
```

The only thing that looks problematic here is the query on the inventories table, which is really slow. This is natural, given that the application is fetching data for thousands of films. We can fix this by reducing the scope of the action so that the application fetches less data. This is typically done with pagination. Beyond that, everything seems fine.

Life is good...but it can be better.

Imagine the following—very reasonable—situation: films in our system only change once a week. Every Thursday at 8 a.m., employees add new films, remove the ones that the company doesn't keep in stores anymore, and update inventories. Again, this happens only once a week when a script is run to update the data. Why is this so relevant?

Well, the thing is that while the data is very rarely updated, our system behaves as if the data could be changed continuously, accessing the database every time that the endpoint is accessed. The result is that while the content of /films is *almost* static, the application is processing it as if it were extremely dynamic. Returning static content is always faster than returning dynamic content because the application won't need to perform any calculations.

So, how do you take advantage of the relative "static-ness" of the data in /films? You cache it. Every time that the endpoint gets hit, the application will check if the response is already present in specialized storage (the cache); if it is, the application will just serve it, making the response way faster.

Caching is a very important feature of web applications, and therefore, Rails is prepared to deal with this, having several useful conventions. Our caching path starts checking the configured cache storage. By default, this configuration depends on the application environment. For our example application, which is using the Rails defaults, this is how it's configured in development in the file config/environments/development.rb:

```
rails-performance-book/config/environments/development.rb
# Enable/disable caching. By default caching is disabled.
# Run rails dev:cache to toggle caching.
if Rails.root.join("tmp/caching-dev.txt").exist?
  config.action_controller.perform_caching = true
  config.action_controller.enable_fragment_cache_logging = true

  config.cache_store = :memory_store
  config.public_file_server.headers = {
    "Cache-Control" => "public, max-age=#{2.days.to_i}"
  }
else
  config.action_controller.perform_caching = false

  config.cache_store = :null_store
end
```

In short, caching is disabled in development by default, and :null_store is the cache store. You won't be able to use any form of caching. But enabling caching is as easy as creating a caching-dev.txt file in the /tmp folder. Let's do that. Run the following in your terminal from the root folder of your Rails application:

```
% touch tmp/caching-dev.txt
```

Alternatively, since Rails 5, you can also execute the following command to toggle the caching on development mode:

```
% rails dev:cache
```

Before moving on to adding the caching to the view, I would like to point to the two other options that are set up in the environment file you just checked. We will comment further on them later, but it's still worth it to give you an idea of what they mean.

The line config.cache_store = :memory_store, specifies that the cached content will be stored in memory. This is something that typically you will want to change, at least on production, and most probably on development, too. Later in this chapter, we will comment on the most common options. Finally, the config.public _file_server.headers option defines the Cache-Control HTTP header that controls caching in both browsers and shared caches, like proxies and CDNs. We will get deeper into this header in the chapter devoted to the full cycle of the request.

Now, let's go to do some caching!

Using Fragment Caching

Historically, Rails has supported different ways of caching. Nowadays, the most popular way of caching that's currently supported by vanilla Rails is fragment caching. Let's use it to make our application a bit better!

Let's go back to our view in app/views/films/index.html.erb. Using fragment caching is as simple as adding a call to the cache[3] method in one line of our file:

```erb
# app/views/films/index.html.erb

<% cache @films do %>
  <% @films.each do |film| %>
    <div class="film">
      <h2><%= film.title %></h2>
      <p>
        <%= "Language: #{film.language.name}" %>
      </p>
      <p>
        <%= "Available at #{film.stores.pluck(:name).join(', ')}" %>
      </p>
    </div>
  <% end %>
<% end %>
```

Accessing /films will execute that call to the cache you just added to the view. Remember that the first time, the cache check will be a miss, and therefore, you won't see any performance improvement. Still, checking the log will show us how the cache method operates.

```
Started GET "/films" for ::1 at 2023-01-08 19:01:02 -0500
Processing by FilmsController#index as HTML
  Rendering layout layouts/application.html.erb
  Rendering films/index.html.erb within layouts/application
   (121.8ms)  SELECT COUNT(*) AS `size`,
    MAX(`films`.`updated_at`) AS timestamp FROM `films`
  ↳ app/views/films/index.html.erb:1
Read fragment views/films/index:9ac9805c2... (140.5ms)
[...]
# Stuff happening here...
[...]
Write fragment views/films/index:9ac9805c2... (0.1ms)
  Rendered films/index.html.erb within layouts/application
    (Duration: 5317.1ms | GC: 668.6ms)
  Rendered layout layouts/application.html.erb
    (Duration: 5393.9ms | GC: 705.8ms)
```

---

3.   https://api.rubyonrails.org/classes/ActionView/Helpers/CacheHelper.html#method-i-cache

```
Completed 200 OK in 5409ms
  (Views: 4391.8ms | ActiveRecord: 1004.5ms (5 queries, 0 cached)
    | GC: 705.8ms)
```

When Rails starts rendering films/index.html.erb the first thing it does is execute this SQL query:

```
SELECT COUNT(*) AS 'size', MAX('films'.'updated_at')
  AS timestamp FROM 'films'
```

This call is necessary to generate the cache version. The cache version is the way for Rails to know that the objects contained in the view have changed, and therefore, the version of the view stored in the cache is invalid. By default, the cache method in Rails will do the following:

- If the parameter passed to cache is a singular object (for example, one film), it will base the cache version only on the updated_at attribute of that object.

- If the parameter passed to cache is a collection, Rails will base the cache version on two things: the max value for updated_at in any of the objects in the collection (so changing one object will invalidate the cache for the whole collection); and the number of objects. You may not immediately see the reason why the second one is necessary. That's normal: most of us who have implemented a caching system from scratch (including yours truly) have encountered the same pitfall. The reason is deleted records. Hard-deleting a record (and, if you use default scopes, also soft-deleting), won't trigger a cache refresh if the cache version is only based on the latest updated_at of the *existing* records.

Changes on those two values, the latest updated_at and the number of records, are not the only ones that can trigger a cache renewal. They are combined with the cache key, which follows this pattern:

> template path + template tree digest + class + (id OR hashed query)

This guarantees that any change on the template will expire the cache. For example, our previous exercise generated the following cache key:

```
views/films/index:9ac9805c2c974b49cd6b0ca190d571a3
  /films/query-04c2bc1ee298cf4ec8a68a79173ae0f6-10395-20241211180338674883
```

That cache key is accessed (Read fragment views/films/index:9ac98...). In this case, the return was a miss. Accordingly, Rails needs to execute the whole view. After that, Rails writes the result of rendering the films#index view in the cache storage (Write fragment views/films/index:9ac9805...) and returns a 200 with the rendered view in the body.

OK, you have just seen what happens when the cache method ends up with a miss. Let's access /films again so you can see what happens when the cache returns a hit:

```
Started GET "/films" for ::1 at 2023-01-08 23:42:27 -0500
Processing by FilmsController#index as HTML
  Rendering layout layouts/application.html.erb
  Rendering films/index.html.erb within layouts/application
   (24.5ms)  SELECT COUNT(*) AS `size`,
    MAX(`films`.`updated_at`) AS timestamp FROM `films`
 ↳ app/views/films/index.html.erb:1
Read fragment views/films/index:9ac9805c2... (34.7ms)
  Rendered films/index.html.erb within layouts/application
    (Duration: 13.8ms | GC: 0.4ms)
  Rendered layout layouts/application.html.erb
    (Duration: 16.5ms | GC: 0.4ms)
Completed 200 OK in 17ms
  (Views: 5.2ms | ActiveRecord: 11.7ms (1 query, 0 cached) | GC: 0.4ms)
```

Astonishingly faster: without the cache, our call took over seven seconds; with it, only 55 milliseconds.

There are a few more quirks on the cache API for you to learn. For example, if you pass an array of ActiveRecord objects instead of one AR object isolated, Rails will use all of them to calculate the cache version. If you set cache like this:

```
<% cache [@films, Store.all] do %>
```

Then, the application will have to check the max updated_at for both the @films collection and the whole stores table.

```
Started GET "/films" for ::1 at 2024-08-05 21:10:15 +0200
Processing by FilmsController#index as HTML
  Rendering layout layouts/application.html.erb
  Rendering films/index.html.erb within layouts/application
   (27.4ms)  SELECT COUNT(*) AS `size`,
    MAX(`films`.`updated_at`) AS timestamp FROM `films`
 ↳ app/views/films/index.html.erb:1
   (0.7ms)  SELECT COUNT(*) AS `size`,
    MAX(`stores`.`updated_at`) AS timestamp FROM `stores`
 ↳ app/views/films/index.html.erb:1
  [...]
```

This can be very useful if your view depends on multiple objects and not only one.

Finally, you can always set up a completely customized cache version by passing a string as a parameter to cache instead of an AR object. In the view, you could replace:

```
<% cache @films do %>
```

with:

```
<% cache "#{@films.max(:updated_at)}-#{@films.count}" do %>
```

and the result would be exactly the same. But remember: the Rails philosophy of "convention over configuration" still applies here. Try to follow the most conventional way possible for your use case.

Before moving on to the next caching topic, one last piece of advice: if you use SQL queries to construct the cache version, it's probably a good idea to make those queries as fast as possible. In our example, it would make sense to set an index on the updated_at column to speed up SELECT MAX(`films`.`updated_at`) query; for the counter (SELECT COUNT(*) AS `size`), you could consider using counter cache.

Using Russian Doll Caching

Fragment caching is very nice, but it has a pretty heavy drawback. Take the view you just improved: as it currently stands, it's enormous, containing a lot of content from thousands of different films. An update on any of the films will expire the cache of the whole fragment, forcing it to reprocess everything. And all that when only a very small piece of the whole response has been modified!

Fortunately, there is a better way. You can break the contents of this huge view into smaller ones that will be cached individually. This is appropriately called Russian doll caching. Like Russian dolls, you can have cached content inside cached content: when the bigger cached content expires, you just move to the smaller pieces of content, which also happen to be cached.

To implement this in our application, you will first need to break our view into partials. A good candidate for being transformed into a partial view is all the content that is rendered into each block in a view. For example, in films#index you have:

rails-performance-book/app/views/films/index.html.erb
```
<% @films.each do |film| %>
  <div class="film">
    <h2><%= film.title %></h2>
    <p>
      <%= "Language: #{film.language.name}" %>
    </p>
    <p>
      <%= "Available at #{film.stores.pluck(:name).join(', ')}" %>
    </p>
  </div>
<% end %>
```

The body of the block can be easily moved to a partial. While using partials is technically not necessary to use Russian doll caching, it can help to clarify the views structure. Create a file app/views/films/_show.html.erb and write the following:

rails-performance-book-completed/app/views/films/_show.html.erb
```erb
<% cache film do %>
  <div class="film">
    <h2><%= film.title %></h2>
    <p>
      <%= "Language: #{film.language.name}" %>
    </p>
    <p>
      <%= "Available at #{film.stores.pluck(:name).join(', ')}" %>
    </p>
  </div>
<% end %>
```

Now, change the original view at app/views/films/index.html.erb so it uses a partial render:

rails-performance-book-completed/app/views/films/index.html.erb
```erb
<% cache @films do %>
  <% @films.each do |film| %>
    <%= render "films/show", film: film %>
  <% end %>
<% end %>
```

Donc! What you just implemented is the most common kind of Russian doll caching, with only two levels. However, as the name suggests, you can have as many levels of caching as you need.

If you restart the Rails app server and call /films in our browser again, you will see in the log that the application now writes the information of each film in an individual cache fragment:

```
[...]
Read fragment views/films/_show:
  a389be7f4983e8861a61ad19c932ccba/films/1-20241211180235360098 (0.1ms)
Write fragment views/films/_show:
  a389be7f4983e8861a61ad19c932ccba/films/1-20241211180235360098 (0.1ms)
  Rendered films/_show.html.erb
    (Duration: 0.1ms | GC: 0.0ms) [cache miss]
[...]
```

Access it again. You will notice that it's really fast. This is because the application gets a hit from the cache of the whole view (our biggest "Russian doll") and therefore, it doesn't need to process anything else.

What would happen if one (and only one) film is updated? Run Film.last.touch on the console and check it out. You will see that the cache for the whole view has expired, and therefore, our application needs to check on each of the smaller caches. All of them will return a hit, except the last one:

```
[...]
Read fragment views/films/_show:
  a389be7f4983e8861a61ad19c932ccba/films/10393-20241211180338660929 (0.0ms)
  Rendered films/_show.html.erb
    (Duration: 0.1ms | GC: 0.0ms) [cache hit]
Read fragment views/films/_show:
  a389be7f4983e8861a61ad19c932ccba/films/10394-20241211180338666855 (0.0ms)
  Rendered films/_show.html.erb
    (Duration: 0.1ms | GC: 0.0ms) [cache hit]
Read fragment views/films/_show:
  a389be7f4983e8861a61ad19c932ccba/films/10395-20230114181101149212 (0.0ms)
Write fragment views/films/_show:
  a389be7f4983e8861a61ad19c932ccba/films/10395-20230114181101149212 (0.0ms)
  Rendered films/_show.html.erb
    (Duration: 0.3ms | GC: 0.0ms) [cache miss]
[...]
```

This style of caching performs better than just caching the whole view on a fragment, but you'll notice the request is still slow. The reason for this is once the "big" cache is expired, the application needs to execute the SQL query fetching all the films, and that is the slowest part of the whole process. Nevertheless, you're still saving time on the rendering side; if the partials were more complex, the improvement would be even more acute.

However, you may ask yourself if there are ways to make this process faster. It does feel like a huge waste to have to reprocess so much when only a small part of the view has changed. The answer is yes. There are ways to make the caching more efficient, but they are a bit out of the default workflow that Rails enables for us. It's time to write a more customized caching mechanism.

Writing Your Own Caching

For our next step, you will improve the performance of the films#index endpoint in the API by implementing your own caching. As always, you can hit the endpoint in api/v1/films to see the current state. Do exactly that and take a look. You should get something like this:

```
Started GET "/api/v1/films" for ::1 at 2023-01-21 10:55:23 -0500
Processing by Api::V1::FilmsController#index as HTML
  Film Load (12.5ms)  SELECT `films`.`id`, `films`.`title`,
    `films`.`updated_at` FROM `films`
  ↳ app/controllers/api/v1/films_controller.rb:7:in `map'
```

```
Completed 200 OK in 159ms
  (Views: 8.0ms | ActiveRecord: 20.2ms (1 query, 0 cached) | GC: 47.6ms)
```

It's not terrible, but it certainly could be better. Let's add caching to the mix. We will follow a Russian doll strategy, and we will start with the smallest element in the response—the individual film presented.

Caching Individual Objects

To complete this task, you will need to modify the logic in the presenter. This is how FilmPresenter (at app/presenters/api/v1/film_presenter.rb) looks currently:

rails-performance-book/app/presenters/api/v1/film_presenter.rb
```
class Api::V1::FilmPresenter
  attr_reader :resource

  def initialize(film)
    @resource = film
  end

  def to_json
    return nil unless resource
    {
      id: resource.id,
      title: resource.title
    }
  end
end
```

The previous class contains some pretty simple logic. The presenter is initialized with an object; this presenter then offers a method to_json containing the schema of the object as a JSON. What you need to implement here is this:

1. If the object is already cached and not expired, return it.
2. If the object is not cached or expired, cache it and then return it.
3. For both previous steps, the application needs a way to determine that the caching has already expired.

This is how it could look:

```
# app/presenters/api/v1/film_presenter.rb

class Api::V1::FilmPresenter
  attr_reader :resource

  def initialize(film)
    @resource = film
  end

  def to_json
    return nil unless resource

    object = Rails.cache.fetch(cache_key)
```

```
    if object && object[:expiration_key] == expiration_key
      return object.tap { |h| h.delete(:expiration_key) }
    end

    as_json.merge(expiration_key: expiration_key).tap do |object|
      Rails.cache.write(cache_key, object)
      object.delete(:expiration_key)
    end
  end

  private

  def cache_key
    "Film-#{resource.id}"
  end

  def as_json
    {
      id: resource.id,
      title: resource.title
    }
  end

  def expiration_key
    resource.updated_at
  end
end
```

Most of the magic in our mechanism happens in the to_json method: it accomplishes the three requirements that were put before. To control expiration, the application adds a new attribute, expiration_key, to the cached object. This attribute is not accessible to our users, as it will be removed when building the response. Beyond to_json, there are methods that clearly encapsulate different concepts in the caching process. as_json is the schema of the JSON object, expiration_key generates the expiration key, and cache_key defines the key under which the application will store the cached object.

You can refactor this in a superclass so that other presenters can use your brand-new caching mechanism. Create a file in app/presenters/api/v1/presenter.rb and extract the appropriate logic. You will also need to modify FilmPresenter. The result for both files should look like the following:

```
# app/presenters/api/v1/film_presenter.rb

class Api::V1::Presenter
  def to_json()
    return nil unless resource

    object = Rails.cache.fetch(cache_key)

    if object && object[:expiration_key] == expiration_key
      return object.tap { |h| h.delete(:expiration_key) }
    end
```

```
      as_json.merge(expiration_key: expiration_key).tap do |object|
        Rails.cache.write(cache_key, object)
        object.delete(:expiring_key)
      end
    end
  end
end
```

rails-performance-book-completed/app/presenters/api/v1/film_presenter.rb
```
class Api::V1::FilmPresenter < Api::V1::Presenter

  private

  def as_json
    {
      id: resource.id,
      title: resource.title
    }
  end
end
```

Neat! With this, writing presenters that use caching is extremely easy. At the bare minimum, they only need to implement one method: as_json—the one that holds the schema. Moreover, you can also overwrite other methods in the subclasses of Api::V1::Presenter, like expiration_key, on a per-need basis.

Caching Collections

You just implemented the caching of the individual records. However, as we saw previously, the most effective caching is the one that holds the whole body of the response. Next, you will write the logic to do exactly that. The place to implement this piece of logic is the controller. You will start with a films#index action that looks like this:

rails-performance-book/app/controllers/api/v1/films_controller.rb
```
def index
  render json: scope.map { |film| Api::V1::FilmPresenter.new(film).to_json }
end
```

In this action, the caching of individual objects has already been implemented. Now, what is missing is something that, following the same pattern, caches the whole collection. As in the previous step, you need to write code that checks if the response is already in the cache and, if that's the case, confirms the value hasn't expired. In that case, the application just returns the cached response; if not, it executes the appropriate logic to generate the response, store it in the cache, and return it. This is a possible implementation:

```
# app/controllers/api/v1/films_controller.rb

class Api::V1::FilmsController < ApplicationController
```

```ruby
  def index
    render json: cached_index_response
  end

  private

  def cached_index_response
    cached_response do
      scope.map { |film| Api::V1::FilmPresenter.new(film).to_json }
    end
  end

  def cached_response
    cache_key = "films/index-cache"
    object = Rails.cache.fetch(cache_key)
    expiration_key = "#{Film.count}-#{Film.maximum(:updated_at)}"

    # If what we find on the cache layer is a Hash
    # and the expiration key in it is the same as the one we calculated
    # remove the expiration key and return it.
    if object&.last&.fetch(:expiration_key) == expiration_key
      object.pop
      return object
    end

    # If the object found on the cache is invalid
    # we execute the block so we calculate a new response,
    # we store on the cache layer with the expiration key mixed in it
    # and then we return it without the expiration key
    # so it can be rendered.
    yield.push(expiration_key: expiration_key).tap do |object|
      Rails.cache.write(cache_key, object)
      object.pop
    end
  end

  [...]
end
```

What does this code do? Well, the whole logic is in the cached_response method. We pass the block that actually calculates the response to cached_response as a parameter. cached_response sets a cache_key and fetches whatever is in our cache layer under that key. If what is under that key is something that "quacks" like a possible response (a Hash with an expiration_key) and the expiration key returned is equal to the new one, then we remove the expiration key from the response and return the value:

```ruby
object.pop
return object
```

If not, we execute the block to calculate the response anew (yield), we mix in it the expiration key (push(expiration_key: expiration_key), we save it to the cache layer (Rails.cache.write(cache_key, object)) and finally, we return it without the expiration key.

Most of this code could be shared with the rest of the controllers, so the cached_response method is available for all actions in our application. You can easily refactor these methods to make this happen:

```ruby
# app/controllers/api/v1/films_controller.rb

class Api::V1::FilmsController < ApplicationController
  [...]

  def index
    expiration_key = "#{Film.count}-#{Film.maximum(:updated_at)}"
    aux = cached_response(expiration_key) do
      scope.map { |film| Api::V1::FilmPresenter.new(film).to_json }
    end
    render json: aux
  end

  def cached_index_response
    expiration_key = "#{Film.count}-#{Film.maximum(:updated_at)}"
    aux = cached_response(expiration_key) do
      scope.map { |film| Api::V1::FilmPresenter.new(film).to_json }
    end
  end

  # Remove the cached_response method

  [...]
end
```

```ruby
# app/controllers/application_controller.rb

class ApplicationController < ActionController::Base
  private

  def cached_response(expiration_key)
    cache_key = request.path
    object = Rails.cache.fetch(cache_key)

    if object&.last&.fetch(:expiration_key) == expiration_key
      object.pop
      return object
    end

    object = yield
    object.push(expiration_key: expiration_key).tap do |object|
      Rails.cache.write(cache_key, object)
      object.pop
    end
  end
end
```

The code is the same as before, but cached_response has been moved to ApplicationController so that it's available for all actions. Also, expiration_key has become a parameter passed by each action, as each action will be storing the cached response in a different space.

And that's it. This was just an example; there are many ways to do it. But, I'd like to highlight a crucial part of the implementation: the definition of the cache_key variable. In the example, it's implemented so it's exactly the same as request.path: in this specific case, it will be /api/v1/films. This means that all hits on that endpoint will return exactly the same. In this use case, this makes total sense. But, it would have been a big mistake if you had implemented the endpoint in a slightly different way. For example, what if the application would support multiple locales, and the locale wasn't set in the path (for example, it could be stored in a cookie)? In this case, the application would cache the response with the locale of the first user that had called that endpoint; the locale of all the following users would simply be ignored. The point here is that the cache key needs to include all the elements that are relevant to the generation of the response.

Another peculiarity of this solution is that each and every film in JSON form is stored twice: one in the "big" cache and another in its individual cache. This may be relevant to you if you have issues with memory space and want to reduce its usage.

Including the Expiration on the Cache Key

One of the drawbacks of the caching mechanism you just implemented is the complexity, particularly the complexity around cache invalidation. One alternative implementation that takes care of this is adding the expiration time to the cache key so it would be impossible for the application to fetch expired data. This method is recommended by DHH (David Heinemeier Hansson, the creator of Ruby on Rails) in his blog.[4] Introducing this in the application will be as simple as modifying the cached_response method:

rails-performance-book-completed/app/controllers/application_controller.rb
```
class ApplicationController < ActionController::Base

  private

  def cached_response(expiration_key)
    cache_key = request.path + "###-expiration_key"
    object = Rails.cache.fetch(cache_key)

    return object if object
```

---

4.   https://signalvnoise.com/posts/3113-how-key-based-cache-expiration-works

```
    object = yield
    object.tap do |object|
      Rails.cache.write(cache_key, object)
    end
  end
end
```

Unfortunately, this implementation will eventually generate a lot of garbage, as the expired objects stay in the cache storage instead of being overwritten. If you want to use this method, your cache storage needs to have a way for content to auto-expire. There are a few options. For example, when Memcached runs out of memory, it removes the least recently used items first. Other storages have the feature of giving an expiration time to cached content. Once that time is reached, the content will automatically be thrown out, giving all our content an expiration time that fits our needs (for example, Time.now + 1.day) would solve the problem.

Using Write-Through Caching

One of the most important mottos of this book, one that you will read again and again on these pages, is that performance improvements are often a matter of trade-offs. The most common trade-off that performance engineers make on web applications is writing time vs. reading time; in other words, make writing slower so reading is faster. This *typically* makes sense in most web applications, because reading is way more common than writing.

The image on page 71 summarizes write-through caching.

You can implement write-through caching in our application easily. In this case, the ActiveModel callbacks will be extremely useful, and you can make use of after_save in particular. Go and modify the Film model so that every time a film is modified, the application updates the cache at the same time:

rails-performance-book-completed/app/models/film.rb
```
class Film < ApplicationRecord
  after_save :write_cache

  def write_cache
    # Updates the cache
    Api::V1::FilmPresenter.new(self).to_json
  end
end
```

The call to Api::V1::FilmPresenter.new(film).to_json works because, as you remember, the to_json method renews the cache if it's expired.

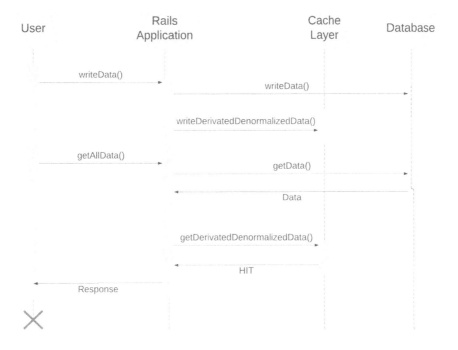

This change has renewed the "smaller doll" in our Russian doll caching. Now, change the code so the application also updates the cache for the whole /api/v1/films response. You can do that by modifying the ActiveModel callback you just created.

```
class Film < ApplicationRecord
  [...]

  def write_cache
    Rails.cache.write("/api/v1/films",
      Film.all.map do |film|
        Api::V1::FilmPresenter.new(film).to_json }.append(
          expiration_key: "#{Film.count}-#{updated_at}"
        )
      end
    )
    true
  end
end
```

I do not recommend implementing the previous block, but it'll be helpful to continue analyzing caching techniques. The previous code replaces the individual update of the cache of one particular for a full refresh of the cache of the endpoint. With this, any access to api/v1/films will *always* result in a cache hit, with obvious performance advantages. The next and final step would be to remove the check of the expiration key—it is not needed anymore. With write-through caching, reading can be an O(1) operation.

Still, write-through caching, as implemented here, has some significant drawbacks. Let's look at them.

First of all, updating a record has become significantly more expensive computationally, and this means it's slower. One way to improve this is to make the call to write_cache asynchronous. Nevertheless, taking this step implies a new set of trade-offs that we will explore together later in the book.

The fact that write-through caching slows down the write is an important issue, but in my opinion, the main drawback of this technique is its impact on the complexity of the application. As a matter of fact, you just *significantly* increased the complexity of the application. The Film model is now entangled with our implementation of the response for a particular endpoint (api/v1/films). Of course, there are ways to make this cleaner: the example you just coded is basically a proof of concept to show the power of write-through caching. All this can be refactored quite deeply. Even from a design perspective, one can separate the updating of the database from the writing of the cache by—again—making it asynchronous. Nevertheless, complexity has increased, and this will just get worse as our application gets more endpoints.

Still, there is more to caching and to write-through caching in particular than a sheer storing of an API response. Next, you will explore a different way of using it: fan-out writing.

Implementing Fan-Out Writing

Yes, our application may sound outdated, being a video store management system, but don't think we are stuck in the 90s. We have implemented a social network on top of it! Our customers can follow each other, X-style. But wait, it gets even cooler than that: customers have a public timeline that shows the latest films rented by the people they follow! You can see it calling api/v1/customers/#{id}/timeline.

Unfortunately, the queries that our application needs to run to fetch the timeline aren't pretty. Let's call the endpoint and check the logs. We'll take a look at Matz's timeline: appropriately for the creator of Ruby, he is the customer with id 1. Hit api/v1/customers/1/timeline, and you will see this database query:

```
Rental Load (43.6ms)  SELECT `rentals`.* FROM `rentals`
  WHERE `rentals`.`customer_id` IN (2, 3, 4, 5, 6, 7, 8,
    9, 10, 2, 3, 4, 5, 6, 7, 8, 9, 10, 11, 12, 13, 14, 15,
    16, 17, 18, 19, 20, 21, 22, 23, 24, 25, 26, 27, 28, 29, 30,
    31, 32, 33, 34, 35, 36, 37, 38, 39, 40, 41, 42, 43, 44, 45,
    46, 47, 48, 49, 50, 51, 52, 53, 54, 55, 56, 57, 58, 59, 60,
    ...)
    ORDER BY `rentals`.`created_at` DESC LIMIT 10
```

The thing is Matz is nice, so he is following thousands of users in our application! This makes for a pretty complex query. To build the timeline, the application needs to order the rentals by created_at, but the issue here is that the customer_id value is arbitrary. Our database will need to pick all the rentals of the customers that Matz is following and then order them. Even if the number of rentals finally fetched is limited, the database still needs to operate with thousands of rentals to select the latest ones. One quick look at the controller action will show the ActiveRecord query seems written well enough:

rails-performance-book/app/controllers/api/v1/customers_controller.rb
```
class Api::V1::CustomersController < ApplicationController

  def timeline
    customer = Customer.find(params[:customer_id])
    rentals = Rental.where
      (customer_id: customer.followings.pluck(:followed_id))
      .order(created_at: :desc).limit(10)
      .includes(inventory: :film)

    render json: rentals.map do |rental|
      Api::V1::RentalPresenter.new(rental).to_json
    end
  end
end
```

Not much to optimize here. There is a way to eliminate the Customer.find call (can you implement it?), but that's small potatoes compared to the crucial method here: the Rental.where. In summary, there's not much you can do here to make this faster by refining the way the application accesses the database.

The suggested solution here isn't changing how the query runs but rather using write-through caching instead. However, in this particular caching the full response would be ill-advised. Imagine what would happen if one of the customers was very popular, being followed by millions of other customers. The application would cache exactly the same JSON Rental objects millions of times. Such a waste! The alternative is for each customer to store the ids of the rentals of the customers she is following. It'd be a bit like having a mailbox: every time a new Rental object is created, the application would store the id of this new rental in the "mailbox" of all the customers following the creator of that rental. Implementing this is very straightforward:

rails-performance-book-completed/app/models/rental.rb

```ruby
class Rental < ApplicationRecord
  after_create :cache_for_followers

  private

  def cache_for_followers
    customer.followers.each do |follower|
      timeline = Rails.cache.read(follower.timeline_cache_key) || []

      Rails.cache.write(
        follower.timeline_cache_key, timeline.unshift(id)[0..9]
      )
    end
  end
end
```

rails-performance-book-completed/app/models/customer.rb

```ruby
class Customer < ApplicationRecord
  def timeline_cache_key
    @timeline_cache_key ||= "rental-timeline-#{id}"
  end
end
```

This implementation seems sane, but it's not thread-safe. If two Rails processes concurrently try to add two different rentals to a user's timeline, chances are one of them would be accidentally wiped out. To fix this, you'll need a storage system that would allow you to append values to an array in an atomic way. Fortunately, you have a few options, including Redis, one of the most popular key-value stores in the market. We will comment on this later in this chapter, in the section dedicated to choosing a storage system for caching purposes.

Thanks to caching on the write, now the query needed to fetch the timeline is *extremely* simple. You just need to get the ids of the Rentals that need to be presented from our cached timeline and load them from the database using the primary key, the id. Fast and simple!

rails-performance-book-completed/app/controllers/api/v1/customers_controller.rb

```ruby
class Api::V1::CustomersController < ApplicationController
  def timeline
    customer = Customer.find(params[:customer_id])
    rentals = Rental.where(id: Rails.cache.read(customer.timeline_cache_key))
    render json: rentals.map do |rental|
      Api::V1::RentalPresenter.new(rental).to_json
    end
  end
end
```

This example, though simplified, illustrates how real systems scale. For instance, many years ago I was the CTO of a startup (aka solo engineer) called Playfulbet, my first company. We had to scale so the application worked for hundreds of thousands of users and with very few resources. The application had a timeline, and I used fan-out writing to make it scale. It's also how Twitter[5] worked, at least until 2012 when the company still used Rails in its stack. Nowadays you can see an implementation of this in Mastodon,[6] a microblogging social network implemented as an open-source Rails application.[7] Fan-out writing is a very useful design pattern that can power many complex operations.

Still, fan-out writing has its own drawbacks. The most obvious is yet another increase in the complexity of the application. The most subtle and dangerous issue is that the increased computational cost of the write may be too expensive in certain specific cases. For example, some social networks[8] have what is called the "Justin Bieber problem." Each post by a user with many followers could become a problem for the infrastructure. During the year 2010, Justin Bieber was using three percent of X resources at any given moment, with the rumor being that there were full servers dedicated to his account.[9] A way around this would be to introduce mixed fan-out, so the vast majority of tweets use fan-out writing but keep the ones written by celebrities exempt. The timeline of a user would be constructed by using her timeline "bucket" created by fan-out writing and mixing it with the tweets of the celebrities she follows, which will be fetched directly from the database—this is called fan-out reading. Nevertheless, despite these inconveniences, fan-out writing can considerably speed up applications that operate at large scale.

Using Action Caching and Page Caching

Once upon a time, when Rails was in version number 3, the framework provided other, more powerful caching methods out of the box. Too "powerful" in fact: it was decided that they were too prone to cause bugs, and they were eventually deprecated in version 4, circa 2013. Still, if you understand what they were, you can better see the trade-offs that you face when using caching. These two deprecated techniques were page caching and action caching.

---

5. https://www.infoq.com/presentations/Twitter-Timeline-Scalability/
6. https://joinmastodon.org/
7. https://github.com/mastodon/mastodon
8. https://www.wired.com/2015/11/how-instagram-solved-its-justin-bieber-problem/
9. https://gizmodo.com/justin-bieber-has-dedicated-servers-at-twitter-5632095

In page caching, the content of a response (typically, a rendered view) is stored in a file. The next time that a request to that same endpoint hits the web server, the web server will return the content of that file without even passing the request to the Rails application. In essence, the page becomes a static asset. While this technique is incredibly powerful, it has limited usability, as it makes the write significantly slower. For any resource that is changed often, it is not a good fit.

Action caching is quite similar but with an important difference: the request does hit the Rails stack, running the whole middleware and the controller filters. The only cached part is the execution of the action itself, including the rendering of the view. This is obviously slower, but it allows much more flexibility. One common use case for action caching is endpoints restricted for authenticated users. Authentication in Rails applications is typically implemented using before filters. Using page caching for a resource that requires authentication would be a mistake, as it would open access to anyone hitting that endpoint, including unauthenticated users.

If you think that these techniques could be useful for your application, you are in luck. While page caching and action caching were removed from vanilla Rails, both are still available through two gems: actionpack-page_caching[10] and actionpack-action_caching.[11] Let's use them in your application. Add both of them to your Gemfile and run bundle. The versions I used in this example are 1.2.2 for actionpack-action_caching and 1.2.4 for actionpack-page_caching.

Using this gem, you are going to cache two endpoints, both of them returning static content. The two endpoints are /home and /happynewyear.

rails-performance-book/app/controllers/home_controller.rb
```
class HomeController < ApplicationController
  before_action :check_new_year, only: [:happy_new_year]

  def home
  end

  def happy_new_year
  end

  private

  def check_new_year
    head :forbidden unless true
  end
end
```

---

10. https://github.com/rails/actionpack-page_caching
11. https://github.com/rails/actionpack-action_caching

The previous explanation would imply that home is a perfect candidate for page caching while happy_new_year is ideal for action caching. Thanks to the magic of programming and open source, using these caching strategies is as simple as adding two lines:

```
# app/controllers/home_controller.rb

class HomeController < ApplicationController

  [...]

  caches_page :home
  caches_action :happy_new_year

  [...]

end
```

Let's compare the logs before and after adding the caching. Before, you had both actions rendering all the components of the page, including the layout:

```
Started GET "/home" for ::1 at 2025-02-25 02:54:37 +0100
Processing by HomeController#home as HTML
  Rendering layout layouts/application.html.erb
  Rendering home/home.html.erb within layouts/application
  Rendered home/home.html.erb within layouts/application
    (Duration: 5.3ms | GC: 0.1ms)
  Rendered layout layouts/application.html.erb
    (Duration: 27.4ms | GC: 0.1ms)
Completed 200 OK in 37ms
  (Views: 29.8ms | ActiveRecord: 0.0ms (0 queries, 0 cached) | GC: 0.2ms)

Started GET "/happynewyear" for ::1 at 2025-02-25 02:54:41 +0100
Processing by HomeController#happy_new_year as HTML
  Rendering layout layouts/application.html.erb
  Rendering home/happy_new_year.html.erb within layouts/application
  Rendered home/happy_new_year.html.erb within layouts/application
    (Duration: 2.6ms | GC: 0.0ms)
  Rendered layout layouts/application.html.erb
    (Duration: 6.1ms | GC: 0.0ms)
Completed 200 OK in 8ms
  (Views: 6.6ms | ActiveRecord: 0.0ms (0 queries, 0 cached) | GC: 0.0ms)
```

And after:

```
Started GET "/happynewyear" for ::1 at 2023-02-25 02:56:57 +0100
Processing by HomeController#happy_new_year as HTML
Read fragment views/localhost:3000/happynewyear (0.2ms)
Completed 200 OK in 1ms
  (ActiveRecord: 0.0ms (0 queries, 0 cached) | GC: 0.0ms)
```

That's not an error: I haven't forgotten about the /home endpoint. What happened is that the request didn't even get to the Rails application, so there was nothing to log. We will discuss further how page caching does this in a moment.

But first, let's try to understand the action caching implementation.

What happened when you called /happynewyear, the endpoint in which you enabled action caching? If you check the log, you will notice that the multiple Rendering ... calls that appeared originally are there no more. In exchange, you got a Read fragment line. This is because actionpack-action_caching is reading the response from the cache and returning it without executing the view. The mechanism is, up to a certain point, similar to what you implemented previously in this chapter.

The following[12] is the most important method of the implementation. This is not the whole logic, but you will be able to understand the functionality of all the methods thanks to their pretty explicit names.

```ruby
module ActionController
  module Caching
    module Actions
      class ActionCacheFilter
        def around(controller)
          cache_layout = expand_option(controller, @cache_layout)
          path_options = expand_option(controller, @cache_path)
          cache_path = ActionCachePath.new(controller, path_options || {})

          body = controller
            .read_fragment(cache_path.path, @store_options)

          unless body
            controller.action_has_layout = false unless cache_layout
            yield
            controller.action_has_layout = true
            body = controller._save_fragment(cache_path.path, @store_options)
          end

          body = render_to_string(controller, body) unless cache_layout

          controller.response_body = body
          controller.content_type = Mime[cache_path.extension || :html]
        end
      end
    end
  end
end
```

The _save_fragment and read_fragment methods write and read from the endpoint path as a key. Fortunately, you can modify this default by passing a cache_path

---

12. https://github.com/rails/actionpack-action_caching/blob/v1.2.2/lib/action_controller/caching/actions.rb#L154

option to the caches_action method. For example, if the view returned by happy_new_year depended on the number of films the system holds on the database, you would need to modify the controller with this:

rails-performance-book-completed/app/controllers/home_controller.rb
```
class HomeController < ApplicationController
  caches_page :home
  caches_action :happy_new_year,
    cache_path: -> { request.path + "#film_count#{Film.count}" }
end
```

This option is very powerful: as you learned in this chapter when we talked about key-based cache expiration, you can control the expiration of the case just by modifying the elements that form the key name. Another useful option for time-sensitive caching is expires_in.

Getting Deep into Page Caching

Now, let's check what happened with the endpoint where you implemented page caching. As you saw, the request was not even getting to the Rails application, as it's being served directly by the web server. And what is being served exactly? Well, check what you have in the /public folder in your Rails application. Surprise, surprise, now there is a home.html file. This is what is being returned by the web server. Remember that the folder in which cached pages are stored is configurable with the page_cache_directory command.

Page caching is extremely fast, but because everything happens outside of the Rails application, expiring it can be a bit more challenging. Still, there are ways to do it. The simplest and most obvious is to manually remove the file in which the cached response is saved. Of course, this is not very convenient. Fortunately, the gem comes with a method to expire the cache from the Rails application in ActionController::Caching::Pages::PageCache.expire_page. Typically, you will want to call it when an action that would modify the cached content has been performed. For example, you could expire the cached page for home every time a new Film is created, like this:

rails-performance-book-completed/app/controllers/films_controller.rb
```
class FilmsController < ApplicationController

  def create
    @film = Film.create params[:film]
    expire_page controller: 'home', action: "home"
    redirect_to film_path(@film)
  end
end
```

The expire_page method is now included in ApplicationController, so you can call it from anywhere in the code. You can use observers or even Active Record callbacks to clear that cache.

We've gotten pretty detailed here, but now let's look at caching from a broader view.

Adding a Cache Layer to ActiveRecord

So far we have focused on caching elements in a request response, or even the full response. However, this is not the only way to use caching. I recommend you design a custom-made solution for the unique architecture and use case of your application. But one common usage of caching is to apply it directly on database accesses, which, in the case of the Rails framework, means adding a caching layer on top of ActiveRecord. The Ruby ecosystem has us covered, and you have a couple of libraries that are ready and available for your benefit. This said, identity_cache,[13] built by Shopify, is currently more popular, so this will be the one you are going to use in this section.

Using IdentityCache

What exactly is IdentityCache? This is how its documentation defines the project:

> Opt in read through ActiveRecord caching used in production and extracted from Shopify. IdentityCache lets you specify how you want to cache your model objects, at the model level, and adds a number of convenience methods for accessing those objects through the cache. Memcached is used as the back-end cache store, and the database is only hit when a copy of the object cannot be found in Memcached.

In essence, IdentityCache is a caching mechanism that allows you to cache whole model objects, using Memcached as a back end. Sounds really useful! (Note it also can work with other back-end stores, like Redis.) How can you get hold of some of those performance improvements? Well, adding identity_cache to our application is simple enough:

- Add it to our Gemfile (gem 'identity_cache). You are going to use IdentityCache with a Memcached back end, so we will also add Dalli to the Gemfile, Memcached's client (gem 'dalli'). You will also need to have Memcached running (memcached restart). Finally, adding Cityhash (gem 'cityhash') will make IdentityCache faster if you are using C-Ruby.

- Define identity_cache_store in your configuration, like this:

---

13. https://github.com/Shopify/identity_cache

rails-performance-book-completed/config/environments/development.rb

```
config.identity_cache_store = :mem_cache_store, {
  expires_in: 6.hours.to_i,
  failover: false,
}
```

- Finally, add an initializer with the following code. You can create a file at (config/initializers/identity_cache.rb) and paste it:

rails-performance-book-completed/config/initializers/identity_cache.rb

```
IdentityCache.cache_backend = ActiveSupport::Cache.lookup_store(
  *Rails.configuration.identity_cache_store
)
```

Once IdentityCache has been added to your application, using it is very simple. You just need to add a module in your model (include IdentityCache). By default, this will cache accesses by the primary index (typically, the id column). Where would it make sense to use it in your application? You typically want models that don't have an extremely high number of instances and that are heavily accessed. Let's cache, for example, the Store model:

rails-performance-book-completed/app/models/store.rb

```
class Store < ApplicationRecord
  include IdentityCache
```

This module has added one new method to the Store class, the method fetch. In essence, fetch implements the cache lookup: it checks if the searched data is already on Memcached, and if so (cache hit), fetches the data and returns the model. If it isn't (cache miss), it retrieves the data from the database, writes it to the cache, and returns the model. Test it on the Rails Console, and you'll get something like this:

```
irb(main):001:0> Store.fetch(1)
Dalli::Server#connect 127.0.0.1:11211
  Store Load (1.0ms)  SELECT `stores`.* FROM `stores`
    WHERE `stores`.`id` = 1 LIMIT 1
[IdentityCache] cache miss for IDC:8:blob:Store:5433489649916790044:1
=>
#<Store:0x00000001065c1320
 id: 1,
 created_at: Fri, 10 Feb 2023 05:07:35.560451000 UTC +00:00,
 updated_at: Fri, 10 Feb 2023 05:07:35.560451000 UTC +00:00,
 name: "Store 1">
irb(main):002:0> Store.fetch(1)
[IdentityCache] (cache_backend)
  cache hit for IDC:8:blob:Store:5433489649916790044:1
```

```
=>
#<Store:0x00000001068a6590
 id: 1,
 created_at: Fri, 10 Feb 2023 05:07:35.560451000 UTC +00:00,
 updated_at: Fri, 10 Feb 2023 05:07:35.560451000 UTC +00:00,
 name: "Store 1">
```

This is not the only feature of IdentityCache. While by default it only caches the access by the primary key, you can add other keys with the method cache_index; with it, the method fetch_by_#{attribute} becomes available:

rails-performance-book-completed/app/models/store.rb
```
class Store < ApplicationRecord
  include IdentityCache
  cache_index :name

> Store.fetch_by_name("Store 1")
```

Another feature of IdentityCache is caching the access to the objects via associations. This is typically the most common way of accessing, so it's quite important. IdentityCache provides you with cache_has_many and cache_has_one to cache has_many and has_one associations, respectively. As in the case of cache_index, the method fetch_#{association_name} becomes available:

rails-performance-book-completed/app/models/language.rb
```
class Language < ApplicationRecord
  include IdentityCache

  has_many :films
  cache_has_many :films
end

> Language.first.fetch_films
```

Useful, isn't it? These were only the basic features of IdentityCache. If you think it could be useful to add it to your application, I encourage you to read its documentation.[14] It's well-written, straightforward, and has plenty of examples.

What is Monkey-Patching?

You may have never heard of the concept of "monkey-patching," particularly if you're new to Ruby or other dynamic languages. The idea is simple: modifying the behavior of an established piece of logic by overwriting it at runtime—specifically, by reopening the class and adding or redefining methods. This is different from overwriting an inherited method in a subclass because the original method is lost. Moreover, all calls to the "old" method will be using the new "monkey-patched" logic. A true double-edged sword!

---

14. https://github.com/Shopify/identity_cache

The origins of the (certainly memorable) "monkey-patching" term are unclear. It may have derived from "guerrilla-patching," and transformed later into "gorilla-patching" to eventually become "monkey-patching." Another theory is that the term came from the idea of "monkeying" with the code (as in messing with it).

Choosing a Storage System for Your Cache

All the techniques you have explored so far depend on one thing: the storage in which the cached contents are saved. The impact that any caching will have on your application depends on your storage, especially at scale. Moreover, choosing the right storage for your specific use case will prove very useful as your applications grow. So, what options do you have?

Rails provides you with a few options out of the box. Changing them is as easy as changing the value of config.cache_store in your environment file. For example, typically, the default on development is memory. This is declared like this on your config environment file, for example, config/environments/development.rb:

```
config.cache_store = :memory_store
```

So, what are the options you can use right off the bat, and what are the consequences of using them? Let's see:

1. The first option is the default one on development: using memory to store cached data. Each Rails process will have its own memory storage, so you may find data will be duplicated across multiple processes, therefore reducing the hit rate. By default, each process will have 32 MB of memory storage, but you can change this with the size option, for example, by declaring it like this: config.cache_store = :memory_store, { size: 128.megabytes }.

2. Another option is to use the file system as cache storage. You can configure it with config.cache_store = :file_store. This has the advantage that multiple processes can share the same storage as long as they are located in the same host. Unfortunately, using :file_store as cache storage is a poor decision from a performance perspective, and if you are reading this book, you probably care about performance, don't you?

3. A third, very use-specific option, is the null store (:null_store). In this storage, the scope is even narrower than in :memory_store. Each web request has "its own" cache, with the stored values being wiped when the request is completed. It makes sense in some cases, particularly when testing.

Those three options are fine, but in scalable systems, you will be expected to use a storage built to serve caching purposes. In Rails 8, the default cache storage on production is SolidCache. Until the release of SolidCache (:solid_cache), the two most commonly used cache storages on production were Memcached (:mem_cache_store) and Redis (:redis_cache_store). Let's analyze their differences.

SolidCache, Memcached, Redis

The idea behind SolidCache's design is quite original and very different from those of both Memcached and Redis. From its README:[15]

> SolidCache is a database-backed Active Support cache store that lets you keep a much larger cache than is typically possible with traditional memory-only Redis or Memcached stores. This is thanks to the speed of modern SSD drives, which makes the access-time penalty of using disk vs. RAM insignificant for most caching purposes. Simply put, you're now usually better off keeping a huge cache on disk rather than a small cache in memory.

In essence, SolidCache's proposal is to read from disk instead of memory, which allows for the maintenance of a significantly larger cache. SolidCache documentation suggests using it with a relational database (SQLite by default, but the documentation also covers MySQL and PostgreSQL) as the store. If you want to set it up, I recommend creating a different database from your primary one (as the creators of SolidCache do in Basecamp and HEY.com),[16] or at least set up a different connection pool so your "source of truth" data layer is not competing for resources with your caching layer. SolidCache has some important advantages, some of which stem from being the default Rails cache store and being deeply integrated into Rails.

Still, there is an important trade-off: speed. Benchmarks show that Solid-Cache, both backed by SQLite and Postgres, is significantly slower than both Redis and Memcached.[17] I think the trade-off was nicely summarized by Donal McBreen, senior programmer at 37Signals (the creator of SolidCache):[18]

> On Basecamp, compared to our old Redis cache, reads are now about 40 percent slower. But the cache is 6 times larger and running on storage that's 80 percent cheaper.

What about the "classic" options, Memcached and Redis? Well, they have a lot in common:

---

15. https://github.com/rails/solid_cache
16. https://github.com/rails/solid_cache/issues/130
17. https://www.bigbinary.com/blog/caching-in-rails-with-redis-vs-alternatives
18. https://dev.37signals.com/solid-cache/

- They are both in-memory data storages, which makes them fast.

- Both Memcached and Redis follow a key-value data model, which is perfect for the typically simpler requirements of cached data access.

- They are also horizontally scalable, as it's easy to add more nodes to the existing setup. This helps them provide high availability and scalability.

Still, there are some key differences:

- Redis allows for data to be persisted to disk; Memcached does not. This is a key difference if you plan to use caching extensively.

- The data structures that these storages implement are very different. Memcached has no datatypes, supporting only simple key-value pairs of strings; meanwhile, Redis supports a wider range of data structures and types like lists, sets, hashes, and sorted sets (ZSET). In my experience, those extra structures can end up becoming very useful.

- Redis supports atomic operations, while Memcached offers no such guarantee.

- Memcached only has one supported eviction policy, LRU (least recently used), while Redis supports six different ones.

- Performance-wise, Memcached can be a bit faster.

In general, Memcached can make more sense for simpler use cases, when you are just caching fragments of your responses (be it HTML or JSON). However, for more complex situations, Redis's versatility makes it the superior choice in many scenarios. Using both is a reasonable option in some cases.

On the client side, Rails will use Dalli[19] as the default client for Memcached. For Redis, Rails documentation suggests two alternatives in the form of two gems: redis[20] and hiredis.[21] The difference is that the second one may be faster, particularly when parsing multi-bulk replies. If you want to know more about all the options you have to configure your Redis client, check their documentation. The following is just an example taken from the Rails guide:

```
cache_servers = %w(redis://cache-01:6379/0 redis://cache-02:6379/0)
config.cache_store = :redis_cache_store, { url: cache_servers,

  connect_timeout:    30,  # Defaults to 20 seconds
  read_timeout:       0.2, # Defaults to 1 second
```

---

19. https://github.com/petergoldstein/dalli
20. https://github.com/redis/redis-rb
21. https://github.com/redis/hiredis-rb

```
  write_timeout:       0.2, # Defaults to 1 second
  reconnect_attempts: 1,    # Defaults to 0

  error_handler: -> (method:, returning:, exception:) {
    # Report errors to Sentry as warnings
    Raven.capture_exception exception, level: 'warning',
      tags: { method: method, returning: returning }
  }
}
```

So, what to make of all this? From my perspective, it's important for a caching layer to have the capacity to be written to disk. This is why my preferred options would be both SolidCache and Redis. In between those two, I think that Redis shines in use cases that are heavier on the read than on the write, while SolidCache may be a better option with more balanced workloads and when simplicity is important.

Before concluding this chapter, let's go back to the idea of data denormalization and its role in systems that require high scalability.

Using Denormalization

Denormalization is so useful it would be hard to get along without it. Still, duplicating data for performance can be seen as a bit of a hack, particularly by less experienced engineers. And they're not exactly wrong. Denormalizing databases comes with two significant disadvantages: data redundancy and (the risk of) inconsistency.

The key to being successful when applying denormalization is to take the architect's point of view. In a complex system, whether data is duplicated in the same database or in two different ones is moot. Typically, data is already duplicated. To give a very common use case, if you index your data in a search engine (like ElasticSearch), you already have redundant data, and you are at risk of data inconsistency. I am not just stating an obvious technicality. As anyone who has managed the search cluster of a big company can tell you, there are plenty of chances for data to become inconsistent, even in a use case apparently as straightforward as indexing data for search purposes. From this perspective, you can see that duplicating data in the same database or in a different data storage (be it a storage dedicated to caching or a search engine) becomes essentially the same.

We saw an example of denormalization when we talked about counter_cache.

Now, we're going to use denormalization by ourselves, without the support of a Rails convention. Our target this time will be an API endpoint: api/v1 /stores/#{id}. This endpoint returns the most rented film for each store. That calculation is implemented in the method Store.most_rented_film, and it isn't simple, or cheap:

rails-performance-book/app/models/store.rb

```
class Store < ApplicationRecord
  def most_rented_film
    Film.find(Rental.joins(:inventory)
      .where(inventory: {store_id: id})
      .group(:film_id).count.max_by { |k, v| v }.last)
  end
end
```

```
irb(main):001:0> Store.first.most_rented_film
Store Load (0.3ms)  SELECT `stores`.* FROM `stores`
  ORDER BY `stores`.`id` ASC LIMIT 1
Rental Count (28.1ms)  SELECT COUNT(*) AS `count_all`, `film_id` AS `film_id`
  FROM `rentals` INNER JOIN `inventories` `inventory`
  ON `inventory`.`id` = `rentals`.`inventory_id`
  WHERE `inventory`.`store_id` = 1 GROUP BY `film_id`
Film Load (2.9ms)
  SELECT `films`.* FROM `films` WHERE `films`.`id` = 1 LIMIT 1
=>
#<Film:0x0000000109b29fa8
 id: 1,
 title: "Breathless"
 ...
```

Fixing this is simple. Add a new column to the stores table—an integer column with the name most_rented_film_id. You can do so with a migration:

```
% rails g migration AddMostRentedFilmIdToStore most_rented_film_id:integer
```

Then, change the Store model, so most_rented_film becomes an association. You will also need to add a method that calculates the most rented film for a store every time a rental is created.

rails-performance-book-completed/app/models/store.rb

```
class Store < ApplicationRecord
  include IdentityCache
  cache_index :name

  has_many :inventories
  has_many :films, through: :inventories
  belongs_to :most_rented_film, class_name: 'Film'

  def set_most_rented_film!
    update_attribute(:most_rented_film_id, Rental.joins(:inventory)
      .where(inventory: {store_id: id}).group(:film_id)
      .count.max_by { |k, v| v }.last)
  end
end
```

```
class Rental < ApplicationRecord
  after_commit :recalculate_store_rentals

  def recalculate_store_rentals
    store.set_most_rented_film!
  end
end
```

In this case, you materialized derived data. But this is just one application of denormalization. Another common pattern is to copy one attribute of one object into an associated one, particularly if the attribute is heavily used and/or the association is complex to calculate, database-wise. A possible example in our application would be to copy the film title into the rentals table itself. This is an example of a heavily used attribute that is coming from an associated object, as we will rarely render anything associated with the rental that does not include the film title.

But, rather than thinking in terms of specific use cases, you should feel empowered to use denormalization as another tool in your performance engineer toolbox.

Summing Up

We are done! We have covered quite a lot in this chapter. We have examined the effects of caching and denormalizing from a software design perspective, seeing the pros and cons of using these techniques. Also, we have explored many different approaches to caching, including:

- Counter-Cache
- Fragment caching
- Russian doll caching
- Write-through caching
- Action caching and page caching
- Caching ActiveRecord

This chapter and the previous one are crucial to understanding performance from an application perspective, particularly a Rails application. Next, we will focus on the point of contact between your application and the client: the API.

## CHAPTER 4

Designing a Scalable API

In the last two chapters, we learned how to speed up our application by finetuning our database access and by adding caching in both our data access and the responses we return to the client, be it an HTML-based view or a JSON API response. This is great, and it is, in fact, what most people understand by improving the performance of an application.

But in this chapter, we're going to shift our focus. So far, we have been focused on the tactics, the individual actions one executes to succeed. Now, we are moving on to the strategy—the action plan that will bring us where we want to go. Therefore, we will stop finetuning an existing application and start changing its design. We'll begin with the gateway to our applications: the API. No amount of finetuning of queries will save you from a malfunctioning API—one that returns megabytes of data when the client is only searching for a string or one that forces a client to run a huge amount of requests against your application for what should have been returned in only one call.

You'll learn different ways to slice and dice the data exposed by your application interface and how to give your users tools so they can get *exactly* the data they need. So, happier customers, fewer resources used, and a faster application. These are all great things to have in an application that scales.

Let's start by taking inspiration from the ancient Romans.

Paginating Your Endpoints

Big applications hold a lot of data. Managing this can be hard, not only from the perspective of the system that "holds" the data but also from the perspective of the consumer. Our example application demonstrates this well. Hit the endpoint api/v1/films/lean. It returns *all* the customers in our database. You'll get something like the following in the log:

```
Started GET "/api/v1/films/lean" for ::1 at 2025-02-12 22:43:16 +0100
Processing by Api::V1::FilmsController#lean as HTML
  Film Pluck (18.7ms)  SELECT `films`.`id`, `films`.`title` FROM `films`
  ↳ app/controllers/api/v1/films_controller.rb:31:in
  'Api::V1::FilmsController#json_response'
Completed 200 OK in 60ms
  (Views: 0.1ms | ActiveRecord: 36.4ms (1 query, 0 cached) | GC: 2.4ms)
```

The issue here is not so much the performance of the endpoint, but its *content*. If you check the end of the response, you will see the number of records the endpoint is returning; a lot of them—over 10,000. The response is relatively heavy, clocking a few hundred kilobytes (376 KB in the version I am running as I write this). In a real-world example, an endpoint returning *all* the data can easily return gigabytes or even terabytes of data. There are legit use cases in which you may want to get a final result like this, for example, when exporting data from the application, but the process will be managed in a very different way: JSON endpoints are not designed with this intention in mind. We need to limit the number of records that one hit to our API endpoints will retrieve.

The problem of having to limit the amount of content to improve maneuverability is hardly exclusive to computer science. The way in which our endpoint returns all the content in one response is similar to how text was recorded in ancient times: with scrolls. Scrolls were bulky and hard to transport, and accessing specific parts of their content could be quite complicated. Finding a specific part of the text implied a whole lot of unrolling. Fortunately, around the second or third century of our era, the Romans invented the codex, a direct ancestor of the modern book, with its innovation of individual pages that were stacked and bound together.

Let's follow this ancient wisdom and introduce pages to our endpoint. For this, we can follow not only the example of the Romans but also of another group full of wise people: the Ruby community. In the context of an API, pagination is dividing a dataset into smaller, more manageable chunks to improve both the user experience and the performance of the endpoint. There are multiple gems that implement pagination on top of Active Record, and we'll use one of those. Historically, the two most popular libraries for this purpose have been Kaminari,[1] created by Akira Matsuda in 2011, and will_paginate,[2] created in 2008. For many years, I preferred will_paginate, but it was put on maintenance mode in 2021, so no new features will be developed for it anymore. So, let's use Kaminari for our application.

---

1.   https://github.com/kaminari/kaminari.
2.   https://github.com/mislav/will_paginate.

Setting Up Pagination with Kaminari

As with all the gems that we include in our application, we need to add Kaminari to our Gemfile (gem 'kaminari') and then run bundle install. To configure it further, run the following on your terminal:

```
% rails g kaminari:config
```

This will create a file in config/initializers/kaminari_config.rb with the following content:

```
rails-performance-book-completed/config/initializers/kaminari_config.rb
# frozen_string_literal: true

Kaminari.configure do |config|
  # config.default_per_page = 25
  # config.max_per_page = nil
  # config.window = 4
  # config.outer_window = 0
  # config.left = 0
  # config.right = 0
  # config.page_method_name = :page
  # config.param_name = :page
  # config.max_pages = nil
  # config.params_on_first_page = false
end
```

The functionality of some of these options is as described. For example, default_per_page defines the default amount of objects that each page will return by default. Other options are more arcane, and some only make sense if you want to use the HTML-generating features of Kaminari, which we will not use in this book. In any case, if you want to know more, I recommend you to read Kaminari's documentation on its GitHub page.[3]

Our target, though, is to implement pagination in the api/v1/films endpoint. Kaminari monkey-patches ActiveRecord relations, adding two new methods to facilitate pagination:

- The method page (the name of this method is an option that can be changed) sets the page that will be returned by the query.[4]

- The method per sets the number of objects that will be returned on that aforementioned page.[5]

---

3. https://github.com/kaminari/kaminari.
4. https://github.com/kaminari/kaminari/blob/master/kaminari-activerecord/lib/kaminari/activerecord/
   active_record_model_extension.rb.
5. https://github.com/kaminari/kaminari/blob/master/kaminari-core/lib/kaminari/models/page_scope_methods.rb.

These two methods combined implement pagination. Take a look at the SQL query that is generated when we use both of them:

```
> Film.page(5).per(10)
  Film Load (10.8ms)  SELECT `films`.* FROM `films` LIMIT 10 OFFSET 40
[...]
```

The crucial part here is the LIMIT 10 OFFSET 40. In plain English, this query returns the first 10 records with an offset of 40—the records that would've been in between the 41st and 50th positions if we had gotten the full collection at once. We just need to add these methods to our controller. In our application, we can do this by modifying the json_response method and adding that call at the end:

rails-performance-book-completed/app/controllers/api/v1/films_controller.rb
```ruby
class Api::V1::FilmsController < ApplicationController
  def lean
    render json: json_response
  end

  def json_response
    films = paginated_scope.pluck(:id, :title)
      .map { |m| {id: m.first, title: m.last} }
  end

  def paginated_scope
    Film.page(params[:page]).per(params[:per_page])
  end
end
```

That's it. By only adding Kaminari to our Gemfile and modifying one line in our controller, we got pagination running in our application. Go hit api/v1/films/lean?page=3&per_page=20.

```
Started GET "/api/v1/films/lean?page=3&per_page=20" for ::1
  at 2025-02-12 22:57:57 +0100
Processing by Api::V1::FilmsController#lean as HTML
  Parameters: {"page" => "3", "per_page" => "20"}
  Film Pluck (2.9ms)  SELECT `films`.`id`, `films`.`title`
    FROM `films` LIMIT 20 OFFSET 40
  ↳ app/controllers/api/v1/films_controller.rb:31:
    in 'Api::V1::FilmsController#json_response'
Completed 200 OK in 45ms (Views: 0.2ms | ActiveRecord: 2.9ms
  (1 query, 0 cached) | GC: 0.0ms)
```

Check the results. You will see that we get back 20 films, from the 41st to the 60th: exactly what we expected.

While we could close the chapter here, it's common to offer our users some tools to navigate the data in a simpler way. In particular, it's common for us to want to expose links to the previous and the next page (like in a book!), as well as the total number of pages. This will make it easier for third parties to consume our data. Again, Kaminari provides us with helper methods that do the job for us. We'll need to include the Kaminari::Helpers::UrlHelper module in our controller so we can access two new methods: prev_page_url and next_page_url. To get the total amount of pages, Kaminari added the total_pages method to ActiveRecord. Try to modify the controller response yourself. You should get something similar to this:

```
rails-performance-book-completed/app/controllers/api/v1/films_controller.rb
require 'kaminari/helpers/helper_methods'

class Api::V1::FilmsController < ApplicationController
  include Kaminari::Helpers::UrlHelper

  def json_response
    films = paginated_scope.pluck(:id, :title)
      .map { |m| {id: m.first, title: m.last} }
    # If you didn't complete the Data Access chapter, this would look like:
    # paginated_scope.map { |m| {id: m.id, title: m.title}.to_json

    {films: films}.merge(paginated_scope_decorations).to_json
  end

  def paginated_scope
    Film.page(params[:page]).per(params[:per_page])
  end

  def paginated_scope_decorations
    {
      count: paginated_scope.total_count,
      previous_page: prev_page_url(paginated_scope),
      next_page: next_page_url(paginated_scope),
      total_pages: paginated_scope.total_pages
    }
  end
end
```

```
# app/controllers/api/v1/films_controller.rb

require 'kaminari/helpers/helper_methods'

class Api::V1::FilmsController < ApplicationController
  include Kaminari::Helpers::UrlHelper

  [...]

  private

  def json_response
    films = paginated_scope.pluck(:id, :title).map do |movie|
      {id: movie.first, title: movie.last} }
    end

    # If you didn't complete the Data Access chapter, this would look like:
    # films = paginated_scope.map { |m| {id: m.id, title: m.title}

    {films: films}.merge(paginated_scope_decorations).to_json
  end
```

```
  def paginated_scope_decorations
    {
      count: paginated_scope.total_count,
      previous_page: prev_page_url(paginated_scope),
      next_page: next_page_url(paginated_scope),
      total_pages: paginated_scope.total_pages
    }
  end
end
```

Hit api/v1/films/lean?page=3&per_page=20 again and you will see the new attributes in the response:

```
{
  [...]
  count: 10395,
  previous_page:
    "http://localhost:3000/api/v1/films/lean?page=2&per_page=20",
  next_page: "http://localhost:3000/api/v1/films/lean?page=4&per_page=20",
  total_pages: 520
}
```

This "simple" pagination (also known as page-based pagination) is just one of the kinds of pagination for an API endpoint. Another is offset pagination, where the API parameter used is the offset directly. For example, a call to the API with parameters page=3&per_page=10 would return the same as offset=20. After all, offset pagination is pretty similar to page-based pagination.

Nevertheless, offset and page-based pagination have a drawback: the possibility of inconsistent and unstable results. Fortunately, there are other options.

Discovering Cursor-Based Pagination

Cursor-based pagination (CBP) solves some of the problems with offset and page-based pagination. Let's look at what CBP is and how it solves the problems present in other kinds of pagination.

The trouble with offset and page-based pagination is that, despite the book analogy, the pages in these methods *change*. Typically, most APIs return the latest records. This is what you want them to do. A chat that offered you the first thing that you ever wrote and made you go all the way through all your messages to see the latest would be very hard to use. But this means that an object currently at the top of the first page will eventually move to other pages as new records are created. As I said, the pages *change*.

This has some implications:

- Caching an endpoint with page-based or offset pagination will be significantly less effective than caching one using cursor-based pagination. This is because every time a new record is created, this may change *all* the pages, thereby forcing us to invalidate the caching for the whole endpoint for any parameters. With cursor-based pagination, the cache will expire less often, to the point that it just won't expire if your objects are immutable.

- Using cursor-based pagination is more performant even when the query is not cached. This is because the SQL query associated with it is significantly more straightforward for the database engine to execute. We will see more of this in an upcoming section, "Benchmarking CBP."

To implement cursor-based pagination, we need to establish a cursor. Continuing the book analogy, the cursor is something like a bookmark, only indicating the last "word" (in our case, the last object) that has been read. Given that we want to be able to traverse the response in two directions, we will also need to establish the direction in which the cursor will point. For example, a "page" exposing all records from ID 21 to ID 40 should have two cursors, one indicating *"ID<21"* and another indicating *"ID>40"*. Note that I put the word "page" in quotes because there will be no such thing as pages in CBP, just cursors that give instructions to the API about what to return in the response. The cursor can be as complex or as simple as the engineer designing it wishes it to be; it's an incredibly flexible solution.

So, should we always use cursor-based pagination?

Not always. Cursor-based pagination is a very powerful form of pagination but one that makes way more sense in applications that have to perform at scale. Picking CBP is also a trade-off. It's more complex and harder to use for clients. This is why it's not that common compared to offset/page-based pagination; it's also why you won't find a popular library ready for you to add to your Gemfile. The few times I have worked with a CBP implementation in Rails, it was custom-made for the application. Still, you can find some gems that implement CBP, such as rails_cursor_pagination,[6] developed by XING, another fairly big company that uses Rails.

---

6.   https://github.com/xing/rails_cursor_pagination

Adding Cursor-Based Pagination to Your Application

While I do encourage you to explore already-made solutions to add to your application, for the purpose of this book, we will create our own implementation. I have encapsulated most of the logic in a Rails concern that you can find in app/controllers/concerns/cursor_based_pagination_support.rb:

```
rails-performance-book-completed/app/controllers/concerns/cursor_based_pagination_support.rb
require 'base64'
require 'json'

module CursorBasedPaginationSupport
  extend ActiveSupport::Concern

  def generate_cursor(attr, value, direction)
    Base64.encode64({
      attr: attr,
      value: value.is_a?(String) ? "'#{value}'" : value,
      direction: direction
    }.to_json)
  end

  def cbp_scope(klass, encoded_cursor)
    results = if params[:cursor]
      cursor = decode_cursor(encoded_cursor)
      klass.where(where_conditions(cursor))
        .order("#{cursor['attr']} #{order(cursor)}")
    else
      klass.order("id asc")
    end.limit(20).to_a

    results.tap do |r|
      if params[:cursor] && order(cursor) == 'desc'
        results.reverse!
      end
    end
  end

  def decode_cursor(cursor)
    JSON.parse(Base64.decode64(cursor))
  end

  private

  def where_conditions(cursor)
    cursor.fetch_values('attr', 'direction', 'value').join(" ")
  end

  def order(cursor)
    cursor['direction'] == '<' ? 'desc' : 'asc'
  end
end
```

In essence, we will have a hash as a parameter indicating how the cursor works. This will be an example:

```
{
  attr: 'id',
  value: 100,
  direction: '>'
}
```

This data can be easily transformed into the query we need: Film.where('id > 100'). This is exactly what the where_conditions method does. Moreover, you'll also see the cursor is encoded in base64. Base64 is useful for us because it helps us obscure the information included in the cursor, prevents users from easily modifying it, guarantees uniformity, and is URL-safe. With this done, you can easily employ CBP in your endpoints. First, let's import the concern into ApplicationController:

rails-performance-book-completed/app/controllers/application_controller.rb
```
class ApplicationController < ActionController::Base
  include CursorBasedPaginationSupport

end

# app/controllers/application_controller.rb

class ApplicationController < ActionController::Base
  include CursorBasedPaginationSupport

  [...]
end
```

Now, let's add the new behavior to the endpoint. We will add a new parameter to it, cbp, so both page-based and CBP pagination will be available in the same endpoint:

rails-performance-book-completed/app/controllers/api/v1/films_controller.rb
```
require 'kaminari/helpers/helper_methods'

class Api::V1::FilmsController < ApplicationController
  include Kaminari::Helpers::UrlHelper

  def lean
    if params[:cbp]
      results = cbp_scope(Film, params[:cursor])
      response = {
        films: results.pluck(:id, :title)
          .map { |m| {id: m.first, title: m.last} }
      }

      if results.count > 0
        response[:previous_page] = api_v1_films_url(
          cbp: true,
          cursor: generate_cursor('id', results&.first&.id, '<')
        )
```

```
        response[:next_page] = api_v1_films_url(
          cbp: true,
          cursor: generate_cursor('id', results&.last&.id, '>')
        )
      end

      render json: response
    else
    render json: json_response
    end
  end
end
```

Hitting our endpoint with the cbp parameter (api/v1/films/lean?cbp=true) will return the same results but with two new URLs at the end of the response:

```
{
  [...],
  previous_page: "http://localhost:3000/api/v1/films/lean?cbp=true
    &cursor=eyJhdHRyIjoiaW...",
  next_page: "http://localhost:3000/api/v1/films/lean?cbp=true
    &cursor=eyJhdHRyIjoiaW..."
}
```

Feel free to navigate the collection of films using the cursors. You got it done!

But is using an ID as a cursor the most efficient way to go? Let's look at an alternative.

Using Dates as a Cursor

While you can build a cursor based on IDs only, it's probably more common to use timestamps to order the records. This is because ordering by time is more significant from a usage perspective. The Rails convention is that all models come with two timestamps, created_at and updated_at, out of the box, so we already have what we need.

This can have a very significant impact on your API performance, and performance is what this book is all about. The issue is that IDs are unique, timestamps are not. You will only have one record with ID 42; you may find any number of records with a created_at of "01-01-2025 00:00:00". This can significantly complicate things.

Take the following scenario: we have a system with a default page size of 100 records, and one of your customers has 10,000 records with the same created_at value. This may seem not very probable to you, but believe me, it happens. This book is dedicated to introducing engineers to problems that appear in applications that have had to scale to millions of users, and events that are rare in most cases happen way more often when you are scaling to a world audience. Moreover, this particular scenario is more common than you may think. For example, a customer may create thousands of records at the same time when they are importing data into your system. Crucially, a CBP query in which results are returned *only* by a non-unique column can be buggy, skipping some objects that have a duplicated value on the ordering attribute.

The most straightforward solution to this is to add a secondary ordering key to the query, one using a unique column, so it can keep the original requirement (order by the first key) while avoiding problems like the one we just commented upon and other shenanigans. For example, even if your database has very few repeated results in one column, ordering two records by a column in which they have the same value has a non-deterministic result, meaning that the database does not guarantee that the order will stay the same if you execute the query multiple times. This does not happen often, but it does happen, particularly when upgrading database versions or changing the database to another SQL database.

Benchmarking CBP

One of the advantages of cursor-based pagination is that it's faster. That's because the query associated with it is just more performant. Page-based and offset paginations generate queries using the OFFSET SQL keyword, like this:

```
SELECT `films`.* FROM `films` LIMIT 25 OFFSET 50
```

In comparison, cursor-based pagination generates queries like this:

```
SELECT `films`.* FROM `films` WHERE (id > 51) LIMIT 25
```

CBP has the edge because of the extra context given by (id > 51). Thanks to that, our SQL engine can traverse the index far faster. As you already know, database access can be *the* crucial element when improving performance; this will obviously trickle down to the speed of our endpoints and processes.

Of course, you don't need to take my word over this; I have a benchmark ready for you to run to see the difference. The benchmark is in lib/tasks /benchmark_paginations.rake, and you can run it on your terminal by executing rake benchmark_paginations. In the exercise, I ran 1000 queries with OFFSET and 1000 queries using a cursor. These are the results:

Query Type	Real Time	User Time	CPU Time	Improvement in User Time
offset	1.097s	391.5ms	51.49ms	-
cursor	0.327ms	163.1ms	22.16ms	2.4x

We have just explored the idea of limiting the number of items that our API endpoints return. But what about the size of an item? What are the consequences of putting more or less data in each item, and how we can finetune this?

Splitting Your Model Data

Performance in an API endpoint is all about measuring the data we are returning in the response. To better exemplify this, we will check another endpoint in our application, the one that returns the films owned by each store: api/v1/stores/:store_id/films. If you hit the endpoint now, you will get only the most basic data of the films owned by that store. For example, this is the response in api/v1/stores/1/films:

```
[
  {
    id: 1,
    title: "La La Land"
  },
  {
    id: 2,
    title: "Breathless"
  },
  {
    id: 3,
    title: "Ordet"
  },
  [...]
]
```

Now, imagine the following use case: for each film in that particular store, we also want to see the history of rentals. In the UI of our future mobile app, there will be a screen in which store managers will be able to see all the store's films, including some basic information about the last five times the movie was rented. Fortunately, we already have an endpoint in our API that exposes that information. The endpoint is api/v1/stores/:store_id/films/:film_id/rentals. You can find the code for it in Api::V1::FilmsController:

rails-performance-book-completed/app/controllers/api/v1/films_controller.rb
```
class Api::V1::FilmsController < ApplicationController

  def rentals
    inventory_ids = Inventory
      .where(film_id: params[:film_id], store_id: params[:store_id])
      .pluck(:id)
    rentals = Rental
      .where(inventory_id: inventory_ids).includes(:film, :customer)
```

```
      render json: rentals.map do |rental|
        Api::V1::RentalPresenter.new(rental).to_json
      end
    end
  end
end
```

This endpoint has already been optimized following the suggestions we shared in Chapter 2, Optimizing Data Access with ActiveRecord, on page 11. We are using pluck and includes to minimize simultaneously the amount of data we fetch from the database, the number of queries we execute, and even memory usage.

Given that all the information we need to fulfill the requirements is already there, we can suggest that our mobile team just fetch the data from those two endpoints. We could make it even easier for them by adding a link to the film JSON object. That's easy enough to do. You could create a new presenter, something like StoreFilmPresenter, that would use our original FilmPresenter and add the rentals_url attribute.

Understanding the Difference Between Linking and Embedding

But, there is an issue with how the films#index action expresses two very different concepts: a film general entity and the ownership of the film by a particular store. At some point, it might be a good idea to segregate them into two different actions. To keep it simple, let's just go for the smallest change that shows you the performance implications of different API designs. You will need to add a key named rentals_url with the link to rentals of the film in that store (api_v1_store_film_rentals_url) for each film. In my implementation, I ended up creating a new method, decorated_film, which replaces the previous calls to Api::V1::FilmPresenter.new:

rails-performance-book-completed/app/controllers/api/v1/films_controller.rb
```
class Api::V1::FilmsController < ApplicationController

  def decorated_film(film)
    presented_film = Api::V1::FilmPresenter.new(film).to_json

    if params['store_id']
      rentals_url = api_v1_store_film_rentals_url(
        film_id: film.id, store_id: params['store_id']
      )
      presented_film[:rental_url] = rentals_url
    end

    presented_film
  end
end
```

If you call that endpoint, you should get something like the following:

```
{
  films: [
    {
      id: 1,
      title: "Breathless",
      rentals_url: "http://localhost:3000/api/v1/stores/1/films/1/rentals"
    },
    {
      id: 2,
      title: "Ordet",
      rentals_url: "http://localhost:3000/api/v1/stores/1/films/2/rentals"
    },
    {
      id: 3,
      title: "Imitation of Life",
      rentals_url: "http://localhost:3000/api/v1/stores/1/films/3/rentals"
    },
    [...]
  ],
  [...]
}
```

Yes, that's it. Or is it? Remember your use case: a list of *all* films including their rentals. What would you need to do to get all that data? First, you would make a call to api/v1/stores/:store_id/films, to get the list of films. Then, you would need to make a call for each to get its rentals.

This is not good. It's basically an n+1 issue at the API level, which has even more dire consequences than when it happens on the application level. Not only are you executing n requests against the database (where n is the number of films), but you're actually running n requests on your application. This means n trips back and forth through the Internet, n executions of the whole Rails middleware, and so on. It's just too expensive, resource-wise. We need to find another way.

The first alternative is just embedding the data. Instead of adding the link, we will just add the list of rentals to the response. Notice that you want to avoid causing an n+1 issue when accessing the rentals. Changing the structure of the logic a bit will help. This is my take:

rails-performance-book-completed/app/controllers/api/v1/films_controller.rb
```
def full_films_json_response
  if params['store_id']
    films = scope.includes(:rentals)
      .where(inventories: { "store_id" => params[:store_id] })
```

```
    films.map do |film|
      decorated_film_with_embedded_rentals(film)
    end
  else
    scope.select(:id, :title).map do |film|
      Api::V1::FilmPresenter.new(film).to_json
    end
  end
end

def decorated_film_with_embedded_rentals
  presented_film = Api::V1::FilmPresenter.new(film).to_json

  if params['store_id']
    json_rentals = film.rentals.map do |rental|
      Api::V1::RentalPresenter.new(rental).to_json
    end
    presented_film[:rentals] = json_rentals
  end

  presented_film
end
```

As you learned in Chapter 2, Optimizing Data Access with ActiveRecord, on page 11, adding includes to the scope helps us fetch all the associated rows in other tables in a much more efficient way.

If you check the endpoint response again, you will see that now all the rentals data is embedded in the original object:

```
[
  {
    id: 1,
    title: "Breathless",
    rentals: [
      {
        movie_name: "Breathless",
        user: 1,
        rental_date: "2024-06-15T00:00:00.000Z",
        returnal_date: "2024-06-18T00:00:00.000Z"
      },
      {
        movie_name: "Breathless",
        user: 2,
        rental_date: "2024-06-22T00:00:00.000Z",
        returnal_date: "2024-06-25T00:00:00.000Z"
      }
    ]
  },
```

```
  {
    id: 2,
    title: "Ordet",
    rentals: [ ]
  },
  [...]
]
```

This approach certainly fixes the issue with our client needing n+1 requests to fetch the films and the rentals. Still, there are significant drawbacks.

First, you've probably noticed that there are duplicated data. Each rental JSON object includes the movie_name attribute, something obviously not necessary when we are fetching this data as an embedded object of the film. We are just making the response heavier and harder to parse. There are some simple solutions to this:

Modifying the base presenter (Api::V1::Presenter) so the to_json method accepts an optional exclude attribute that removes the attributes included in that field. In general, at this point, we should refactor the presenters. So, for example, including the rentals of a film becomes something we can add as an option in the FilmPresenter instead of a logic included in the controller. This is a work I leave for you to do, but still, here, you have the exclude option added in the base presenter as we implemented it in Chapter 3, Understanding All the Faces of Caching, on page 47. The new logic is in the last lines:

rails-performance-book-completed/app/presenters/api/v1/presenter.rb
```ruby
class Api::V1::Presenter
  def to_json(exclude: [])
    return nil unless resource

    object = Rails.cache.fetch(cache_key)

    if object && object[:expiration_key] == expiration_key
      return object.tap { |h| h.delete(:expiration_key) }
    end

    as_json.merge(expiration_key: expiration_key).tap do |object|
      Rails.cache.write(cache_key, object)
      object.delete(:expiring_key)

      exclude.each do |excluded_attr|
        object.delete(excluded_attr)
      end
    end
  end
end
```

Second, the issue is the number of rentals that are included in each film. In the previous section of this chapter, we discussed pagination. We are already familiar with the consequences of not setting limits to the number of records returned by an API endpoint. A reasonable alternative would be to change the response so we only return, for example, the latest five rentals of a film. We would also include a link to api/v1/stores/:store_id/films/:film_id/rentals so clients can easily access the complete list of rentals. By the way, that list should also be paginated.

The third and final issue is the one that has the hardest solution: even with limits, we are significantly increasing the payload of the response. It's reasonable to assume that most clients calling films#index are just interested in data on films. Adding rentals adds computational complexity and makes our response overall slower. And yet, it's also unreasonable to ask the clients that need the rentals of each and every film to make n+1 calls. What can we do? Well, fortunately, there is an established answer to this. We can just add sideloads to our endpoint.

Implementing Sideloads

Sideloads allow our clients to decide the extra information they want from our endpoints on a per-need basis using a parameter. It's optional embedding: a call to api/v1/stores/:store_id/films should not return the rentals; a call to api/v1/stores/:store_id/films?include=rentals should return the rentals in the exact same way we discussed when describing the embedded option in the previous section.

Adding this option to our current implementation is really simple. As with the exclude option, it's something that would make sense to move out of the controller and into the presenter. Again, I leave it to you to make the refactoring. This is the minimum implementation that would work:

```ruby
# app/controllers/api/v1/films_controller.rb

class Api::V1::FilmsController < ApplicationController
  [...]

  def full_films_json_response
    if params['store_id'] && params[:include]&.include?('rentals')
      [...]
    end
  end

  [...]
end
```

Sideloads and Caching

> There are only two hard things in Computer Science: cache invalidation and naming things.
>
> – Phil Karlton

Sideloading is a powerful technique, but it adds another layer of complexity to our very finetuned Rails application: suddenly, cache expiration becomes harder. Everything is fine if we only use caching at the level of the individual record. This is what the current implementation of the endpoint supports. But things get trickier if we try to apply caching on a higher level, like the whole collection. Given the include parameter dramatically changes the data returned by any given endpoint, this also changes when the cache is expired. To continue with the example we have been using, a call to api/v1/stores /:store_id/films with the parameter includes?rentals will expire more often than one without it. Any new rental at the store should expire the collection-level caching.

What's the problem with this? Well, expiring the cache every time there is a new rental can be *incredibly inefficient* if 99 percent of the calls to the endpoint are not using the rentals sideload. Moreover, our example has only one sideload, but real businesses can be way more complicated. As your API endpoints get more complex, it's normal to accumulate more and more sideloads that will expire the cache more and more often. A maximalist approach ("any update on any sideload should expire the cache") will backfire pretty fast, as the cache becomes almost irrelevant.

The lesson of this is to think of a sideload as a basic element of the request, at the same level as the path, when thinking about performance. Collection-level caches and CDN-level ones are heavily affected by it. Take this into account when designing your API.

Using GraphQL

There are more options to give clients flexibility when fetching data from your endpoints beyond sideloading. A very popular one is GraphQL.

GraphQL is a query language and runtime that was developed by Facebook in 2012. The idea behind its creation was to allow clients to request and retrieve the exact data they need. With GraphQL, clients have to specify exactly what fields they want for each object they retrieve.

The Ruby ecosystem has a popular and well-maintained GraphQL implementation that we'll use for our example. You can find it on GitHub.[7] It has great documentation[8] that I strongly suggest you read. To install it, do the following:

- Add gem "graphql" to your Gemfile.

- Run bundle install from your terminal.

- Execute the installation. This is because graphql-ruby adds multiple files to your Rails application. You can install it by running rails g graphql:install from the terminal.

- Finally, you will have to run bundle install again because the installation has added a new gem (graphiql-rails) to the Gemfile.

Have you done the installation? Good. But before moving on, check the log you got in your terminal after installing graphql. You will see that the installation has created a lot of files in the subfolder app/graphql/types: those are types, and we will talk about them when we write the schema. But please note that we have a new controller in app/controllers/graphql_controller.rb and have added two new routes to our config/routes.rb:

rails-performance-book-completed/config/routes.rb
```
Rails.application.routes.draw do
  if Rails.env.development?
    mount GraphiQL::Rails::Engine, at: "/graphiql", graphql_path: "/graphql"
  end
  post "/graphql", to: "graphql#execute"
```

The first one, /graphiql, is a development tool that will allow us to test our GraphQL queries in a more straightforward way without interacting with the API. The second one, /graphql, is the *unique* endpoint for our GraphQL interface. Yes, this is one of the main differences between GraphQL and a REST API: while REST tends to express its schema by the path called (for example, we request the films owned by a store calling /api/v1/stores/:store_id/films), in GraphQL the schema is found in the payload sent to the server. This means that GraphQL only needs one single endpoint that is able, by itself, to express all the capabilities of the service.

Of course, to enable all these capabilities, we need to define the resources that will be fetched by our brand-new GraphQL endpoint. In this example, we won't create types for all the models already existing on our application,

7. https://github.com/rmosolgo/graphql-ruby
8. https://graphql-ruby.org/getting_started.html

but we will at least create the "a store has many films" relation that we have been working on in this section.

Let's start with the child object in the association, Film. The graphql-ruby gem comes with generators that will automatically pick up the structure of a model based on its table in your relational database. Just execute the following on your terminal and you'll get a GraphQL schema:

```
% rails g graphql:object Film
```

You should get a Types::FilmType class at app/graphql/types/film_type.rb looking like this:

rails-performance-book-completed/app/graphql/types/film_type.rb
```
module Types
  class FilmType < Types::BaseObject
    field :id, ID, null: false
    field :title, String
    field :created_at, GraphQL::Types::ISO8601DateTime, null: false
    field :updated_at, GraphQL::Types::ISO8601DateTime, null: false
    field :language_id, Integer
    field :big_text_column, String
  end
end
```

Yes, everything is included. But remember, this doesn't mean that everything will be returned in the API response by default. In GraphQL, there is no default.

Next, we will define entry points to the system so that clients can fetch data. We will define two: one that would work like films#index and another that will be akin to films#show. For this purpose, we will have to modify our QueryType. In GraphQL, the QueryType defines the entry points that clients can use to request data from the server; each field in the QueryType will define the type of queries that a client can execute. Next, create two new fields in the QueryType (app/graphql/types/query_type.rb): film (for fetching an individual Film record), and films (for fetching the collection):

rails-performance-book-completed/app/graphql/types/query_type.rb
```
module Types
  class QueryType < Types::BaseObject
    include GraphQL::Types::Relay::HasNodeField
    include GraphQL::Types::Relay::HasNodesField

    field :film, FilmType, null: false do
      argument :id, Integer
    end

    field :films, [FilmType] do
      argument :ids, [Integer], required: false
    end
```

```
    def film(id: )
      Film.find(id)
    end

    def films(ids: nil)
      ids ? Film.where(id: ids) : Film.all
    end
  end
end
```

This will be enough. Note also that films is not only able to return *all* films, but it also allows you to pass an Array of ids, so you can fetch multiple objects with a single query. You can test it by opening your browser and going to http://localhost:3000/graphiql. This will provide you with a nice UI in which to execute queries. For example, the following will return you the id and the title of all the films in the database:

```
{
  films {
    id
    title
  }
}
```

The following query will return you the title and the timestamps for the film with ID 1:

```
{
  film(id:1) {
    title
    createdAt
    updatedAt
  }
}
```

Finally, let's see how to implement an association on GraphQL. For this, we will use the "store-has-many-films" relation.

```
% rails g graphql:object Store films:[Film]
```

This will generate a StoreType with all the attributes directly coming from the stores table, plus a store-films relation. You can see all this in the newly created StoreType class at app/graphql/types/store_type.rb:

rails-performance-book-completed/app/graphql/types/store_type.rb
```
# frozen_string_literal: true

module Types
  class StoreType < Types::BaseObject
    field :id, ID, null: false
```

```
      field :created_at, GraphQL::Types::ISO8601DateTime, null: false
      field :updated_at, GraphQL::Types::ISO8601DateTime, null: false
      field :name, String
      field :most_rented_film_id, Integer
      field :films, [Types::FilmType]
    end
end
```

Ruby is a magical language indeed. The only thing left is to implement a couple of entry points to fetch store data, including the films:

rails-performance-book-completed/app/graphql/types/query_type.rb
```
# frozen_string_literal: true

module Types
  class QueryType < Types::BaseObject
    include GraphQL::Types::Relay::HasNodeField
    include GraphQL::Types::Relay::HasNodesField

    field :film, FilmType, null: false do
      argument :id, Integer
    end

    field :films, [FilmType] do
      argument :ids, [Integer], required: false
    end

    def film(id: )
      Film.find(id)
    end

    def films(ids: nil)
      ids ? Film.where(id: ids) : Film.all
    end

    field :store, StoreType, null: false do
      argument :id, Integer
    end

    field :stores, [StoreType] do
      argument :ids, [Integer], required: false
    end

    def store(id: )
      Store.find(id)
    end

    def stores(ids: nil)
      ids ? Store.where(id: ids) : Store.all
    end
  end
end
```

Only, with this, a query like the following will work:

```
{
  store(id: 1){
        name
    films {
      title
    }
  }
}
```

Done! I'll leave to you the details of the implementation of the "a film has many rentals" association. At this point, you should have got the gist: create a new RentalType:

```
% rails g graphql:object rental
```

Then add the association in FilmType:

rails-performance-book-completed/app/graphql/types/film_type.rb
```
module Types
  class FilmType < Types::BaseObject
    field :id, ID, null: false
    field :title, String
    field :created_at, GraphQL::Types::ISO8601DateTime, null: false
    field :updated_at, GraphQL::Types::ISO8601DateTime, null: false
    field :language_id, Integer
    field :big_text_column, String
    field :rentals, [Types::RentalType]
  end
end
```

Improving Performance on GraphQL APIs

The previous section offered an introduction to implementing GraphQL in a Ruby on Rails application. This does not guarantee a scalable application. While GraphQL really helps to establish an incredibly flexible interface for clients to fetch exactly the data they need, it won't solve performance issues by itself. For example, the implementation we just wrote suffers from an n+1 issue when fetching the films of each store. Fortunately, once you get command over the general issues of performance work, improving performance is a matter of applying those common techniques to the specifics of the implementation you are running.

Finetuning the queries executed by an API controller might look a bit hard in this case, given that graphql-ruby abstracts/hides those database accesses in a way that the typical Rails-based REST API does not. Under the hood, GraphQL is running a function called the resolver[9] to generate the data assigned to each field. You are free to write your own Resolver classes in graphql-ruby.[10]

We are not going to get into the specifics of how to apply the lessons of this book to a GraphQL Ruby implementation, but believe me, you are already equipped with the basics. Moreover, you'll find plenty of good resources.[11] In particular, I recommend the step-by-step guide, *GraphQL for Rails Developers*.[12] GraphQL and Ruby on Rails pair well, powering complex clients like React applications. I'm sure that you will find a way to write incredibly performant GraphQL interfaces.

Summing Up

Time for another recap. In this chapter, we have focused on modifying the structure of your APIs to favor good performance. You learned how to adjust the API response in two ways: with the number of records returned by request and with the amount of data embedded in each object.

To optimize the number of records in an application response, you explored applying pagination to API payloads. You learned about offset-based pagination and page-based pagination and implemented them in a real Rails application using Kaminari. You explored cursor-based pagination, seeing how it is especially useful on applications that operate on a large scale.

You looked at the difference between linking and embedding data to finetune the amount of data included in each object. You saw how sideloading allows clients to choose which data they want to fetch when calling an API endpoint. Finally, you got a brief introduction to GraphQL, a system that allows incredible flexibility in an API.

---

9.   https://graphql.org/learn/execution/

10. https://graphql-ruby.org/fields/resolvers.html

11. https://evilmartians.com/chronicles/how-to-graphql-with-ruby-rails-active-record-and-no-n-plus-one

12. https://pragprog.com/titles/d-rbgql/graphql-for-rails-developers/

## CHAPTER 5

Tracking the Lifecycle of a Request

The Internet isn't exactly a series of tubes,[1] but a network of cables around the whole globe. Making a simple request with your browser triggers a truly global tour that would make Phileas Fogg jealous. Unfortunately, this isn't taken into consideration by the vast majority of engineers working on web and mobile applications. Having a better understanding of what happens to web traffic will help you find opportunities to make your application more scalable.

Crossing the Internet with One Request

What happens when a user writes the name of your domain in the address bar of their browser and hits "Return"? Turns out, a lot. The following is a summary of everything that takes place for you to fetch a website from the Internet:

1. The client initiates the request. For example, the URL is entered into the browser address bar, and the user hits "Return."

2. A DNS Lookup is performed. This means that the browser needs to find the IP address corresponding to the domain name. On the Internet, there are specialized DNS servers that resolve domain names, return IP addresses, and allow the browser to send requests to the right place.

3. A TCP connection is established with the server found in the IP address obtained from the DNS lookup.

4. The HTTP(S) request is sent to the server. This request will include the HTTP method (GET, PUT, POST, and so on), the URL path, the headers, and an optional payload.

5. Server Processing. The request gets to the server and is processed by it. In a typical Rails application, this process will have the application

---

1. https://en.wikipedia.org/wiki/Series_of_tubes

crossing multiple layers in the server. Commonly, the request will be processed by a web server (like Nginx), which will forward the request to an application server (like Puma). Eventually, the application server will send the request to our Rails application, first crossing its middleware, being processed, and returning a response. The response also goes through the application server and the web server.

6. The client receives the response. If there are no further requests, the TCP connection is closed.

7. The response is processed. For example, if the client is a browser and the response is an HTML page, a web page will be rendered.

This chapter is going to focus on improving performance by optimizing the trip that we just described. There are two main techniques:

- Reduce the amount of requests by using HTTP headers. HTTP headers can also help the server by indicating that the body of the response is not necessary and, therefore, the request does not need to be processed.

- Shortening the trip by using CDNs. CDNs (Content Delivery Networks) are systems of distributed servers that deliver different kinds of content, like images, scripts, videos, and so on. For certain resources, a CDN can set itself in between the DNS lookup and the application server in a geographical location closer to the client, hastening the request resolution.

Using HTTP Headers to Speed Up Your Application

HTTP headers add crucial information to both requests and responses. They are central for tons of basic functionalities of the web, like authentication (both the Authentication and the Cookie header), localization (the Accept-language header), tracking (User-Agent, Referral...), and many others. In this section, we are going to explore the most important headers related to performance, in particular, the ones that define caching mechanisms. Thanks to them, a client (typically from the browser) can decide to skip requests, as the server has stated that no change in the response will be found. On the server side, it can also make the application more performant. The client can pass a header (If-None-Match) that establishes the version of the last response. If the server has a quick mechanism to determine that the response has not changed, it can directly return a "304 Not Modified" response with an empty body, avoiding having to recalculate the response and return the payload.

The headers you can use to improve the performance of your application on the server side (the response) are:

The Cache-Control header.[2] It was introduced with the HTTP/1.1 specification. Both the server and the client can establish multiple cache directives in it. In the response, the server can define 13 directives:

Header	Description
max-age	Indicates the number of seconds that the response will remain fresh, aka it can be cached
s-max-age	Similar to max-age, but applying only for shared caches
no-cache	It indicates that the response can be cached, but it requires validation by the origin server.
must-revalidate	It indicates that the response can be cached and used with no validation while fresh; when it becomes stale, it must be validated with the origin server.
proxy-revalidate	The same as must-revalidate, but applies only for shared caches
no-store	It indicates that the response should not be stored under any circumstances
private	It indicates that the response can only be stored on private caches, like at the browser level
public	It indicates that the response can be stored in a shared cache.
must-understand	This directive indicates that the response should only be cached if the requirements for caching are understood based on the returned status.
no-transform	It indicates that the response can be stored in a shared cache
immutable	It indicates that the response will not be modified while it's considered fresh
stale-while-revalidate	This directive is designed to be used in combination with max-age. With it, the response will first have a period of freshness (the period defined by max_age) and then a period in the state of must-revalidate (the time in between max-age and state-while-revalidate).
stale-if-error	It indicates that the client can use the cached response despite it being stale if the server returns an error

---

2.   https://developer.mozilla.org/en-US/docs/Web/HTTP/Headers/Cache-Control.

On the request, the following seven directives can be established by the client:

Header	Description
no-cache	It asks to validate the response with the origin server even if the cache has a fresh response
no-store	It requests caches not to store both the request and its corresponding response
max-age	It indicates that the client allows storage of the generated response within N seconds.
max-stale	It requests caches not to store both the request and its corresponding response
min-fresh	It indicates that the client allows a stored response that is fresh for at least N seconds
no-transform	It indicates that the response can be stored in a shared cache
only-if-cached	The client indicates that an already-cached response needs to be returned by the server. If none is available, a 504 response is returned instead.

In summary, the Cache-Control header offers plenty of different utilities to improve the performance of your application. The Cache-Control header was created to simplify and unify browser directives related to caching. It supersedes previous headers.

Before the existence of the Cache-Control header, the most commonly used header to work with the caching of HTTP responses was the Expires[3] header. Expires defines the maximum amount of time after which the cache for the resource fetched will be considered expired. This means that once that time arrives, the data returned in the response must be considered stale and should be re-fetched.

Still, while understanding that the Expires header can be useful when working with legacy systems, the Cache-Control header is a complete tool, and, as it has already been said, it supersedes Expires. For example, if a response returns both an Expires header and a Cache-Control with a max-age directive, the latter is supposed to take precedence over the former.

Finally, we have the ETag.[4] An ETag (or entity tag) is an HTTP response header containing an identifier for a specific version of a resource. This means that the ETag has to change every time that the body of the response (be it

---

3.   https://developer.mozilla.org/en-US/docs/Web/HTTP/Headers/Expires
4.   https://developer.mozilla.org/en-US/docs/Web/HTTP/Headers/ETag

an HTML page, a JSON, or something else) changes. For performance purposes, the client will need to send an If-None-Match header in the request containing the value of the ETag header the client received the last time it requested the resource. With the value of the If-None-Match header, the server can check if the resource has changed since the last time the client received the source. If the resource has not changed, the server can just send back a "304 Not Modified" status without a body, telling the client that its cached version is fresh. If the server makes this check early enough in the process (you can do it even before the request hits the Rails app), you will be saving the application from a lot of needless processing, plus you will be returning a response way faster.

Enough theory! Let's use some of these headers in the application.

Applying Cache-Control Headers to Your Application

You can check what headers your application is currently returning using, such as Chrome Tools. Go to the Network tab and click the "stores" request. Under "Response Headers," check the value for "Cache-Control." It's "max-age=0, private, must-revalidate."

Name		X	Headers	Preview	Response	Initiator	Timing	Cookies
stores		▼General						
application-e0cf9d8fcb1...		Request URL:				http://localhost:3000/stores		
application-37f365cbecf...		Request Method:				GET		
turbo.min-cd3ce4205ea...		Status Code:				200 OK		
stimulus.min-dd364f16e...		Remote Address:				[::1]:3000		
stimulus-loading-3576ce...		Referrer Policy:				strict-origin-when-cross-origin		
application-368d98631b...								
hello_controller-549135e...		▼Response Headers		Raw				
index-2db729dddcc5b97...		Cache-Control:				max-age=0, private, must-revalidate		
gps.js		Content-Length:				3062		
content_script_vite-148e...		Content-Type:				text/html; charset=utf-8		
favicon.ico		Etag:				W/"b1bd8df3655e2532706c750bbd97661b"		

In the previous section, you learned what those three directives mean, but in summary, the "max-age=0" already shows there is absolutely no caching going on. Let's change this. You will modify the Cache-Control max-age header in the stores#index endpoint. You can find the action in app/controllers/stores_controller.rb. The action currently is pretty simple:

rails-performance-book/app/controllers/stores_controller.rb
```
def index
  @stores = Store.all
end
```

You have to modify this so the application returns a different value for max-age: the current default, 0, establishes that the response is fresh for 0 seconds, so we have no caching at all. Rails offers you two different ways to configure this value. One is a little bit more magic and easier to understand; the other is closer to the HTTP header themselves.

The first option is using expires_in in the action that we want to be cached. In our case, if we want the response to be cached for 60 seconds, it would look like this:

```
# app/controllers/stores_controller.rb

def index
  @stores = Store.all
  expires_in 60.seconds
end
```

Alternatively, you can directly manipulate the response headers using response.headers. If you go this route, the action will look like this:

```
# app/controllers/stores_controller.rb

def index
  @stores = Store.all
  response.headers["Cache-Control"] = "max-age=60"
end
```

I personally prefer the second, in part because you will eventually need more granular control of the directives for more complex cache setups. Still, I have to admit that it's hard to beat the clarity and straightforwardness of just writing expires_in. Either way, the resulting response and client behavior will be the same.

Time to test it. Load your Rails application, open your browser, and hit http://localhost:3000. Check the server log: you will see that the browser request hit the application:

```
Started GET "/stores" for ::1 at 2025-02-17 12:48:35 +0100
Processing by StoresController#index as HTML
  Rendering layout layouts/application.html.erb
  Rendering stores/index.html.erb within layouts/application
  Store Load (0.4ms)  SELECT `stores`.* FROM `stores`
  ↳ app/views/stores/index.html.erb:5
  Rendered stores/index.html.erb within layouts/application
    (Duration: 13.8ms | GC: 0.0ms)
  Rendered layout layouts/application.html.erb
    (Duration: 15.8ms | GC: 0.0ms)
Completed 200 OK in 18ms
  (Views: 15.9ms | ActiveRecord: 0.4ms (1 query, 0 cached) | GC: 0.0ms)
```

Go back to the browser. At the top of the page, there is a link named "Reload." It goes to http://localhost:3000/stores. Hit it. If less than 60 seconds have passed since you loaded the page for the first time, you will see that...nothing happens. The browser has followed the max-age directive and has not reloaded the page. You can confirm this by checking the Rails application log again. There is nothing new. During 60 seconds, you can hit "Reload" as many times as you want, but the browser will abstain from launching a request.

This technique is great, particularly for resources that do not change much or change in very precise intervals. However, most of the endpoints in an API are not like this. In many cases, you will want to have some sort of control on the server side so you can return a full response only when the resource has changed. This is something you can do with our next technique, ETags.

Unlocking the Power of 304s with ETags

As we stated before, an ETag or Entity Tag is an HTTP response header containing an identifier for a specific version of a resource. By itself, it does not change the behavior of the browser, but it is expected that the browser will use that ETag in subsequent requests of the same resource. The client can set the ETag in an "If-None-Match" header, so the server saves time and does not fully process the request, returning a 304 instead. This mechanism is called a conditional GET; there's a pretty good explanation in the Ruby on Rails guides.[5]

Let's implement this behavior in your application. For example, you will improve the performance of the api/v1/stores/:id endpoint you worked with in the chapter we dedicated to caching. You should start by noticing that Rails already adds ETag headers. You can check this by hitting api/v1/stores/1 with the Network tab of Chrome Tools open. You can see that ETag is one of the response headers.

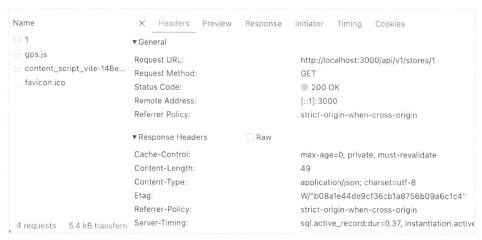

Rails generates the Etags by default. Moreover, it's not only the server that does this automatically. If you recheck the Network tab of Chrome Tools, you will see that Chrome is already sending back the ETag under the header "If-None-Match."

Strong vs. Weak ETags

There are two kinds of ETags: weak and strong. This adjective refers to the relation they have. When a response comes with a weak ETag header, it means that the body may have some *minor* changes despite not having changed. On the other hand, a strong ETag implies that the body of the response is exactly the same, byte per byte. Weak ETags are better for performance; strong ETags are more precise.

Rails, by default, generates weak ETags. You can always identify a weak ETag because they always start with the prefix "W/", like in the previous screenshot.

The only thing is to change the server's behavior so that if the "If-None-Match" header matches our Entity Tag, we don't process anything. Fortunately, there

---

5.   https://guides.rubyonrails.org/caching_with_rails.html#conditional-get-support

is a bit of Rails magic here that makes it super simple. It's a method called stale?. Adding it to your action would look like this:

```
rails-performance-book-completed/app/controllers/api/v1/stores_controller.rb
class Api::V1::StoresController < ApplicationController
  def show
    store = Store.find params['id']

    if stale? store
      render json: Api::V1::StorePresenter.new(store).to_json
    end
  end
end
```

An alternative, more magical way of applying caching headers in your endpoint is using fresh_when. This method sets the caching headers and automatically returns a "304 Not Modified" if the resource hasn't changed. If we wanted to apply this technique to this kind of endpoint, it would look a bit different. As an example, I applied it to Films#show:

```
# app/controllers/films_controller.rb

class FilmsController < ApplicationController
  def show
    @film = Film.find(params[:id])
    fresh_when last_modified: @film.updated_at, etag: @film
  end
```

Now that you have seen how to speed up your Rails application using ETags, let's check the effects of your optimization. The best way to see this is to run two consecutive requests: one before the browser sends back the right ETag (the base case) and one in which the browser already forwards the ETag. To get to this state, you can clear the cache of your browser. Anyway, this is what I got running the same exercise on my machine:

```
Started GET "/api/v1/stores/1" for ::1 at 2025-02-13 01:24:46 +0100
Processing by Api::V1::StoresController#show as HTML
  Parameters: {"id" => "1"}
  Store Load (0.3ms)  SELECT `stores`.* FROM `stores`
    WHERE `stores`.`id` = 1 LIMIT 1
    /*action:show,application:Moviestore,controller:stores*/
  ↳ app/controllers/api/v1/stores_controller.rb:3:in
    'Api::V1::StoresController#show'
  Film Load (0.8ms)  SELECT `films`.* FROM `films` WHERE `films`.`id` = 1
    LIMIT 1 /*action:show,application:Moviestore,controller:stores*/
  ↳ app/presenters/api/v1/store_presenter.rb:12:in
    'Api::V1::StorePresenter#to_json'
Completed 200 OK in 21ms (Views: 0.1ms | ActiveRecord: 9.6ms
  (2 queries, 0 cached) | GC: 0.0ms
```

```
Started GET "/api/v1/stores/1" for ::1 at 2025-02-13 01:24:52 +0100
Processing by Api::V1::StoresController#show as HTML
  Parameters: {"id" => "1"}
  Store Load (1.7ms)  SELECT `stores`.* FROM `stores`
    WHERE `stores`.`id` = 1 LIMIT 1
    /*action:show,application:Moviestore,controller:stores*/
  ↳ app/controllers/api/v1/stores_controller.rb:3:in
    'Api::V1::StoresController#show'
Completed 304 Not Modified in 6ms (ActiveRecord: 1.7ms
  (1 query, 0 cached) | GC: 0.0ms)
```

The difference is astonishing. The first request was quite fast, taking only 21 milliseconds. However, the second request is way better: it took only six milliseconds. Moreover, it also used far less memory. Notice that the second response is not a 200 OK but a 304 Not Modified. Moreover, feel free to refresh the page as many times as you want. So long as you don't modify the store object, you will always get an almost immediate 304.

Finally, consider that you could return this 304 response much earlier in the process. If your application has very bloated middleware, and you have an endpoint that does not change much and has a lot of traffic, you could intercept the call before it crosses most of the middleware (or even earlier), check if the requested resource is stale, and directly return a 304 if it isn't. There is no simple way to do this natively on Rails, as the logic of stale? and fresh_when is defined in ActionController,[6] making it a bit hard to access from outside a controller.

Still, this idea of intercepting a request earlier in its processing brings us to our next section. What if we could respond even before the request hit the application? Let's talk about CDNs.

Introducing CDNs

A CDN, or Content Delivery Network, is a network of geographically distributed servers with the goal of providing high availability and performance. Requests that would typically be resolved in your application server can be responded to faster thanks to the CDN edge server. An edge server is a server that is placed geographically closer to the user (as shown in the image on page 123).

Imagine the following situation: your application is located on the U.S. West Coast; however, a good chunk of your users happen to be located in Europe. A CDN can provide you with an edge server that can cache and serve certain resources (typically static assets like images, stylesheets, and others). The

---

6. https://github.com/rails/rails/blob/main/actionpack/lib/action_controller/metal/conditional_get.rb

The first time

The second time

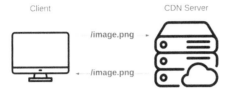

The nth time

request does not need to cross the Atlantic to get to your application server; take into account that a typical transatlantic round trip might add around 60 to 100 milliseconds of latency, depending on various factors. A hundred milliseconds might not sound like much to you, but for many operations, it can be way more than the processing time of the request itself; moreover, this latency "bonus" will be added to all requests. If your application executes many API calls, this latency can pile up. There is another advantage of using CDNs: they distribute the load across more servers. Requests that are resolved by the CDN are requests that your application server does not respond to, improving its performance. The most common use of CDNs is caching resources that are identified as static, like images or stylesheets, but you can configure it to do full pages or even API responses. Nevertheless, in the example in this chapter, we will focus on static assets.

The usage of CDNs on production is common enough for it to have its own section in the Rails official guide.[7] Most typically, you will want to serve your

---

7. https://guides.rubyonrails.org/asset_pipeline.html#cdns

static assets from the CDN using a subdomain provided by the CDN itself. You will need to go to the panel in your CDN and configure it so the subdomain points to the domain from which you are serving your Rails application. For example, if your application is served from the domain *railsperformancebook.com* you will have to configure the CDN so the "origin" of the CDN points back to that domain.

Next, you will need to change your environment configuration so that the assets in production point to the CDN first. You can do so by editing the file config/environments/production.rb and adding the custom subdomain provided by your CDN as the asset host. For example:

```
# config/environments/production.rb
```

```
config.asset_host = 'mycdnsubdomain.mycdnprovider.com'
```

Finally, we need to configure how long the assets can be cached by the CDN. Remember the Cache-Control headers we discussed at the beginning of this chapter? Well, that's exactly what we need to modify. You can change the headers for all assets by adding something like the following to the config/environments/production.rb:

```
# config/environments/production.rb
```

```
config.public_file_server.headers = {
  'Cache-Control' => 'public, max-age=31536000'
}
```

This configuration allows the CDN to cache the resource (the "public" directive) and it sets a caching expiration date of one year (the "max-age=31536000"), which is the max recommended. If you do this, the only way to clear the cache will be to do it manually in the CDN itself or change the name of the assets, so the cache key becomes invalid and the resource needs to be fetched anew from the server by the CDN. Fortunately, this is done by default by the Rails asset pipeline when using a CDN.

Summing Up

We started the chapter by commenting briefly on everything that happens when a user hits "Return" on the address bar of the browser. With this knowledge, the possibility of having a more performant application appeared by just reducing the number of trips from the client to the server, or at least by reducing the distance of those trips.

The first way was using Cache-Control headers, which allow you to configure what, when, and how the client will cache the resources delivered by the server. You have seen a brief definition of all the directives that are available to you, and you have seen an example with two of the most commonly used ones: max-age and ETag. The second way was using CDNs, which are particularly appropriate for static assets of any kind. CDNs improve performance and scalability by reducing the load on the server and by being able to return resources to the client faster, being closer geographically to it.

Next, you will enter perhaps the most essential chapter of the whole book. There are no performance issues to be solved if there is no visibility into them. Let's talk about monitoring.

## CHAPTER 6

Thinking Architecture for Performance

Rails is well-known as the ideal framework for building a startup. Thanks to Ruby on Rails, it's not impossible to get pretty far in the startup game with an incredibly small engineering team. In other words, Rails is a fantastic tool for going from zero to one. This is not a coincidence: Rails scaffolding, generators, a wide array of opinionated libraries, and in general, the "convention over configuration" approach incredibly empower both the solo developer and the small team.

However, the "batteries included" approach of Rails can mean that you may need to introduce significant design changes to jump to the planetary scale. The convention will finally need to be replaced by a configuration tailored for performance. These conventions are ubiquitous in Rails, and we have discussed how to change many of them in this book. In this chapter, we will focus on the architecture of the typical Rails application and how to make it iterate to a system prepared to manage higher workloads.

Discovering Sharding

When a successful product is online for some years, the amount of data stored in the relational database will get very big. In a company I worked for, a single table occupied a grand total of 600 TB. Yes, TB as in terabytes, like 1000 GB. Good luck trying to do anything with that!

While that scale is not that common, having issues with tables that have grown too big is certainly not infrequent. Whenever you find yourself in a situation like that, you will probably feel the temptation to modify the tables—and with them, the data model—not for syntactical reasons, but just to make the data "fit." For example, some information that is embedded in the model table is sent to a different table, becoming an associated object instead. That can be reasonable, but it will only take you so far. Fortunately, there is a better way.

With sharding, you keep the exact same data model (with the same table and column structure). The reduction in data is achieved by dividing the data and sending it to new databases (the shards) with the exact same schema as the original one. For example, if you have a one TB database and you create five shards, you can transform it into five databases of around 200 GB each. The process of deciding which data stays in which cluster, and if sharding is possible with no data duplication, will depend on the peculiarities of your application domain. For example, there are some specific use cases in which the scope of any operation can be the whole dataset. Having to execute operations through all the shards becomes more complex, and having to do so often would complicate things. Still, if you can break your database into smaller shards, that will be a total game-changer for the scalability of your application: your application will go back to the days in which the database was smaller because, in fact, you will be able to make it smaller!

Introducing Horizontal Sharding

If this is the first time that you have read about sharding, you may be wondering how it works in practice. What is the exact strategy used to define the data held by each one of those shards? How can you implement sharding without utterly breaking the functionality of your application?

There is a very common scenario in modern web applications, particularly in B2B services: datasets in which the whole data "hangs" on the account. For example, when a company opens an account in a cloud-based SaaS to manage its human resources, it doesn't expect its data to interact in any way with the data of other accounts. In fact, it would create a huge issue if there was any kind of data leak between accounts! In products like the one we are commenting on—an HR management service—the vast majority of the data can be easily partitioned with no feature loss. In this case, it would be acceptable from a product perspective—even somehow ideal—if each account had its own totally isolated database.

Let's take our movie business as an example. Fortunately, the data model you have in your hands is perfect for applying some sharding. The key you want to use to generate the shards is store_id. Still, so far, none of the features in the application seem to require the usage of sharding...until now. Our new requirement has arrived—we are going to introduce auditing in our application. Every time something relevant to the store occurs, we will create an object and store it. This is how it could look in the figure on page 129.

What you have just seen described is an ideal sharding scenario. It is so ideal that it rarely happens in reality, even in use cases in which data sharding is

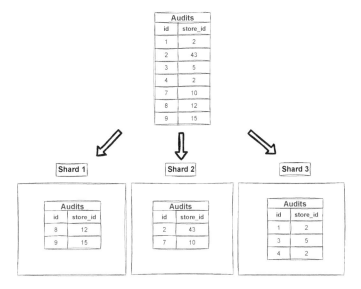

commonly used. The thing is, even if all the data introduced by the customer can be completely sharded, there will be data that is shared. The most common example is that all instances of the application will probably need to connect to a complete accounts table that at least allows them to know the shard assigned to a given account, but there are many others. Fortunately, this kind of "global" data tends not to suffer volume issues in the same way that customer-associated data does, and therefore you can replicate it across all shards without causing scalability problems.

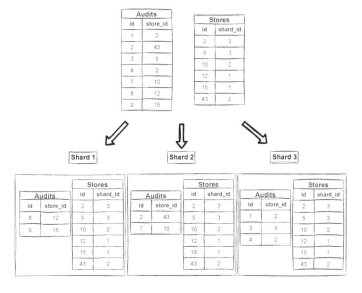

After this explanation, you may think that sharding is an obvious choice, almost something that you should implement preemptively in all your applications. That's not the case. The reality of the tech world is not the massive scale that we are discussing here; it's significantly smaller volumes of data. Moreover, sharding notably increases complexity, and complexity is the silent killer of tech businesses. Maybe that's why Rails didn't support sharding out of the box until fairly recently.

Vertical Sharding

Yes, the term "horizontal sharding" implies the existence of "vertical sharding." While vertical sharding is less useful for scalability purposes, it's still a technique that deserves to be explained.

The difference between horizontal and vertical sharding is the following: as we have seen, in horizontal sharding, we "break" the table by creating multiple tables with the same schema as the original one and dividing the rows between them. In other words, the rows are divided, but the columns stay the same. Vertical sharding is the other way around: we break the original table into multiple tables that have a part of the original schema while maintaining all the rows in all the tables. This can make sense, particularly in tables with many columns.

For example, take the films' table. In our application, it's still quite small. It only has five columns. However, imagine the following situation: in the future, we have implemented multilanguage capability, introducing two columns per language in the films' table: one holding the title (en_title', es_title, fr_title and so on) and another holding the plot (en_plot, es_plot, fr_plot...). Eventually, as more languages are introduced to the application, our 'films' table holds over 100 columns, the majority of those related to maintaining data on over 40 languages. Applying vertical sharding, we could create new tables to keep the data in each language (en_film_data, es_film_data, fr_film_data): each of those tables would require only three columns ('title', 'plot', and film_id to maintain the association with the original record on 'films'). With this, we can reduce the size of the 'films' table without reducing the amount of rows.

Implementing Sharding

It's time to bring all that theory into practice. As I just said, the Rails core team took their time to make sharding a native Rails feature. For a long while, implementing sharding in your Rails application meant supporting it yourself—a feat that required extensive ActiveRecord knowledge—or using a gem like active_record_shards,[1] rails_sharding[2] or, in more recent times, octopus.[3]

---

1.   https://github.com/zendesk/active_record_shards
2.   https://github.com/hsgubert/rails-sharding
3.   https://github.com/thiagopradi/octopus

Fortunately, this is not the case anymore. I remember the day that Eileen Uchitelle explained at RailsConf that the Rails Core team was working on adding sharding support out of the box. That was in her talk, "The Future of Rails 6: Scalable by Default."[4] One of my favorite things in the Rails community is to be able to follow the development of new features in a quite transparent way. In the case we are talking about, the PR that enabled sharding natively is "Part 4: Multi db improvements, Basic API for connection switching".[5]

After this bit of history, it's time for you to create those shiny new shards in your application. By the way, a good part of this section is based on Rails documentation,[6] so feel free to check it out. Let's modify the database configuration existing at config/database.yml. In this example, we only add shards to the development environment, but this should be enough for you to get the gist:

```
# config/database.yml
development:
  primary:
    <<: <%= "*" + ENV.fetch('DB_MODE', 'mysql') %>
    database: moviestore_development
  shard_one:
    <<: <%= "*" + ENV.fetch('DB_MODE', 'mysql') %>
    database: moviestore_development_shard_one
    migrations_paths: db/migrate_shards
  shard_two:
    <<: <%= "*" + ENV.fetch('DB_MODE', 'mysql') %>
    database: moviestore_development_shard_two
    migrations_paths: db/migrate_shards
  shard_three:
    <<: <%= "*" + ENV.fetch('DB_MODE', 'mysql') %>
    database: moviestore_development_shard_three
    migrations_paths: db/migrate_shards
```

Now, let's apply those changes to our database instance:

```
% rails db:create
```

That command you just executed has created three new databases (the shards) in your local SQL server. It has also created schema files under the db folder of your Rails application: db/shard_one_schema.rb, db/shard_two_schema.rb, and db/shard_three_schema.rb. With our databases ready, it's time to create the first model that will be stored in the sharded databases (aka *the shards*). You will start by creating your first sharded table:

4.   https://www.youtube.com/watch?v=8evXWvM4oXM
5.   https://github.com/rails/rails/pull/34052
6.   https://edgeguides.rubyonrails.org/active_record_multiple_databases.html

```
% rails g migration CreateAudits store_id:integer actor_id:integer
  actor_type:string subject_id:integer subject_type:string
  event:string --database shard_one
% rails db:migrate
```

That was a pretty typical migration generation, except for the --database shard_one parameter. You need this so the migration is created in the db/migrate_shards folder. You will also notice that in the db folder, three files have changed: db/shard_one_schema.rb, db/shard_two_schema.rb, and db/shard_three_schema.rb. This is because the migration only changes the sharded databases; meanwhile, db/schema.rb remains exactly the same. Also, you will have noticed that you specified "shard_one" as the database; in fact, you could have also put "shard_two" or "shard_three". Given that the migration path is the same, the result of executing that migration generation would also be the same.

Next, you need some setup so our brand new Audit model connects to the shards. You could just write some code specific for Audit, but it would be smarter to set up a superclass that manages this for all sharded models: ShardRecord. It will be a new model located in app/models and it should look like this:

rails-performance-book-completed/app/models/shard_record.rb
```ruby
class ShardRecord < ApplicationRecord
  self.abstract_class = true

  connects_to shards: {
    shard_one: { writing: :shard_one, reading: :shard_one },
    shard_two: { writing: :shard_two, reading: :shard_two },
    shard_three: { writing: :shard_three, reading: :shard_three }
  }
end
```

Next, you will need to change Audit so it becomes a direct subclass of ShardRecord instead of ApplicationRecord. Here, you have how Audit should look, with a couple of associations that will be useful along the way:

rails-performance-book-completed/components/audit/app/models/audit.rb
```ruby
class Audit < ShardRecord
  belongs_to :store
  belongs_to :actor, polymorphic: true
  belongs_to :subject, polymorphic: true
end
```

Now, before interacting with the data in the shards, you need to tell your application which one of the shards exactly you want to use. You can make this scoped to a block using connected_to, or you can make it in effect until the next change by using connecting_to. For example:

```
> Audit.count
[...]  No connection pool for 'ShardRecord' found.
  (ActiveRecord::ConnectionNotEstablished)
> ShardRecord.connected_to(shard: :shard_one) do
  Audit.count
end
  Audit Count (11.7ms)  SELECT COUNT(*) FROM `audits`
=> 0
> Audit.count
[...]  No connection pool for 'ShardRecord' found.
  (ActiveRecord::ConnectionNotEstablished)
> ShardRecord.connecting_to(:shard_two)
> Audit.count
  Audit Count (10.0ms)  SELECT COUNT(*) FROM `audits`
=> 0
```

It's time to put all this setup to work. Modify your application so that every time a rental gets created, an audit is also added. This is my take:

rails-performance-book-completed/app/models/rental.rb
```ruby
class Rental < ApplicationRecord
  after_create :generate_create_audit

  def self.backfill_audits
    all.each(&:generate_audit)
  end

  def generate_create_audit
    store.generate_audit('Rental creation', self, customer) unless audit
  end
end

# app/models/store.rb

class Store

  [...]

  def generate_audit(event, subject, actor)
    ActiveRecord::Base.connected_to(shard: shard) do
      Audit.create(
        event: event,
        subject: subject,
        actor: actor,
        store: self
      )
    end
  end

  def shard
    [:shard_one, :shard_two, :shard_three]
  end
end
```

The previous code adds an after_create hook to the Rental class that calls the generate_audit method on the store associated with that rental. The Store.generate_audit method just creates an audit (Audit.create(...)), but it does that on a block in which the associated database is a shard. This is what the call to ActiveRecord::Base.connected_to does. Finally, the shard is selected in a simple way that you can observe in the method Store.shard: it's just a mod on the store ID. This means that the audits of the store with ID 1 will end up in shard_two, the ones of ID 2 in shard_three, the ones of ID 3 in shard_one, the ones of ID 4 again in shard_two...and so on. This strategy is called modular hashing, and despite its simplicity, it can be quite powerful, particularly if the groups by which you are dividing have a somewhat similar amount of records. Before moving on to the next point, backfill audits for all existing rentals. In my proposed solution, there is a method Rental.backfill_audits. If you add this method to your implementation and call it from the Rails console, you will get all the audits you need.

Next, expose your brand-new audits with a new API endpoint. The path should include the store_id—something like api/v1/stores/:store_id/audits. You will need to create a new controller (app/controllers/api/v1/audits_controller.rb) and add the route to config/routes.rb.

rails-performance-book-completed/components/audit/app/controllers/api/v1/audits_controller.rb
```ruby
class Api::V1::AuditsController < ApplicationController
  def index
    store = Store.find(params[:store_id])
    audits = Audit.where(store_id: params[:store_id])
    render json: audits.all.map do |store|
      Api::V1::AuditPresenter.new(store).to_json
    end
  end
end
```

rails-performance-book-completed/config/routes.rb
```ruby
  namespace :api do
    namespace :v1 do
      resources :stores, only: [:show] do
        resources :audits, only: [:index]
      end
    end
  end
end
```

```ruby
# app/presenters/api/v1/audit_presenter.rb

class Api::V1::AuditPresenter < Api::V1::Presenter
  def to_json
    {
      id: resource.id,
      created_at: resource.created_at,
      event: resource.event,
      store_id: resource.id
    }
  end
end
```

Now, you can hit api/v1/stores/1/audits and you should get a list of audits, coming not from the main database but from the sharded one.

Supporting Non-Sharded Features

The use case you just experienced is a completely valid one. However, many applications—particularly in the B2B space—are able to take sharding up a notch and have most, if not all, their data sharded. This is not possible (or is at least much harder) in your application because you built some features that fetch data across shards. Users can rent films from different stores; while you could still build a system that would work with those requirements, we have some endpoints that offer data across stores. Those endpoints are:

- /api/v1/customers/:id/rentals: This endpoint exposes all the rentals of a particular customer in all the stores. In the current data model, the only way to check from which store a customer has rented a film is to fetch from the rentals table itself. This would mean that we would need to fetch data from each and every shard. This can get even worse if we want the endpoint to support sorting; we would need to sort the rentals in memory.

- /api/v1/customers/:id/timeline: This endpoint exposes the rentals for all the customers followed by the customer referenced by :id. The same difficulties we just described for the previous endpoint also apply to this one.

These issues show how intertwined scalable architecture and feature design are. Once a feature is released, dropping functionality (aka, breaking it) will be way more traumatic. When introducing sharding, some functionalities can be more or less restored. For example, api/v1/customers/:id/rentals could give place to api/v1/customers/:id/stores/:store_id/rentals, thereby limiting queries to the shard where the store with ID :store_id is found. The timeline feature, though, is far harder and would probably require adding new storage in which data from different shards can be kept. The sharded databases can stay as the source of truth, but data will need to be duplicated to support non-sharded functionalities.

Selecting Shards Based on Subdomain

A very common pattern in B2B is to offer customers their own subdomain. This is good for customers, as they get a more tailored feel. But, most importantly, it's useful for the application to detect to which shard it needs to connect. This switch can happen in the middleware before the controller action gets executed. The middleware is the layer of software that is located between the web server and the Rails application, processing both requests from the client to the server and responses from the server to the client. It's the ideal layer to run logic that is common for all requests (or responses) going into or out of the Rails application.

Rails brings automatic database connection switching out of the box, but unfortunately, it doesn't support our use case. It switches all connections to the shards, and we want to keep connected to both the primary database (where most of our tables are located) and the shards (where we find the audits table). You can read more about it in the Rails 7 documentation.[7] In any case, Rails enables you to set up your own customized connection switch in the middleware. The idea is quite simple: to detect if the request is going to execute a "sharded" action, and if so, call the action inside of a connected_to block. This can be a little bit harder if you are not familiar with the syntax of Rails middleware. This is how your middleware should look:

rails-performance-book-completed/app/middleware/shard_switcher.rb
```ruby
module Middleware
  class ShardSwitcher
    def initialize(app)
      @app = app
    end

    def call(env)
      request = Rack::Request.new(env)
      request.path =~ /.*stores\/(\d+).*/
      store_id = $1

      if store_id
        store = Store.find(store_id.to_i)
        ShardRecord.connected_to(shard: store.shard) do
          @app.call(env)
        end
      else
        @app.call(env)
      end
    end
  end
end
```

---

7. https://guides.rubyonrails.org/v7.2/active_record_multiple_databases.html

Look at the Middleware::ShardSwitcher.call method. This method checks if the request path includes a pattern like stores/(number). If that's the case, it captures the number since it's the ID of the store we want to operate with. After that, it loads the selected store from the database, and it connects to the shard associated with that store with ShardRecord.connected_to.

You will also need to add the middleware to config/application.rb, so this logic is executed with every incoming request to your Rails application:

rails-performance-book-completed/config/application.rb
```
require_relative '../app/middleware/shard_switcher'
module Moviestore
  class Application < Rails::Application

    config.middleware.use Middleware::ShardSwitcher

  end
end
```

You are done. Now you can remove those ugly connected_to calls from AuditsController. You have successfully abstracted the shard switch outside of the controller action, which is an extremely important (I may even say *basic*) refactor on any Rails application using sharding.

The Cost of Sharding

In the process of getting this book to the readers, the text was reviewed by some fellow engineers—professionals whom I deeply respect. One of them gave me some pretty brutal feedback about the section you have just read: to remove it. His reasoning was that sharding is a technique that comes with a heavy penalty: the vast majority of projects do not need it, and many software engineers out there may shoot themselves in the foot by implementing it in their projects.

My reviewer is right in his observation: the cost of adding sharding to a project can be staggering. By "cost," I am not talking about money, but about the increase in complexity. Doing something as simple as running some analytics will be way harder, as you will need to harmonize the process through all the shards. You will need to calculate the results for all shards and then add them up. It's probable that you may also need to move accounts from shard to shard, for example, if one shard becomes imbalanced (with significantly more data than the average). This can also be quite complicated. Moreover, if none of your instances can access all the shards at the same time because data is segregated by region (for example, U.S. instances cannot access data in the EU and vice versa), the complexity of manipulating sharded data increases even more.

And yet, I decided to keep this section in the book anyway. One thing I have always loved about Ruby is how it gives so much power to developers, even if it implies that some will make mistakes; metaprogramming is a fantastic example of this. I can guarantee that, for many companies, sharding is one of the key decisions that allowed them to scale. It is a steep price, but one worth paying sometimes.

Improving Your Response Time with Asynchronous Processing

Feature bloat is a common fate for applications that have been around for a while; this may be even more common for Rails applications, given the speed of development that Rails provides to its users. Even if the product has not added new *features* for the customers, it's probable that the application complexity has increased in other ways. Take the following diagram as an example: years ago, you had a simple function (writeData()) that performed something simple (writeA()). Time passed, and complexity piled up; now, the same action does writeB(), writeC(), writeD(), writeE(), and writeF(). All those actions can be whatever: recalculating statistics, emitting events, generating derived data, sending emails, or anything that makes sense in the domain of the application.

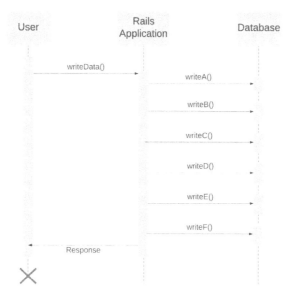

From a product perspective, this may be fine and dandy, but from a performance perspective, it may not. Of course, all those new actions could be very important, and they may be also extremely optimized so they are executed as fast as possible. Nevertheless, writeData() is way slower than it used to be when it only executed writeA(). This can be particularly problematic if it ends up affecting the user experience (think a slow endpoint).

What to do? Well, even if you have decided that everything that this function does is completely necessary, do you really need it to happen synchronously with its primary action? Could you perform writeB(), writeC(), and so on asynchronously? Of course, you may decide that the application needs synchronicity. For example, you may decide that making an API call needs to be performed before the SQL transaction of a database change gets committed so that the change can be canceled if the API call fails. However, making some actions asynchronous can make your function look like this:

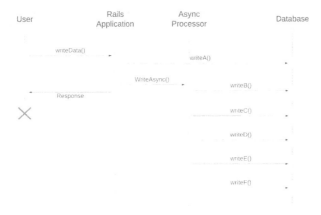

In this section, we'll be moving part of the logic of an endpoint to an asynchronous processor.

Before moving on to the implementation, I'd like to share with you my experience breaking down actions into multiple asynchronous processes. In my opinion, software engineers start their careers with a very idealized view of how an application should run, and this view includes total synchronicity. As one gets experience, the necessity of accepting certain trade-offs becomes apparent. Still, one concern remains: how will users react to the effects of their actions becoming asynchronous? My advice is to be deeply empathic to your users and respect their intelligence. Your users will expect the primary change that they executed to take place immediately (at least to them; "read your own write" can be a solution here), but the effects of their actions can happen asynchronously. Having clear targets (this effect will take place in under a second 99.99 percent of the time) is important. Having a clear product direction is even more important.

Designing a system that is asynchronous from the start is way easier than transitioning a synchronous system to being asynchronous.

Processing Asynchronously with Background Jobs

Rails 4.2 included a new piece of the *Active* ecosystem: ActiveJob.

For engineers who had been using Rails for a while, this action by the Rails core team was a nod to the reality that many, many Rails teams around the world were already using asynchronous jobs. Maybe this is why ActiveJob is agnostic on the precise job runner you use. From the Rails documentation:[8]

> ActiveJob is a framework for declaring jobs and making them run on a variety of queuing backends. The main point is to ensure that all Rails apps will have a job infrastructure in place. We can then have framework features and other gems built on top of that without having to worry about API differences between various job runners, such as Delayed Job and Resque. Picking your queuing backend becomes more of an operational concern, then. And you'll be able to switch between them without having to rewrite your jobs.

In other words, ActiveJob offers us a common API for background jobs. Still, the architecture behind ActiveJob is completely customizable. There are some quite popular gems at your disposal. For example, resque,[9] Delayed::Job,[10] or bunny.[11] However, the most used and the one that we are going to employ in this exercise is sidekiq.[12] Apart from that, in Rails 8, solid_queue[13] was introduced; this is the new default for running background jobs in Rails. After implementing our job queue with Sidekiq, we will do the same with Solid Queue so you can appreciate their differences and pick the solution that better fits your needs.

Setting Up ActiveJob and Sidekiq

You can start off by adding Sidekiq to your application. As always, add the gem to your Gemfile:

rails-performance-book-completed/Gemfile
```
gem "sidekiq"
```

For this section, we are going to use ActiveJob. Remember, you can also use Sidekiq *solo*. Doing so will make sense if you want to gain a tiny bit

---

8.   https://guides.rubyonrails.org/active_job_basics.html
9.   https://github.com/resque/resque
10. https://github.com/collectiveidea/delayed_job
11. https://github.com/ruby-amqp/bunny
12. https://github.com/sidekiq/sidekiq
13. https://github.com/rails/solid_queue

of performance and if you are sure that you will not switch to another background job management system in the future. To use ActiveJob, you need to declare which is your queue adapter: in our case, sidekiq. We are going to try this on development, so you have to add the following to config/environments/development.rb:

```
# config/environments/development.rb

Rails.application.configure do
  [...]
  config.active_job.queue_adapter = :sidekiq
  [...]
end
```

Sidekiq will execute jobs by running a new instance of your application. This means that just calling rails server will not initiate sidekiq. For that, you will need an instance that will run Sidekiq alone without listening to HTTP requests. To initiate that instance, just run bundle exec sidekiq in the console.

```
% bundle exec sidekiq

                m,
               `$b
       .ss,   $$:          .,d$
      `$$P,d$P'       .,md$P"'
       ,$$$$$b/md$$$P^'
     .d$$$$$$/$$$P'
     $$^'  `"/$$$'      ____  _     _        _             _
     $:      ',$$:     / ___|(_) __| | ___  | | _ (_) __ _
     `b      :$$       \___ \| |/ _` |/ _ \ | |/ / | |/ _` |
             $$:        ___) | | (_| |  __/ |   <| | | (_| |
             $$        |____/|_|\__,_|\___|_|\_\_|_|\__, |
            .d$$                                       |_|

2024-03-16T12:15:37.088Z pid=21359 tid=d77 INFO:
  Booted Rails 7.1.3.4 application in development environment
2024-03-16T12:15:37.088Z pid=21359 tid=d77 INFO:
  Running in ruby 3.3.4 (2024-07-09 revision be1089c8ec) [arm64-darwin22]
2024-03-16T12:15:37.088Z pid=21359 tid=d77 INFO:
  See LICENSE and the LGPL-3.0 for licensing details.
2024-03-16T12:15:37.088Z pid=21359 tid=d77 INFO:
  Upgrade to Sidekiq Pro for more features and support: https://sidekiq.org
2024-03-16T12:15:37.088Z pid=21359 tid=d77
  INFO: Sidekiq 7.2.2 connecting to Redis with options
  {:size=>10, :pool_name=>"internal", :url=>nil}
2024-03-16T12:15:37.091Z pid=21359 tid=d77 INFO:
  Sidekiq 7.2.2 connecting to Redis with options
  {:size=>5, :pool_name=>"default", :url=>nil}
2024-03-16T12:15:37.091Z pid=21359 tid=d77 INFO:
  Starting processing, hit Ctrl-C to stop
```

Creating Your First Asynchronous Job

It's time for you to put this new pipeline to work. In this case, you are not going to refactor a piece of existing logic; you are going to write a new feature. The feature will be to recalculate some stats about our customers every time they perform certain actions. Fret not—you are going to start very small, and almost everything is ready for you to add it. The application already has a CustomerStatsProfile with its corresponding table in the database. Its structure is incredibly simple: a customer_id integer to column to associate the object with a customer and a text column named data to store the stats in whatever format you decide.

Initially, the requirement is that the system needs a way to check the number of rentals per language that every customer has made. We could calculate this on the fly with some SQL queries, but we want to materialize this counting into the associated CustomerStatsProfile. This calculation needs to be re-executed every time that a new rental is created. Moreover, it is expected that the number of stats will increase with time. You need to design this in a way that the stats calculations don't increase the latency of whatever triggered the recalculation. In other words, you need to move this calculation to a background job.

In my experience, it can make sense to first write the background job as synchronous logic and then move it to the job. It makes that logic much easier to test. Let's do exactly that! You can start by adding a method in CustomerStatsProfile that makes that calculation. After that, add an after_save hook to Rental to trigger the recalculation. It should look something like this:

```
rails-performance-book-completed/app/models/customer_stats_profile.rb
class CustomerStatsProfile < ApplicationRecord
  serialize :data
  belongs_to :customer

  def recalculate!
    update_attribute(
      :data,
      rentals_by_language: customer.rentals.includes(:film)
        .group(:language_id).count(:id)
    )
  end
end

class Rental < ApplicationRecord
  after_save :recalculate_customer_stats_profile
  [...]

  private
```

```ruby
  def recalculate_customer_stats_profile
    CustomerStatsProfile.find_or_create_by(customer_id: customer_id)
      .recalculate!
  end

  [...]
end
```

In the example, I added an after_save hook (recalculate_customer_stats_profile) that gets the CustomerStatsProfile associated with the customer that made the rental (or creates a new one if it doesn't exist yet). Then, it calls recalculate!. That method uses some ActiveRecord syntactic sugar, so our SQL database makes the whole work for us. In particular, the .group(:language_id).count(:id) groups the films from the rentals from the user by language id and then counts them.

The "only" issue left is…the actual reason why you are reading this—to make the call to recalculate! asynchronous. Once again, Rails provides an easy-to-use platform to write our code: just execute rails generate job RecalculateCustomerStatsProfile and you will have a new file in app/jobs/recalculate_customer_stats_profile_job.rb. It will have an empty perform method. Fill that method with logic that, given the ID of a customer, recalculates the corresponding CustomerStatsProfile—something like this:

```ruby
# app/jobs/recalculate_customer_stats_profile_job.rb

class RecalculateCustomerStatsProfileJob < ApplicationJob
  queue_as :default

  def perform(customer_id)
    CustomerStatsProfile.find_or_create_by(customer_id: customer_id)
      .recalculate!
  end
end
```

Now, you need to change that after_save hook so it enqueues the job instead of running the recalculation synchronously. ActiveJob offers you two ways of executing a job: perform will run the job right away, while perform_later will put the job into the queue from where it will be eventually picked up by the Rails process and executed. Let's go with perform_later:

```ruby
rails-performance-book-completed/app/models/rental.rb
class Rental < ApplicationRecord
  after_save :recalculate_customer_stats_profile

  def recalculate_customer_stats_profile
    RecalculateCustomerStatsProfileJob.perform_later(customer_id)
  end
end
```

This will work. As a last step, let's try this out. Create a new rental using the Rails console. You will see some new lines logging the enqueueing of your job:

```
> Rental.create(customer: Customer.last, inventory: Inventory.first)
[...]
2024-03-24T21:51:31.756Z pid=46787 tid=wwn INFO:
  Sidekiq 7.2.2 connecting to Redis with options
  {:size=>10, :pool_name=>"internal", :url=>nil}
Enqueued RecalculateCustomerStatsProfileJob
  (Job ID: a0855cf0-580d-4322-a4a5-515ae3aaba74)
  to Sidekiq(default) with arguments: 3010
```

Once you have done that, check what happened in the process that is running Sidekiq:

```
2024-03-24T21:58:57.442Z pid=47051 tid=1bfv
  class=RecalculateCustomerStatsProfileJob
  jid=784afb3a35ed635e2bef6825 INFO: start
2024-03-24T21:58:57.464Z pid=47051 tid=1bfv
  class=RecalculateCustomerStatsProfileJob
  jid=784afb3a35ed635e2bef6825
  INFO: Performing RecalculateCustomerStatsProfileJob
  (Job ID: 85cc8a11-b916-4e5c-ba17-5b1ee8ce124e) from Sidekiq(default)
  enqueued at 2024-03-24T21:58:57Z with arguments: 3010
2024-03-24T21:58:57.521Z pid=47051 tid=1bfv
  class=RecalculateCustomerStatsProfileJob
  jid=784afb3a35ed635e2bef6825
  INFO: Performed RecalculateCustomerStatsProfileJob
  (Job ID: 85cc8a11-b916-4e5c-ba17-5b1ee8ce124e)
  from Sidekiq(default) in 56.76ms
2024-03-24T21:58:57.521Z pid=47051 tid=1bfv
  class=RecalculateCustomerStatsProfileJob
  jid=784afb3a35ed635e2bef6825 elapsed=0.079 INFO: done
```

Congratulations, you have successfully detached part of the logic of rental.save. Believe it or not, the performance wins that you can achieve through this technique are incalculable. If you want to know more, I recommend you read the book *Ruby on Rails Background Jobs with Sidekiq*[14] by David Bryant Copeland, also published by Pragmatic Bookshelf.

---

14. https://pragprog.com/titles/dcsidekiq/ruby-on-rails-background-jobs-with-sidekiq/

ActiveJob, Sidekiq, and Performance

While ActiveJob offers us a common API to run background jobs with whichever system we desire, it may very well be that this could come with a loss on the performance side. According to the Sidekiq README, using ActiveJob will "add a notable amount of CPU overhead due to argument deserialization and callbacks." In my opinion, the effect of this will be negligible if your jobs are processing stuff "heavy" enough. If your architecture has brought you to a place where you have a very high number of jobs running extremely small tasks, using Sidekiq directly without the ActiveJob wrapper could be an option to earn a little bit of speed. The change shouldn't be very hard, as Sidekiq and ActiveJob APIs are quite similar.

Setting Job Priorities and Queues

Once you start breaking down the logic that your application executes into chunks that can be processed asynchronously, you will realize that not all tasks are created equal. Even similar ones! Let's use an example of a task typically processed asynchronously: sending emails. You probably do not care much if an email summarizing the actions of a user during a given year is sent 30 minutes after the job was originally enqueued. On the other hand, if the email that will allow a user to register into your application takes 30 minutes to be sent, that is a big problem since the user will most probably not be engaged anymore. You obviously want to give more priority to the latter.

The solution to this problem is dividing the job into different priorities; each priority is assigned a different queue. When you configure the consumers that will actually perform the jobs, you can add more consumers to the high-priority jobs so they are executed as soon as possible. Meanwhile, the low-priority queue can have fewer consumers, given that they can take longer to execute without any issues. Alternatively, you can have a common pool of consumers but have them fetching jobs more frequently. This is a very important feature for background job processing, and both ActiveJob and Sidekiq support using queues. On the "enqueueing" side, you have probably noticed that the job you created already declared its queue in the second line:

```
# app/jobs/recalculate_customer_stats_profile_job.rb

class RecalculateCustomerStatsProfileJob < ApplicationJob
  queue_as :default
```

:default is the, well, default name for queues in Sidekiq. You are going to give up that simple naming and establish two clearly named queues: :low_priority and :high_priority. Changing the queue to which your job is assigned is very simple:

```
rails-performance-book-completed/app/jobs/recalculate_customer_stats_profile_job.rb
class RecalculateCustomerStatsProfileJob < ApplicationJob
  queue_as :low_priority

  def perform(customer_id)
    CustomerStatsProfile.find_or_create_by(customer_id: customer_id)
      .recalculate!
  end
end
```

That's it for the "enqueueing" side, now for the processing one. You are going to modify Sidekiq's configuration. Sidekiq's configuration is stored in a YAML file in config/sidekiq.yml. However, Sidekiq, by default, doesn't create a file; you will need to do it yourself if you want to use something different from the out-of-the-box configuration, which for queues will mean that only jobs in the default queue will be performed. Not a problem. Create the file with the following content:

```
# config/sidekiq.yml

:queues:
  - [high_priority, 3]
  - [default, 2]
  - [low_priority, 1]
```

With this, you just set up a configuration with weighted queues. A task in the default queue will have twice the chance of being picked up as one in the low_priority queue. Meanwhile, a job in the high_priority one will have three times the chance.

Monitoring Sidekiq Processing

Being able to monitor the state of your job queues is basic to understanding the state of your system. You can set up your own mechanisms to perform that check-up, but Sidekiq offers you a nice web UI to control how your asynchronous jobs are being executed. I personally find it incredibly useful, particularly when in an environment short on resources, like most startups are.

Adding this web UI to your application is quite simple. Just add the following lines to the top of your config/routes.rb:

rails-performance-book-completed/config/routes.rb

```
require 'sidekiq/web'

Rails.application.routes.draw do
  mount Sidekiq::Web => "/sidekiq"
end
```

You can now access the Sidekiq web UI for your application at http://local-host:3000/sidekiq:

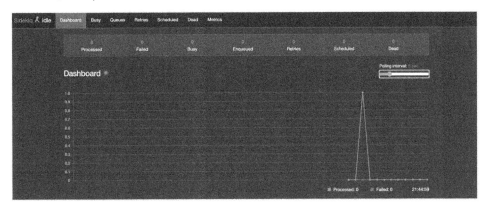

Remember that, by default, the web UI will have no authentication; this means that it will be accessible to everyone. You will need to control access with it—maybe in the routes.rb file itself—using whatever authentication system you choose. Finally, remember that you can learn more about this in Sidekiq's documentation.[15]

Using Solid Queue

In 2024, Solid Queue was released[16] as the default queuing back end for ActiveJob. Following the same philosophy as Solid Cache, it proposes to replace in-memory storage (like Redis) with using disk via the database. This makes the system simpler, as one doesn't need a separate queueing system and can even use the same database that powers the Rails application itself. Another advantage of Solid Queue is that it's persistent by default, while Sidekiq will depend on Redis configuration for durability guarantees. On the other hand, Solid Queue has a disadvantage, something similar to what happened with Solid Cache; performance-wise, Redis is still a faster option. I personally find Solid Queue's trade-off way more acceptable than Solid Cache's: the storage system for a queueing system is less impactful on its performance than the whole caching layer. Moreover, in

15. https://github.com/sidekiq/sidekiq/wiki/Monitoring
16. https://dev.37signals.com/solid-queue-v1-0/

asynchronous processing, performance can be less crucial than when processing a synchronous request.

Setting Up Solid Queue

In this section, we will move the Sidekiq implementation we just completed to Solid Queue while commenting on the differences between APIs. Here, the existence of ActiveJob shows its usefulness. Having that shared abstraction makes the migration from Sidekiq to Solid Queue way easier.

You can start by replacing the ActiveJob Queue Adapter in the configuration:

rails-performance-book-completed/config/environments/development.rb
```
# config.active_job.queue_adapter = :sidekiq
config.active_job.queue_adapter = :solid_queue
config.solid_queue.connects_to = { database: { writing: :queue } }
```

Next, you need to run Solid Queue itself so the jobs get executed. You can do so by just running bin/jobs. You can also run it together with Puma. Just add the following to config/puma.rb:

rails-performance-book-completed/config/puma.rb
```
plugin :solid_queue if ENV["SOLID_QUEUE_IN_PUMA"] || Rails.env.development?
```

With this, you already have the basic setup for Solid Queue ready. Trigger a job execution by creating a new rental and then check your server log. You should see how the job has been executed and how it has been marked as completed in the queue database:

```
[ActiveJob] [RecalculateCustomerStatsProfileJob]
  [86557581-68ca-463d-806b-cbafb311dfbe]
  Performed RecalculateCustomerStatsProfileJob
  (Job ID: 86557581-68ca-463d-806b-cbafb311dfbe)
  from SolidQueue(low_priority) in 47.14ms

[...]

SolidQueue::Job Update (1.4ms)
  UPDATE `solid_queue_jobs`
  SET `solid_queue_jobs`.`updated_at` = '2025-02-16 15:56:00.459568',
  `solid_queue_jobs`.`finished_at` = '2025-02-16 15:56:00.459568'
  WHERE `solid_queue_jobs`.`id` = 1
  SolidQueue::ClaimedExecution Destroy (0.3ms)
  DELETE FROM `solid_queue_claimed_executions`
  WHERE `solid_queue_claimed_executions`.`id` = 1
```

Scheduling Recurring Tasks with Solid Queue

One of my favorite features of Solid Queue is that it supports scheduled tasks out of the box. You can configure those jobs at config/recurring.yml. The example provided by default is quite complete and explanatory, so I will use it to show you how you can set up your own jobs:

```
rails-performance-book-completed/config/recurring.yml
# production:
#   periodic_cleanup:
#     class: CleanSoftDeletedRecordsJob
#     queue: background
#     args: [ 1000, { batch_size: 500 } ]
#     schedule: every hour
#   periodic_command:
#     command: "SoftDeletedRecord.due.delete_all"
#     priority: 2
#     schedule: at 5am every day
```

The top key is the environment in which the jobs are being configured: in the example, production. If you want to test it in your dev environment, change this to development. The second-level key is the value that will identify the task internally. In the prior example, there are two tasks: periodic_cleanup and periodic_command. On the third level, you finally get to the configuration of the task itself. There are two ways to configure a task:

- As a job class: To configure a task like this, you will need to add two keys: class and args. class should correspond to an ActiveJob class in the applications; args are the arguments passed to the perform method in that job.

- As a command: In this case, you set up a command key: the value is Ruby code that will be executed by Solid Queue. This is the case of periodic_command in the example.

Finally, both types of tasks share some attributes:

- schedule: This key defines how often the task will be executed. This parameter accepts any value that can be parsed by fugit,[17] including very natural-language-looking values like "at 5 a.m. every day."

- queue: The queue to which the task will be added

- priority: The priority for execution of the task inside of a queue, expressed as a number. The smaller the value, the higher the priority.

How queues are managed is defined in Solid Queue's configuration. Let's take a look at it.

---

17. https://github.com/floraison/fugit

Configuring Solid Queue

You can check Solid Queue's default configuration at config/queue.yml. This is how it looks:

rails-performance-book/config/recurring.yml
```
# production:
#   periodic_cleanup:
#     class: CleanSoftDeletedRecordsJob
#     queue: background
#     args: [ 1000, { batch_size: 500 } ]
#     schedule: every hour
#   periodic_command:
#     command: "SoftDeletedRecord.due.delete_all"
#     priority: 2
#     schedule: at 5am every day
```

The configuration is divided into two parts: dispatchers and workers. Dispatchers are in charge of scheduled tasks, moving them from "scheduled execution" to "ready for execution." Workers are in charge of actually executing the tasks. There are two other kinds of actors that do not appear in this configuration: the scheduler (that manages recurring tasks) and the supervisor (that orchestrates both workers and dispatchers).

The most important options are:

- polling_interval: How often (in seconds) will both workers or dispatchers check if there are new jobs

- batch_size: How many jobs are dispatched by the dispatcher at once. Only dispatchers have this option.

- threads: The max size of the thread pool running a specific worker. Only workers have this option. The default is 3; having less than three will not work, as workers require two threads for maintenance issues (polling and heartbeat) and at least one to execute the tasks.

- processes: The number of processes forked to run a specific worker. Only workers have this option.

- queues: The queues from which the worker being configured will pick jobs. You can pass a specific queue (low_priority), all of them (*), or an array of queues ([high_priority, low_priority]). If you set up an array, the worker will prioritize all the jobs of the first queue before moving on to jobs of subsequent queues; in my experience, configuring job priority like this can be problematic, as some jobs may not get ever executed. To summarize, the following configuration sets up three processes for high_priority tasks and one for low_priority:

rails-performance-book-completed/config/recurring.yml
```
# production:
#   periodic_cleanup:
#     class: CleanSoftDeletedRecordsJob
#     queue: background
#     args: [ 1000, { batch_size: 500 } ]
#     schedule: every hour
#   periodic_command:
#     command: "SoftDeletedRecord.due.delete_all"
#     priority: 2
#     schedule: at 5am every day
```

You can check more in the Solid Queue README, particularly in the section dedicated to the configuration.[18] You will find more options to configure dispatchers and workers there.

Getting Started with Event-Driven Microservice Architectures

It is not a big secret that microservice architectures have gained a lot of traction in the last decade. This is typically seen as bad news for the Ruby community and, more specifically, for Ruby on Rails adoption. Rails is one of the best tools in the market to build a web application or an API in the form of a monolith. In my opinion, the continued appeal of Rails is because it empowers developers to achieve a lot with very little—the power of "convention over configuration." A monolithic architecture is also part of this vision of simplifying systems.

However, lately, it seems that the engineering community has become addicted to unjustified complexity. During the latter half of the 2010s, as the tech market made more and more money available to founders—particularly in the United States—starting a tech project with an architecture that established tens of microservices from the get-go became a possibility. It's not a wise decision if you ask me. There is a natural growth progression, a process of adaptation, for both businesses and systems, something that I believe has been ignored in the last few years. My point of view is quite similar to the one expressed by Jason Warner, the CTO of GitHub, in an X thread in 2022:[19] "I'm convinced that one of the biggest architectural mistakes of the past decade was going full microservice. On a spectrum of monolith to microservices, I suggest the following: Monolith > apps > services > microservices [...] If you are reading this at a 5-50 person company...just stick with a monolith. Trust me."

18. https://github.com/rails/solid_queue?tab=readme-ov-file#configuration
19. https://twitter.com/jasoncwarner/status/1592227285024636928

Staying with a monolith for as long as possible (and no longer) is a good idea. A small organization with a limited business scope and a few engineers very rarely makes a good decision if they start with tens of microservices. The complexity can crush the business. But still, this leaves a clear path in which microservices work fantastically well: projects that need to scale by business logic scope and/or volume of work.

In this section, we are going to talk about microservices and, particularly, about how microservices can communicate with each other through events. For that, you are going to first write a producer and a consumer in your Rails monolith; later, you will write a tiny service that will feed from the events coming from the Rails application.

Learning How Microservices Communicate with Each Other

Before plunging into building, let's talk a bit about the different methods in which microservices can communicate. There are three main ways for microservices to "talk":

- Synchronous HTTP requests
- Asynchronous messaging
- Event-driven architecture

At this point, you should be more than familiar with the first one. It typically involves a service calling another using a REST API. It's the most common and the best way if you need a synchronous response. For example, if you have an authentication service, you will need to get the identity of the user that originated the interaction before allowing access to data.

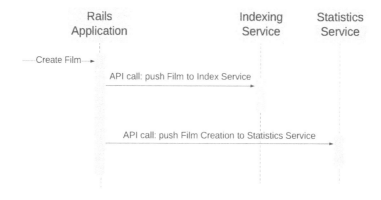

Synchronous HTTP requests

The other two, asynchronous messaging and event-driven architecture, are tightly connected. Both allow services that talk to each other in an asynchronous way, avoiding API calls. In asynchronous messaging, microservices use message brokers—like Apache Kafka—to communicate via message queues. Those messages can be read by the receiving service at any point, making the communication asynchronous. An event-driven architecture takes that concept and replaces the idea of one service communicating explicitly with another through event sourcing. Services will not be producing messages that explicitly tell another what to do but just create events, messages that encapsulate significant changes in the system.

Asynchronous Messaging

Event-Driven Architecture

Let's illustrate this with an example. Imagine that you have multiple services that need to do something every time a new film is created in your Rails application. With asynchronous messaging, you would emit a different message for each service: "Add to Elastic Search Cluster" for the Indexing Service, "Recalculate statistics" for the Statistics Service, and so on. With an event-driven architecture, the Rails application would only produce one message (the log-like event). All services subscribed to that topic will be able to consume that event and decide if they need to do something. Of course, there are drawbacks to using an event-driven architecture. The most obvious for me is the increased complexity. Processes that previously happened in one application and were recorded in one database on one transaction are now spread across many stakeholders; debugging, in particular, can become challenging. Tracing why anything happens in an event-based system can be quite hard! Other drawbacks are related to the nitty-gritty of the design. In many cases, services will need different data to perform their actions. With customized messages, you can add the required data to each service. With events, you may have to add data that will not be useful for the vast majority of cases, or alternatively, not add it and provide the service with another way to access that data. As you can see, software engineering is a game of trade-offs.

Setting Up Kafka and Karafka

Let's start by running Kafka on your machine. I decided not to add the installation of Kafka to the setup chapter because you will be only using Kafka in this section. I did this because you are going to run Kafka in a bit of a different way: using a Docker container. Of course, this means that you need to have Docker running on your machine. If you don't have it, I recommend you take a look at the Docker docs.[20]

Once you have Docker running, you need to run the Docker image provided by the Karafka team:

```
% git clone git@github.com:karafka/karafka.git
% cd karafka
% docker-compose up
```

Done. Next, you are going to add Karafka[21] to your application. Karafka is a very feature-rich library for using Kafka with Ruby. There are other options in the Ruby space, like racecar, created by Daniel Schierbeck. Still, Karafka offers some features out of the box that can be very useful when running with limited engineering resources.

Add karafka to your Gemfile, and then run bundle install and bundle exec karafka install from the terminal. This will result in the creation of a few files, including karafka.rb (Karafka's configuration) and the app/consumers folder, in which you

---

20. https://docs.docker.com/desktop/
21. https://github.com/karafka/karafka

will find ApplicationConsumer—the superclass for all your consumers—and ExampleConsumer—self-explanatory.

Producing and Consuming Messages

Now, it's time to use Karafka to build something. I do not want to increase the complexity of the project, so you are not going to build a new feature. Instead, you are going to move the customer stats feature from running on background jobs to using consumers. In this case, the consumer will be located in the same Rails application that produced the consumed message; however, it could be in a different application. What you build here points to the construction in the future of a stats service with its own database that could update in real time via Kafka messages.

Start by adding a new hook that produces a Kafka message every time that a rental is saved. Use Karafka's producer class for it. You will need to specify the topic in which the message will be written and the payload (the message itself). My take looks like this:

```
rails-performance-book-completed/app/models/rental.rb
class Rental < ApplicationRecord
  after_save :produce_kafka_message

  private

  def produce_kafka_message
    Karafka.producer.produce_sync(
      topic: 'rentals',
      payload: {
        rental: Api::V1::RentalPresenter.new(self).as_json
      }.to_json
    )
  end
end
```

If you test this via the console, you will get the following message:

```
[23d45f0fdc39] Sync producing of a message
  to 'rentals' topic took 17.41899999976158 ms
```

Producing messages wasn't very hard, and consuming them is not going to be much harder. Creating a new consumer is very simple, you just need to create a subclass of ApplicationConsumer and define a consume method. This new class will have access to the messages consumed via a messages attribute. Now, create a RentalsConsumer in app/consumers/rentals_consumer.rb. Its consume method should call CustomerStatsProfile#recalculate!.

```ruby
# app/consumers/rentals_consumer.rb

class RentalsConsumer < ApplicationConsumer
  def consume
    messages.each do |message|
      customer_id = message.payload.dig("rental", "resource", "customer_id")
      CustomerStatsProfile
        .find_or_create_by(customer_id: customer_id).recalculate!
    end
  end
end
```

Finally, you will need to declare the connection between RentalsConsumer and the rentals topic. You can do so in Karafka's configuration, in karafka.rb:

```ruby
# karafka.rb

class KarafkaApp < Karafka::App
  [...]

  routes.draw do
    [...]

    topic :rentals do
      consumer RentalsConsumer
    end
  end
end
```

With everything set up, you can start the Karafka server so your new consumer can start working. You can do so by opening a new terminal and running bundle exec karafka server. You will be able to see how the topic is polled and messages are consumed, triggering whichever logic you wrote in the consume method:

```
% bundle exec karafka server

@@@                                        @@@@@  @@@
@@@                                        @@@    @@@
@@@   @@@    @@@@@@@@@   @@@ @@@   @@@@@@@@@ @@@@@@@@@  @@@  @@@@   @@@@@@@@@
@@@@@@       @@@    @@@  @@@@@     @@@   @@@   @@@     @@@@@@@  @@@    @@@
@@@@@@@      @@@    @@@  @@@    @@@@   @@@   @@@     @@@@@@@  @@@    @@@
@@@  @@@@    @@@@@@@@@@   @@@       @@@@@@@@@@   @@@     @@@  @@@@  @@@@@@@@@

Upgrade to Karafka Pro for more features and support: https://karafka.io
Running in ruby 3.1.2p20 (2022-04-12 revision 4491bb740a) [arm64-darwin21]
Running Karafka 2.3.3 server
See LICENSE and the LGPL-3.0 for licensing details
[3e2df03d68bd] Polling messages...
[3e2df03d68bd] Polled 0 messages in 1005.6029999926686ms
[3e2df03d68bd] Polling messages...
[3e2df03d68bd] Polled 0 messages in 1005.1280000060797ms
[3e2df03d68bd] Polling messages...
```

```
[3e2df03d68bd] Polled 1 messages in 956.7039999961853ms
[6c7231368d80] Consume job for RentalsConsumer on rentals/0 started
  CustomerStatsProfile Load (0.6ms)  SELECT `customer_stats_profiles`.*
    FROM `customer_stats_profiles`
    WHERE `customer_stats_profiles`.`customer_id` = 1010 LIMIT 1
    ↳ app/consumers/rentals_consumer.rb:8:in
      'block in RentalsConsumer#consume'
  Customer Load (0.2ms)  SELECT `customers`.* FROM `customers`
    WHERE `customers`.`id` = 1010 LIMIT 1
    ↳ app/models/customer_stats_profile.rb:8:
      in 'CustomerStatsProfile#recalculate!'
  Rental Count (0.9ms)  SELECT COUNT(DISTINCT `rentals`.`id`) AS `count_id`,
    `language_id` AS `language_id` FROM `rentals`
    LEFT OUTER JOIN `inventories`
      ON `inventories`.`id` = `rentals`.`inventory_id`
    LEFT OUTER JOIN `films` ON `films`.`id` = `inventories`.`film_id`
    WHERE `rentals`.`customer_id` = 1010 GROUP BY `language_id`
    ↳ app/models/customer_stats_profile.rb:9:
      in 'CustomerStatsProfile#recalculate!'
[0c05027b29ac] Consume job for RentalsConsumer on rentals/0
  finished in 9.97 ms
[3e2df03d68bd] Polling messages...
[3e2df03d68bd] Polled 0 messages in 1005.1730000004172ms
```

Creating a Microservice

What you just did already shows all the basics of producing and consuming Kafka messages, but you haven't created an independent service, as both the producing and the consuming were happening in the Rails monolith. For simplicity's sake, this service that you are going to create will do something very straightforward: count the number of rentals each customer has done. You will store that data in Redis.

Create a new folder in the folder that contains your Rails application (I named it counter_consumer). Open a Gemfile file and add karafka and redis:

rails-performance-book-completed/counter_consumer/Gemfile
```
source "https://rubygems.org"
git_source(:github) { |repo| "https://github.com/#{repo}.git" }

gem 'karafka'
gem 'redis'
```

Install everything with bundle install and bundle exec karafka install. Write a new consumer at counter_consumer/app/consumers/rentals_consumer.rb. This consumer needs to increase a counter every time that a rental is consumed. The key for that counter needs to be associated with the user ID. This is my take.

```
rails-performance-book-completed/counter_consumer/app/consumers/rentals_consumer.rb
# frozen_string_literal: true
require 'redis'
class RentalsConsumer < ApplicationConsumer
  def consume
    messages.each do |message|
      customer_id = message.payload['rental']['user']
      redis_client.incr("customer_rentals_counter_#{customer_id}")
    end
  end

  private

  def redis_client
    @redis_client ||= Redis.new
  end
end
```

Like the one that you wrote before, this consumer looks deceptively simple, and this is because a lot of the heavy lifting is done by code that RentalsConsumer is inheriting from ApplicationConsumer, which is a subclass of Karafka::BaseConsumer.

Now, connect RentalsConsumer to the rentals topic in the karafka.rb of our microservice (counter_consumer/karafka.rb) in exactly the same way you did in the previous section:

```
rails-performance-book-completed/counter_consumer/karafka.rb
class KarafkaApp < Karafka::App

    topic :rentals do
      consumer RentalsConsumer
    end
  end
end
```

And…you are done: you can test this by starting the karafka server from the counter_consumer folder by executing bundle exec karafka server. You just wrote a completely independent service that consumes events generated by your Rails application.

Monitoring Your Kafka Topics with Karafka

We will finish this section by going back to your Rails application. In the same spirit as Sidekiq, Karafka also offers some monitoring capabilities right out of the box, including a pretty nice web dashboard. Installing it is also very similar to what you did with Sidekiq. Run bundle add karafka-web and bundle exec karafka-web install from the root folder of your Rails application. The installation step will add some new topics that will be used to hold the data that will be exposed in the UI; this means that nothing that happened before the installation will be reported.

The last step is adding the web UI to routes.rb:

```ruby
# config/routes.rb
require 'karafka/web'

Rails.application.routes.draw do
  mount Karafka::Web::App, at: '/karafka'

  # All your routes here...
end
```

That's it. You have the Karafka web UI at http://localhost:3000/karafka.

Summing Up

Done! This chapter is probably the most far-sighted in this whole book. It is also the one that brings to the table the most important decisions that you can make with your system. Optimizing queries is great, but you will only achieve massive scale by having a solid architecture that allows for this to happen. Of course, changing your architecture comes with very significant trade-offs.

The first concept that we dove into was sharding. Being able to break your database into multiple smaller databases is incredibly useful and can bring you to the next level. However, it's important for you to remember that it will greatly increase the complexity of your systems and add a lot of new ways for things to go wrong.

Later, we talked about asynchronous processing and background jobs. Introducing asynchronicity to your system will change how you think about your application and will bring disruption everywhere, including to the product side of the enterprise.

Finally, following the themes that started in our discussion about asynchronous processing, we briefly talked about event-driven microservice architecture and Kafka messaging. It is true that Rails is designed for a monolithic architecture, but in my opinion, when a project achieves a certain growth, a progressive transition to a service-oriented architecture can make a lot of sense. Kafka is a great option for these services to communicate with each other while keeping the Rails monolith as a central part of the system architecture.

## CHAPTER 7

Designing Product for Performance

So far in this book, we have focused on how to make an existing *product* faster. This is incredibly useful and, on many occasions, will be enough to bring you to the global level. However, scaling one of the biggest applications in the world is an exercise that goes beyond software engineering. Applications like that are not made scalable; they are conceived, or at least reimagined, to be scalable. This means that, when defining features, the requirements of managing petabytes of data were taken into account. You may be thinking I am referring to trade-offs, to drop features in exchange for a better performance. That's a valid perspective, but scalable product design is not only about a trade-off; it's about thinking about the product in a way that makes sense when working at scale.

In this chapter, we will explore some of these ideas. A few of them may seem fairly obvious even to engineers without much experience; others are far less common and are typically only applied in products that hold a lot of data and have been running for years. All of them have in common that they change the characteristics of the product, going beyond the scope of simple performance enhancements.

Setting Product Limits

One common problem in the mindset of engineers without much experience is trying to build *perfect* systems. This means many engineers believe that if the system is not responsive enough to *any* kind of demand from the user, the system is somehow badly designed or even broken. This way of thinking is wrong. Systems are built around requirements that they should accomplish; systems should be extensible, so they can be modified if those requirements change. In any case, requirements should be specific and realistic. No system can sustain an infinite amount of load. The Golden Gate Bridge may be a masterpiece of engineering, but I guarantee that even that would fall with enough load. This is not a flaw in its design but a logical trait of building systems in the real world.

The consequence of this is that good products have reasonable product limits. Nevertheless, many startups resist this idea. I understand why product managers may not like discussing product limits: their target is to bring more value to customers and product limits are, well, limiting. On the other hand, everyone agrees that products should not be *abused*. And what is abuse, exactly? Well, that is an interesting question. It is defined as "the improper use of something," but that just brings us to the next question: what is using an application in an "improper way"? It is true that, in many cases, there is a certain level of arbitrariness. Figuring out the point at which your application stops being used in the right way and the usage becomes "improper" is hard, if not impossible. Still, there are cases in which the abuse becomes evident.

Take an example: in the customer support industry, you have employees (called agents) who respond to customers' questions, complaints, and incidents. All these customer interactions are called "tickets." Most customer-support PaaS charge by agent seat (how many agents can work on tickets). Of course, the idea is that the number of agents responding to tickets is directly proportional to the number of agents. You need more agents to solve more tickets. Unfortunately, companies in this space have found that some of their biggest customers by number of tickets (billions of them) have an extremely small number of agents—sometimes the minimum number (one) to have an account at all. The reason for this was that those customers were not using the platform for what it was designed (customer support) but as storage—clunky storage for general purposes, but one that had no limits at all. If one does not pay attention to this, it can hurt a company. In this example, you could have your scalability team try to optimize for use cases that bring minimum value to the company. Successful PaaS companies agree with this idea, as they all have anti-abuse teams.

Still, on many occasions, you may find that the line between abuse and fair usage of your application ends up becoming a point of debate. Sometimes a paying customer may find an alternative way to use your product, one that may not be inherently *wrong*, but that may not make sense for you from a business perspective. For example, in one big corporation I worked for, we found out that one customer was using our platform to track all activity that was happening in their own business. They were using our product in a manner that was much more data-intensive than what we expected for an account of their size. These kinds of situations are common in successful products and should be taken into account. Like with many other issues at the product level, there are no silver bullets I can offer you. Decisions should be made taking into account all factors, and many of those go way beyond engineering. Still, there are some tools and techniques that will help you make the decisions necessary to defend your application.

Introducing Rate Limits

The most direct way to set product limits on your system is to control the number of times your users can utilize your application. This may sound like a very radical idea, but as often happens with radical ideas, they are the most effective ones. We want to set up a mechanism so that if a specific resource is being used excessively, access to that resource will be denied. Of course, the specifics of that mechanism will vary depending on the business logic of your product. In any case, you want this process to happen as early in the lifecycle of the request as possible so it uses as few computational resources as possible. Ideally, a request like this should not even hit the application layer at all; we have talked about this in the chapter dedicated to the life of the request. Still, on many occasions, the logic involved in setting the rate limit will be complex enough that the request will need to be processed by the application.

Our purpose will be to introduce a mechanism in our application middleware so we can accomplish the following:

- Calculate the rate limit for this specific request
- Reject the request and return an appropriate error if it has crossed the rate limit threshold.

Implementing this by yourself is possible but unnecessary. Let's not reinvent the wheel and just pick a robust library ready to be added to our application. In this case, we will use Rack::Attack.[1] While according to its description, Rack::Attack has been designed to fight against abuse, we can easily use it to set up rate limits.

As always, let's start by adding the gem to our Gemfile:

rails-performance-book-completed/Gemfile
```
gem 'rack-attack'
```

Run bundle on your terminal. By doing this, we have added a Rack::Attack module to the end of our middleware. You can do this by running rails middleware in your terminal:

---

1. https://github.com/rack/rack-attack

```
% rails middleware
[...]
use Rack::ETag
use Rack::TempfileReaper
use Warden::Manager
use Middleware::ShardSwitcher
use Rack::Attack
run Moviestore::Application.routes
```

Next, we need to configure the throttling. We can do this by creating a new file at config/initializers/rack_attack.rb. In it, you will configure your rate limits. At this point, I would suggest you read the Rack::Attack README,[2] but its API is straightforward enough to build very readable configurations like the following one. Take a look at it; after the code block, there's a brief explanation of what it does:

rails-performance-book-completed/config/initializers/rack_attack.rb

```
Rack::Attack.throttle("requests by ip", limit: 10, period: 1) do |request|
  request.ip
end

Rack::Attack
  .throttle('limit timeline access', limit: 100, period: 60) do |req|

  if req.path =~ /api\/v1\/customers\/\d+\/timeline/
    req.env['rack.session']['warden.user.user.key']&.first&.first
  end
end
```

This configuration adds two throttles. The first is on all our endpoints, and it's based on the IP originating the request. In essence, each IP is limited to 10 requests per second. The second is centered on the logged user: each user can only access the timeline endpoint 100 times per minute. The call to req.env['rack.session'] allows us to fetch data from the user because our application has an authentication system based on Warden (in our case, Devise). Warden is a "general Rack authentication framework" that gives developers the basic blocks to build their own authentication logic. Developing an authentication system based on Warden typically involves creating strategies (like email and password, or tokens). Devise is built "on top" of Warden as it already implements many common authentication strategies and a set of common behaviors for authenticating. Warden (and therefore Devise) stores session data in req.env['rack.session'].

Going back to our throttling efforts, you can check their effects by modifying the first throttle. Temporarily change the limit parameter to a 1 and hit the

---

endpoint using your browser a couple of times. You will get back a 429 status, "Too Many Requests."

This is most of it. Beyond this, it's a good idea to customize your response, so the client receives full information about why she has been rate limited and how they can go back to being on "good terms" with your application. Rack::Attack offers a pretty configurable API that should allow you to customize your throttling logic. In the version that I used for this example (6.6.1), you have a couple of options to customize your response. The first is a Boolean option to add information about the retry times in the headers, throttled_response_retry_after_header; if you want to completely customize the response, you have throttled_responder, an attribute of Rack::Attack that, using a lambda, will allow you complete flexibility on your response. Those were only a couple of the options available for you. Again, I advise you to check the documentation.

One final recommendation before we move on: you will appreciate having as much manual control over your limitations as possible. If your rate limits depend exclusively on code, you will need to do a deployment every time you need to modify them. It's a good idea to connect your configuration to data storage that you can modify at any moment. That data storage can very well be the database of the application itself. For example, something like this:

```
# config/initializers/rack_attack.rb

Rack::Attack
  .throttle('marked users throttle', limit: 10, period: 60) do |req|
    user_id = req.env['rack.session']['warden.user.user.key']
      &.first&.first

    if user_id
      user = User.find(user_id)
      return user_id if user.rate_limited
    end
end
```

The rate_limited user attribute would be a new column on the users table, defaulting to false. Admins in the application would be able to toggle that attribute on a per-need basis. You can vary this formula in multiple ways. You can even set a list of throttled users somewhere outside the database (like an environment variable). In this case, the throttle would look like this:

```
# config/initializers/rack_attack.rb

Rack::Attack
  .throttle('marked users throttle', limit: 10, period: 60) do |req|
  user_id = req.env['rack.session']['warden.user.user.key']
    &.first&.first
```

```
  if user_id
    if JSON.parse(ENV["RATE_LIMITED_USER_IDS"]).include? user_id
      return_user_id
    end
  end
end
```

Of course, those were just examples. Product limits, by their own essence, depend a lot on the nature of the application in which they are applied, and not only the application but also the targets of the product and the company from a business perspective. The most important thing for us as engineers is to understand that we can implement product limits that are as malleable and versatile as our application may need.

Limiting the Number of Records

Throttling the number of requests is just one kind of product limit. It's extremely useful to control short-term issues, like customers running scripts against your API endpoints. However, we also need product limits that work with a long-term approach. Specifically, you want to set limits to how much data customers can store in your platform.

Why set limits? Well, one thing that I can tell you about scaling a successful online application is that once you hit a certain number of users, you have no clue what they are doing with your product. Sometimes they will use a specific feature in a very heavy way, to an extent that you didn't prepare your systems for. Other times, the customer will use your product in a completely unexpected way. It's for the product people in the business to decide what's fair use of an application and what isn't, but it's undoubtedly a good practice to set a limit on the number of certain records in your system, at the very least as a sanity check on how clients are interacting with the product.

For the use case of our application (a system for a movie rental place), it's not easy to find an obvious place in which to set a limitation like this, but believe me, if this hit production successfully, we would eventually find a need for these kinds of product limits. Anyway, as an example, I have decided to limit the amount of inventory a store can have. You can implement this limitation in multiple layers of your application. You can start at the model level with a simple Rails validation:

rails-performance-book-completed/app/models/inventory.rb
```
class Inventory < ApplicationRecord
  MAX_AMOUNT_PER_STORE = 10000

  belongs_to :film
  belongs_to :store
```

```
  has_many :rentals

  validate :max_amount_of_inventory_per_store

  private

  def max_amount_of_films_per_store
    if store.inventories.count >= MAX_AMOUNT_PER_STORE
      errors.add(:store, 'Store has the max amount of items.')
    end
  end
end
```

This will work, but we also need to be efficient in communicating with the customer when applying a product limit. Any API endpoint that is susceptible to creating new inventory needs to be reviewed so it returns the correct status and message, and the message should be properly localized so your users can understand what is happening. The same applies if your application offers a UI: every time that a user hits a product limit, a thorough and clear message needs to be returned. Confused users are rarely happy, particularly when you are limiting functionalities for them.

Making Them Pay

In the previous two sections, we discussed the idea of product limits. A limit is, by definition, something binary; one is in it or out of it. That's fine and dandy, but most typically, our product will be part of a business, and that means that making money is a pretty enticing idea to us. The logical conclusion is that product limits need to be set with a business perspective in mind.

The central idea here is that businesses that scale need to be flexible with their monetization process, finding mechanisms that encapsulate correctly both the value that is being generated for the customer and the costs that are being taken by you, the vendor. This is particularly important when building a SaaS.

For example, in one major SaaS company in which I worked, we established a process to check which clients were our "whale" customers on different aspects to understand better how our resources were being used. We found out that three of the five customers that used the most data-related resources were using our cheapest plan. I remember in particular that a customer paying around $100 a month was storing more data than our biggest paying customer, who was paying well into seven figures a month. The reason for this is that our pricing model was completely detached from data usage. It was focused exclusively on selling licenses. Of course, there was the fair assumption that the number of licenses sold to a customer would be directly proportional to their data usage—an assumption that, to this day, I still believe to be true. Still, at a certain scale, exceptions can damage, if not kill, both the performance of your application and your viability as a business. It is of paramount importance for you to first detect cost, both in direct money you pay for the platform and in engineering hours needed to maintain use cases and customers. Second, a formula to direct this cost to the customers needs to be established.

Managing the Life of Your Data

Let me tell you a story. When I was in the middle of writing this book, my wife and I relocated from New York City to my hometown, Barcelona. We started searching for a place to buy. In the meantime, my wife and I settled into what used to be my grandparents' apartment. I am writing these lines from there. The apartment had been empty for almost two years after my grandfather's death. Of course, "empty" in this context only means no one was living there; in fact, the apartment was *full* of stuff. It was so full that it became clear to us that, even if this was a temporary refuge, we would have to do a deep cleaning of the place if we wanted to live comfortably in it. Having to dispose of the personal belongings of a deceased family member is strange, particularly if you had a close relationship with the person. I thought I knew my grandfather, and indeed I knew *the grandfather* that he eventually became, but I quickly realized that I didn't know the man. For obvious reasons, I barely knew anything about him before my first childhood memories in the early 90s. I discovered a man who liked to wear stylish clothes until well into his 30s. In one particular picture, he reminded me of some photographs of Jean-Luc Godard in the 60s: a sharp-looking man wearing dark glasses and with a tweed jacket and a nonchalant pose. That picture is one of the coolest things I found at that place, but there were so many others. Most of them had no discernable value, at least not to me. Old-fashioned souvenirs bought in France in the early 80s, utility bills from the 70s, photographs of people whose identity was a mystery to me—or anybody else in the family. All of those items had a meaning and importance enough to be kept for years, but this meaning was now lost. In some cases, even the things that they referred to didn't exist anymore. There was an item I thought was particularly representative in that regard. It was a check with the following text:

Quantity: 10,000 pesetas

Issuer: Industrial Bank of Bilbao

Receiver: Antonio Planas Nou

Date: 7/21/1982

This check fascinated me because nothing on it existed anymore. My grand-father passed away in 2020. The Industrial Bank of Bilbao was acquired and eventually absorbed by another bank in the 2010s. Even the currency, the "peseta," has not been used for more than 20 years since most of the European Union members replaced their national currencies in 2001 with the Euro. Time had done its thing.

As the new inhabitants of the apartment, it was our responsibility to decide what to do with everything that was stored there. Some items had value, maybe even more than they had 30 years ago: a *paella* that belonged to my grandmother and is, in my opinion, a family heirloom now. Others still had some minor sentimental value and could be kept. In many other cases, stuff had to just be thrown away. We cannot store an indefinite number of things, passing them from one generation to another, expecting them to have the same value forever.

Here's another example. Imagine that you work for the police in a big city, in the department that manages the storage facilities in which countless items related to a multitude of cases are kept. Yes, in this case, all the items *can* be accessed at any point, but at the same time, you *know* that some items have a much higher probability of being requested than others. You would logically expect that the file for an obscure case of the 1950s would be harder to access than the record of an ongoing, high-stakes case.

Similar dynamics can be found in software engineering, specifically when managing data. This becomes particularly obvious—and painful—when an application has to scale. The sheer amount of data makes it impossible to maintain a "democratic" stance in which all data is equal and stays in the same state as on the day it was written to the database. Data archival and retention policies are necessary for applications that scale.

In this section, we will explore how a product can manage the lifecycle of the data. As in other product design issues, there are no right positions; each product has its own strategy. We can only share techniques, so you are able to decide your own path.

Archiving Data

Relational databases are incredible tools. This said, even the best-indexed table in the world will eventually have issues operating when it contains bil-lions of rows. In a previous section, we shared some techniques on how to refine the way you access your database, but all those queries would get even faster if they had less data to scan.

You may be thinking, "Come on, Cristian, you cannot have your cake and eat it, too. I cannot have all the data and have less data." Later, we will discuss if you really need to have *all* the data, but we will start by keeping it, just move part of it to different storage. This may have an impact on our features, but we think it's worth it.

Let's try to apply this concept to our example application. In particular, we will target the rentals table. First, we will need to make a couple of product decisions:

- *Is there a subgroup of rentals we could limit access to without impacting the customer significantly?* Yes. Rentals that were returned a long time ago are only in the system for historical purposes.

- *What defines that subgroup of rentals?* We would need to define what is meant by "returned a long time ago." Choosing a cutoff is always somewhat arbitrary. In this case, we will define rentals to be archived as those that had a return date of at least a year ago.

- *What would be the impact on the UX?* Archived rentals will still be available for the user, just from a different endpoint.

As you can see, this is a point at which the collaboration between engineering and product is crucial. If product takes an all-or-nothing position, archiving as an option is basically off the table. At the same time, engineering needs to be able to communicate that archiving does not need to be seen as cutting features. Archiving is an incredibly flexible approach to scaling, and in many cases, the product can retain exactly the same features, just with a different organization.

Next, we will implement an archiving process as we defined in the previous three questions. We will start writing an ActiveRecord scope that fits our definition of a rental to be archived:

rails-performance-book-completed/app/models/rental.rb
```
  scope :to_be_archived, -> { where("returnal_date < ?", Time.now - 1.year) }
end
```

This was simple enough. The next step is not so straightforward: choosing an alternative storage. This is crucial, and it should be taken into account from the beginning of the project. The reason is that different data stores have different capabilities that, in turn, will affect the features offered by your product. For this example, we are going to search for persistent key-value storage. There are plenty of good options on the market. I have directly used—and had good experiences with—Amazon DynamoDB, Riak, and Redis.

To keep things straightforward, and given that we are already using Redis, we will avoid adding a new technology to our stack. For our purposes, we need more persistence than typical memory-only storage would offer, and this means we will enable the AOF (Append Only File) option in our Redis configuration. Redis has multiple options for persistence; you can read about them in the section dedicated to this in the Redis documentation,[3] but it's enough to say that AOF is currently the most durable way to make Redis persistent out of the box. It does so by logging every write operation to a file in real time. This allows Redis to reconstruct the dataset by replaying the log if there is any issue with the server. To enable it, you need to change it in your Redis configuration file. If you cannot find it, running the following in the terminal will get it for you (MacOS only):

```
% redis-cli INFO | grep config_file
config_file:/opt/homebrew/etc/redis.conf # (in my case)
```

Now, you need to find the appendonly option and turn it on:

```
# opt/homebrew/etc/redis.conf

[...]

appendonly yes
```

Finally, restart Redis and you've got it:

```
% brew services restart redis
Stopping `redis`... (might take a while)
==> Successfully stopped `redis` (label: homebrew.mxcl.redis)
==> Successfully started `redis` (label: homebrew.mxcl.redis)
```

Now that we have our data storage ready, it's time to write a mechanism that removes the data from our relational database and pushes it into our archived data storage. You can go multiple ways here: you can run a cron job periodically, or you can have an infinite loop always trying to detect new rentals to be archived. We will go for the first option, and we will use another of the goodies that Rails offers us to accomplish this target—one that we have already discussed in a previous chapter: ActiveJob.[4] You can create a new job running rails g job rentals_archival on the terminal. It should look more or less like this:

rails-performance-book-completed/app/jobs/rentals_archival_job.rb
```
require 'redis'

class RentalsArchivalJob < ApplicationJob
  queue_as :default
```

---

3. https://redis.io/docs/management/persistence/
4. https://guides.rubyonrails.org/active_job_basics.html

```ruby
  def perform(*args)
    Rental.to_be_archived.each do |rental|
      redis_client.rpush(
        Rental.archived_rentals_bucket_key(rental.customer_id),
        rental.attributes.to_json
      )

      rental.delete
    end
  end

  private

  def redis_client
    @redis_client ||= Redis.new
  end
end
```

You'll also need to add the archived_rentals_bucket_key method to the Rental model:

rails-performance-book-completed/app/models/rental.rb

```ruby
  def self.archived_rentals_bucket_key(customer_id)
    "archived_rentals_for_user_#{customer_id}"
  end

  private

  def cache_for_followers
    customer.followers.each do |follower|
      timeline = Rails.cache.read(follower.timeline_cache_key) || []

      Rails.cache.write(
        follower.timeline_cache_key, timeline.unshift(id)[0..9]
      )
    end
  end

  def recalculate_store_rentals
    store.set_most_rented_film!
  end

  def recalculate_customer_stats_profile
    RecalculateCustomerStatsProfileJob.perform_later(customer_id)
  end

  def produce_kafka_message
    Karafka.producer.produce_sync(
      topic: 'rentals',
      payload: {
        rental: Api::V1::RentalPresenter.new(self).as_json
      }.to_json
    )
  end
end
```

Now, you need to schedule your job to be executed periodically. There are multiple options. As we commented in the previous chapter, Solid Queue comes with this feature out of the box, so this is probably the most convenient way to do it. However, there are other options if you do not want to use Solid Queue. If you use a cloud platform (like, for example, Heroku), it's possible that they'll provide you with a tool to schedule job execution. If you run your own servers or just want to know how to do this by yourself, you need to add the job to crontab.[5] You can learn to do this by reading the documentation,[6] or you can use a Ruby tool that will facilitate the task with a simpler API—I'm talking about whenever.[7] This gem provides you with clear syntax and, I would dare to say, some syntactic sugar for scheduling jobs.

Other options, if you are already using Sidekiq for scheduled jobs, are Sidekiq Scheduler[8] and Resque Scheduler.[9]

Beyond the tool you pick to schedule the job, if you want to test the job execution itself, you can also go to the Rails console and execute the job synchronously:

```
irb(main):001:0> RentalsArchivalJob.perform_now
Performing RentalsArchivalJob
  (Job ID: ddaf8df4-fc47-43ef-bfbe-ad35a554f8fa)
    from Async(default) enqueued at
  Rental Load (3.8ms)  SELECT `rentals`.* FROM `rentals`
    WHERE (returnal_date < '2024-07-09 17:29:45.952185')
  Rental Destroy (5.6ms)  DELETE FROM `rentals`
    WHERE `rentals`.`id` = 105277
  Rental Destroy (1.0ms)  DELETE FROM `rentals`
    WHERE `rentals`.`id` = 105278
  Rental Destroy (0.9ms)  DELETE FROM `rentals`
    WHERE `rentals`.`id` = 105279
[...]
```

The last step is quite simple. As things are right now, users have no way to access their archived rentals. There are two ways to proceed here:

• The existence of an archive could be completely invisible to the user. In other words, it's just an implementation characteristic.

---

5.   http://crontab.org/
6.   http://crontab.org/
7.   https://github.com/javan/whenever
8.   https://github.com/sidekiq-scheduler/sidekiq-scheduler
9.   https://github.com/resque/resque-scheduler

- The archive becomes part of the user experience. Archived items may have different features, and they may be accessed in different ways than non-archived items.

The second option is very flexible since the degree to which an archived item is transformed can vary significantly. For example, archived items can have the whole feature set of non-archived items but be accessed in a different way. Product can even establish features that only work on archived items (for example, some analytics). However, most commonly, archived items lose some features, particularly those related to modifying the item. While this isn't the case with Redis, it's common to archive data in a storage that is designed for a higher amount of reads than writes.

For our application, we will just segregate archived rentals from non-archived ones. We will build a new endpoint that will return archived rentals and fetch them from Redis. Add an api/v1/customers/:customer_id/archived_rentals route to routes.rb. The action should look like this:

rails-performance-book-completed/app/controllers/api/v1/customers_controller.rb
```ruby
class Api::V1::CustomersController < ApplicationController

  def archived_rentals
    key = Rental.archived_rentals_bucket_key(params[:customer_id])
    if redis_client.exists? key
      rentals = redis_client.lrange(key, 0, -1).map do |archived_rental|
        Rental.new(JSON.parse(archived_rental))
      end

      render json: rentals.map do |rental|
        Api::V1::RentalPresenter.new(rental).to_json
      end
    else
      render json: []
    end
  end

  private

  def redis_client
    @redis_client ||= Redis.new
  end
end
```

There are a few issues with this logic: for example, we instantiate a Rental object just to pass it as a parameter to the presenter, where it's transformed back into a slightly different JSON. We could make this a tad more efficient memory-wise by manipulating the JSON directly without the presenter or the Rental object; it would probably be a bit faster too. Still, we will leave it as it is. We have been able to demonstrate a very simple implementation of archiving, and it's time for us to move on.

Improving Our Archival Design

The approach we just implemented would improve access to more recent rentals, but ironically, the structure we have defined for archived rentals won't scale very well. For example, the archived_rentals endpoint doesn't support pagination. This will become an issue when customers start having thousands of archived rentals. Moreover, the real issue is not implementing pagination; that should be simple enough. The underlying problem is that we are storing what can potentially be a lot of data under only one key. If we modify the endpoint to support exclusively pages of 10 items, we still have to fetch the whole collection of archived rentals from Redis. That can potentially mean fetching hundreds of megabytes of data to return a few hundred bytes. Worse yet, Redis has a limit size value of 512 MB, so you will eventually hit a barrier there.

There are a few ways around this. You can change the structure of the archival "buckets," so instead of all rentals dwelling in the same space, each bucket works as a "page." Archived rentals buckets would have a name like archived _rentals_for_user_#{customer_id}_page_#{page}. When the archived_rentals endpoint would get called, we'd have to calculate the bucket from which we'd fetch the data based on the pagination parameters provided in the request. Another option would be to store each archived rental in its own Redis key, so, in the archived_rentals key, we'd only store an array with the ids. Each individual rental could be saved in a key like archived_rental_#{id}; fetching a set of integers is less onerous than fetching a list of full-fletched JSON objects. For example, these are the ids of the rentals made by one of the customers in my application instance:

```
irb(main):001> ids = Rental.where(customer_id: Customer.last).pluck(:id)
  Customer Load (8.7ms)  SELECT `customers`.* FROM `customers`
    ORDER BY `customers`.`id` DESC LIMIT 1
  Rental Pluck (2.1ms)  SELECT `rentals`.`id` FROM `rentals`
    WHERE `rentals`.`customer_id` = 3010
=> [3001, 3002, 3005, 3006, 3007, 3009, 3010, 3011, 3012, 3013]
```

Stored as a JSON, that array occupies a grand total of 51 characters:

```
irb(main):002> ids.to_json
=> "[3001,3002,3005,3006,3007,3009,3010,3011,3012,3013]"
irb(main):003> ids.to_json.length
=> 51
```

Storing all of the rental objects occupies almost 2000 characters or 20 times more than storing the ids:

```
irb(main):004> rentals = Rental.where(customer_id: Customer.last)
  .map(&:to_json)
  Customer Load (8.7ms)  SELECT `customers`.* FROM `customers`
    ORDER BY `customers`.`id` DESC LIMIT 1
  Rental Load (1.9ms)  SELECT `rentals`.* FROM `rentals`
    WHERE `rentals`.`customer_id` = 3010
irb(main):005> rentals.to_json.length
=> 1931
```

All the options we have explored so far heavily limit how one can manipulate archived items, particularly if one needs them to be seamlessly mixed with non-archived ones. For example, sorting all the rentals of a store independently from the customer would become a very expensive operation given that archived rentals are stored on a key depending on the customer_id. This is the trade-off we are taking when archiving, particularly when using the strategy we just used. In my experience, archiving can become very simple if the options to filter and sort archived items are very limited, and this is what we have done. However, archival is more of a general idea, and one can opt for less intrusive techniques that still offer performance benefits.

Regulating the "Temperature" of Your Data

An alternative name for the archive is *cold storage*. This is because we divide our data into two types: the "hot" data, ready to be accessed at any time, and the "cold" data, which has more limited and/or slower access. I like this terminology a lot because it suggests that the archival solution is flexible: temperature is not binary and neither are the features of the archive. We can design our archive to be warmer or colder. We can even have multiple levels of archive, with data becoming colder and colder as time passes and access to it becomes more unlikely.

For example, sometimes it can be necessary to leave a part of the object we want to archive on the relational database. This particularly makes sense when you have very heavy objects in which most of the data could perfectly well be archived, but removing that object would cut associations all across your data model. If the associated object only depends on the one we want to archive, it makes a lot of sense to archive them together, almost as if the object would just be a set of attributes. However, that won't work in many cases, especially in more complex data models. A solution would be to create a new model associated with a new table that would keep only the most important information: the id of the original object and others, depending on the use case. It's common to also keep the timestamps so you can easily keep track of the history of the object. If we wanted to apply this idea to the model Film of our application, we could create a new model and table (ArchivedFilmStub). This new model would not keep all the attributes of Film, just the ones we deem necessary. The others would be stored in the archival storage. For example, we probably want the big_text_column out of Film. The most important part of this design, though, is to keep the original id. You can do so by creating a new attribute that keeps track of the original film id, or you can pass the original film id as a parameter when creating the ArchivedFilmStub, something like this:

```
> ArchivedFilmStub.create(id: film.id, title: film.title, ...)
```

Still, you may want to have even "colder" data. This can happen with very big datasets, particularly those related to audit or logging. In this case, the access may be so uncommon that it would be reasonable to allow access only via exporting data tools. There are multiple options you can pick as the "freezer" (as I like to call this very cold storage), but one of the most used is Amazon S3. S3 is the most popular cloud-based storage service in the world, allowing you to store and retrieve data of any size. There is an AWS SDK for Ruby[10] from where you can take the S3 module (gem 'aws-sdk-s3'). The following job would push any archived rental object older than two years into S3 and remove it from Redis. There are a few things missing (like authentication), but it will give you an idea of how yours should look:

rails-performance-book-completed/app/jobs/old_archived_rentals_to_s3_job.rb
```
class OldArchivedRentalsToS3Job < ApplicationJob
  queue_as :default

  def perform(*args)
    time = Time.now - 2.years
    Customer.all.pluck(:id).each do |customer_id|
      bucket_key = Rental.archived_rentals_bucket_key(customer_id)
      rentals = redis_client.lrange(bucket_key, 0, -1)
      folder = "customer_#{customer_id}"

      rentals.each do |rental|
        if rental[:returned_date] > time
          break
        else
          redis_client.lpop(bucket_key)
        end
```

----

10. https://github.com/aws/aws-sdk-ruby

```ruby
      s3_client.put_object(
        bucket: "archived_rentals",
        key: folder + "/" + "archived_rental_#{rental[:id]}",
        body: rental,
        content_type: 'text/json'
      )
    end
  end
end

private

def redis_client
  @redis_client ||= Redis.new
end

def s3_client
  @s3_client ||= Aws::S3::Client.new
end
end
```

You can use it by scheduling a certain period, for example, once a day or every hour.

Going back to the architecture of the system, the design of this new archival space is crucial, as it can have long-term consequences. In the previous example, each archived rental would have its own file, which can be problematic in the long term. Another option would be to hold many archived rentals in one file, but this has the drawback that S3 doesn't support append operations, so modifying a file would imply deleting it and rewriting it anew. Anyway, this should be sufficient for you to get the gist of the alternatives you have when designing an archive.

Destroying Data

This chapter has been full of stories. Now that we're getting close to the end, I would like to share a final one. It's a story that illustrates a certain attitude I believe is very important for performance work—a position that many times is very far from the default ways of a typical software engineer. This time, I'm not going to bother you with my personal life; I am going to tell you a classical tale. Classical, indeed: we're talking about ancient Greece. This is the story of Alexander the Great and The Gordian Knot.

Alexander the Great may have been the most important figure in the golden era of Greece. Born in 356 BCE, he became the king of Macedonia at 20, and he embarked on an unprecedented conquest that transformed the ancient world. A strategic and military genius comparable to Julius Caesar and

Napoleon, he forged one of the largest empires in history, stretching from Greece to Egypt and as far east as India.

The other main character in this story is not a person but an object: the Gordian Knot. This was a knot that could be found in the city of Gordium in Phrygia (modern Turkey). The knot was supposedly created by the first king of the city, Gordias. The knot was incredibly complex, comprising "several knots all so tightly entangled that it was impossible to see how they were fastened," according to the Roman historian Quintus Curtius Rufus.

Alexander's interest in the Gordian Knot starts with a prophecy: an oracle had announced any man who could untie the knot would become the ruler of all of Asia. To someone with Alexander's ambitions, the challenge of undoing the Gordian Knot was, of course, more than accepted. And yet, Alexander couldn't find a way to untie the knot. He struggled. He just wasn't able to undo the knot. Maybe he wasn't destined to become king of Asia after all.

That is, until he found a way. He decided he would never be able to untangle this diabolically complicated knot, so he drew his sword and just sliced it in half with a single stroke. The Gordian Knot was no more, and Alexander became the ruler of all of Asia.

I read this story when I was a kid, but I must admit that it didn't make that much sense to me. I felt that Alexander *cheated* somehow. Things changed when I became an adult. At that point in my life, I had to get used to facing all kinds of problems, so the direct, extreme, no-nonsense take from Alexander began to appeal to me.

Still, the story became more nuanced when I became a software engineer in a big organization. Alexander's act is much more shocking when your working life is more focused on searching for alignments across multiple teams than on writing code as an individual contributor. For example, the idea Alexander had to untie the knot without destroying it was what I call an *assumed* requirement. In all aspects of our lives, we have these tacit assumptions about all kinds of situations. Disruption starts when we're conscious of these requirements and are brave enough to challenge them. Moreover, the story of the Gordian Knot also hints at something incredibly important when building systems: creative destruction. The idea of creative destruction, in general, refers to destroying something (a product, industry, or business model) to give space for new opportunities for growth.

While the idea of "creative destruction" is typically focused on the destructive component of a creative process, it can also be used for the liberating effects of destroying something. And there is no more radical expression of this than, well, just destroying an item that has lost its purpose while still adding complexity to the system. This applies particularly well to data.

Of course, the temptation of following a data policy of holding everything, everywhere, forever, exists. This sometimes happens even in organizations that are legally required to remove data in certain circumstances. I want to argue that storing data can be hard, particularly when there is no established policy around data retention. This, in essence, means you are going to store all data for an infinite amount of time. Of course, the counterpoint to this is that, in many cases, companies are required to *keep* data. Finding the balance between bringing value to the user and maintaining a sustainable system while following the law of each country and/or state can be daunting. Still, maintaining an unchallenged default of keeping everything forever is a mistake that will eventually have consequences.

The antidote to all this is something we have discussed since the beginning of the chapter: product limits. And no product limit *feels* more problematic to software engineers than deleting data. And yet, there is no more radical solution to many problems, particularly scalability problems, than using the sword and cutting the Gordian Knot. One does this by stating a clear data retention policy and then executing it.

Doing Things That Don't Scale

One central idea when building a startup—and really, any kind of technological company—is to establish a business that scales. This is what differentiates successful startups from regular tech businesses. While a regular business takes a specific fee to solve a specific problem (I'm thinking specifically of most consultancies), a startup builds a general solution that can be used again and again to generate income. Sometimes, a company may start consulting and end up building this solution. For example, a firm dedicated to building websites may end up using all that experience to create a tool so anyone can subscribe and make their own site. This was the case with 37signals, the creators of Rails and their flagship product, Basecamp. Individual, specialized work does not scale; general tools do. This is a truth that comes easily for engineers, as engineering is, in many cases, the art of finding general patterns and building upon them.

And yet, this is a rule that, like many other rules, needs to be broken from time to time. We have already talked about the importance of detecting abuse, including abusive action from otherwise legit users. However, some workflows, especially when working with "big" users/accounts (whatever big may mean in the context of your application) will bring completely legitimate scalability issues. At this point, you will face a dilemma: building a general solution to fixing that scalability problem would probably not give a good return on investment. At the same time, you don't want to reject customers or give them a bad experience. Moreover, in many cases, scaling can imply changing the architecture of your system, and this can be a significant engineering effort, one that could take years. That's way too long for your users to wait.

It's in this scenario when *doing things that don't scale* makes sense. Admittedly, the idea for this chapter came from an article by Paul Graham.[11] The article is focused on practices that startups can do to grow business-wise: things like recruiting users individually, finetuning their experience to the extreme, and even "the canonical example of work that doesn't scale"... consulting for them (as long as it's for free). Paul Graham's general point is "to do something unscalably laborious to get started," and not only because those "unscalably laborious" tasks help you to find market fit but also because they may change the company DNA:

> If you have to be aggressive about user acquisition when you're small, you'll probably still be aggressive when you're big. If you have to manufacture your own hardware or use your software on users' behalf, you'll learn things you couldn't have learned otherwise. And most importantly, if you have to work hard to delight users when you only have a handful of them, you'll keep doing it when you have a lot.

The same way of thinking works for scaling, too. Working on the scalability of a particular edge case will help you in the long term. First of all, you will learn. A deep dive into a very specific problem will teach you lessons you'll eventually be able to generalize into a broader perspective. Moreover, constant work on scalability problems, something beyond particular projects, will set up a culture of care for performance. Finally, and most importantly, you will be able to give a quick response to the problems of some of your biggest users.

Some of the special interventions I had to execute during my years were:

- Writing user-specific logic. In the chapter about caching, we have commented on X and the "Justin Bieber problem": how X users with massive amounts of followers forced the platform to use a different algorithm altogether when managing their tweets. Sometimes these kinds of solutions are found when working with a particular user or edge case in mind, and they become extendable to a bigger part of your user base.

- Dividing massive accounts. Working on SaaS or PaaS, you will have to work with customers of extremely different sizes. Some of them are what

---

11. http://paulgraham.com/ds.html

are commonly called "elephant" accounts, which work with huge amounts of data. It's common for these accounts to contain very different use cases that can be easily divided. Sometimes, a special agreement can be made so some data is shared. In our case, we created a "dummy" third account whose only purpose was that anything created there would be automatically copied to the multiple real accounts of the customer. Really, the sky is the limit. Obviously, all this can only be done after discussing it with the customer in an effort that goes clearly beyond engineering and becomes a collaboration between engineering, product, and advocacy.

- Manual rebalancing. We have talked before about sharding. In that chapter, the default way of sharding the database would be round-robin, meaning that all shards would end up with a similar number of accounts or users (depending on the nature of your application). However, this does not mean that each shard will have approximately the same amount of data: user 41 may generate a couple of KBs and user 42 may use GBs. Eventually, you may find users so massive that a manual intervention to set them up in a less busy shard would make a lot of sense. Sometimes, even having a one-user-only shard would totally make sense.

These are just a few examples. As with many other things about this chapter, the strategies you can pursue will change a lot depending on your product. However, one thing that I have found useful is to have a system that allows you to enable and disable logic at will depending on certain conditions, like the specific user executing the request, the account, or even the location of the user. A feature flag system[12] will come in handy for this kind of work, as it allows us to enable or disable certain code paths depending on dynamic variables. We will go deeper into feature flags in Chapter 9, Scaling, Beyond Performance, on page 213.

Increasing Your Usability Time

We have spent a lot of pages discussing performance, but I don't think we have pondered on why we care about it so much. While performance can help in many areas, including cost control, one of the main reasons why we pay so much attention to it is because of its dramatic impact on user experience. Load time (also called page speed) is one of the main factors that decide the SEO ranking of a website for Google. Google even offers a set of tools[13] to help

---

12. https://en.wikipedia.org/wiki/Feature_toggle
13. https://developers.google.com/speed

you make your site as fast as possible, including an analyzer[14] you can apply to any URL.

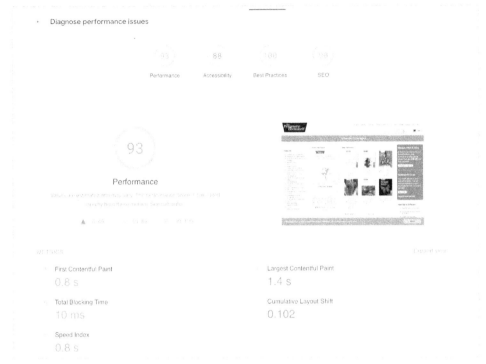

I personally find the second section in the PageSpeed Analyzer, *Diagnose performance issues*, very practical. "Metrics" tells you how long the page takes to get to certain basic milestones, performance-wise:

- First Contentful Paint: The time it took to render the first text or image

- Largest Contentful Paint: The time it took to render the largest text or image

- Total Blocking Time: The sum of all time periods of long tasks (over 50ms) from FCP (First Contentful Paint) to TTI (Time To Interactive). It measures how long your users need to wait to interact with the page after it becomes visible to them.

- Cumulative Layout Shift: It measures the movement of elements within the viewport. You have probably experienced it: you are reading an article (or worse, trying to click a link!), and suddenly, an element renders, moving the whole site down.

- Speed Index: How quickly the contents of the page were visibly populated

---

14. https://pagespeed.web.dev/

It provides a list of "Opportunities" in which it recommends simple actions you can take so your page becomes as fast as possible. For example, I just analyzed the desktop version (desktop and mobile versions of every site get a different score) of https://pragprog.com/. The analyzer gives us some suggestions like "Eliminate render-blocking resources," "Reduce unused JavaScript," "Serve images in next-gen formats," and "Enable text compression."

All this attention paid to page load time makes sense if you put your user hat on: isn't it annoying when a website just takes too long to load? What about when every internal link you hit takes half a second longer than it should? Slow websites have much higher bounce rates compared to more performant ones. According to a 2017 study by Google,[15] the probability of bounce increases 32 percent as page load time goes from one second to three seconds. Having a slow load time can be the difference between a successful product and a failed one.

Applying (Smart) Asynchronous Loading

This book is full of techniques to make your application faster and, therefore, reduce the page loading time. However, here, we will share a way to reduce that blocking time without improving our application response benchmark. In a way, our application won't be faster at all. Arguably, it may become a little bit slower, but it will look faster and provide a better user experience. And isn't this what we are really striving for?

When the Internet started becoming popular in the 90s, traditional websites were static pages or, at least, server-side rendered (SSR). This meant that you got all the functionality only when the response was completed and nothing at all until then. Of course, this started changing with the introduction of scripting languages in the late 90s, a process that would eventually coalesce in the ECMAScript standard and JavaScript. This, added to the creation of AJAX (Asynchronous JavaScript and XML), allowed browsers to load or fetch content from the back-end application in an asynchronous fashion. Nowadays, while AJAX has long disappeared from the tech stack used in almost any web application, the concept of loading asynchronously is ubiquitous.

In this section, we are not going to explain how to do asynchronous loading, but we are going to suggest to be smart about it and strategize for getting the best possible experience. This can be done by splitting data fetching. Imagine that you are developing an SSR web application, and one of your pages is really slow. After taking a look at it, you find that the bottleneck is the

---

15. https://www.thinkwithgoogle.com/marketing-strategies/app-and-mobile/page-load-time-statistics/

database. Typically, in many applications, the latency comes from time spent fetching the data (which will eventually be rendered by the browser) from the database. The next step here would be to investigate the queries performed and see if they can be finetuned to go significantly faster. Another possibility would be to try to cache the data. You have learned quite a lot about those techniques in this book. Assume that there is no way to improve performance directly, but still, you *need* to make that page faster. What could you do here? Well, you can move part of the data fetching out of the loading of the page so the user can start interacting with your site while the cumbersome part of the original request happens in a new request, asynchronously from the first one.

Our application also has an example of this use case. You will find it in CustomersController#show. It's a simple page designed to give some basic functionality to the user. It includes the rental history of a customer—the movie rentals a customer has done in his lifetime. This can be substantial and is indeed what we spend the most time doing when rendering the page. Check the page at /users/1 and take a look at the log:

```
Started GET "/customers/1" for ::1 at 2025-02-17 15:13:01 +0100
Processing by CustomersController#show as HTML
  Parameters: {"id" => "1"}
  Customer Load (23.0ms)  SELECT `customers`.*
    FROM `customers` WHERE `customers`.`id` = 1 LIMIT 1
  ↳ app/controllers/customers_controller.rb:3:in 'CustomersController#show'
  Rendering layout layouts/application.html.erb
  Rendering customers/show.html.erb within layouts/application
  Rental Load (2.0ms)  SELECT `rentals`.* FROM `rentals`
    WHERE `rentals`.`customer_id` = 1 ORDER BY `rentals`.`created_at` DESC
  ↳ app/views/customers/show.html.erb:8
  Inventory Load (1.5ms)  SELECT `inventories`.* FROM `inventories`
    WHERE `inventories`.`id` IN (...)
  ↳ app/views/customers/show.html.erb:8
  Film Load (101.9ms)  SELECT `films`.* FROM `films`
    WHERE `films`.`id` IN (...)
  ↳ app/views/customers/show.html.erb:8
  Rendered customers/show.html.erb within layouts/application
    (Duration: 124.4ms | GC: 0.6ms)
  Rendered layout layouts/application.html.erb
    (Duration: 178.9ms | GC: 5.2ms)
Completed 200 OK in 219ms
  (Views: 75.4ms | ActiveRecord: 136.4ms (4 queries, 0 cached) | GC: 5.7ms)
```

All the SQL queries here except the one on the customers table at the beginning are working on building the rental history. It's true that currently, this is not terribly slow, but eventually, as the number of items in the history increases and each item becomes more complex, this may not scale. Also, the rental history is not the main point of customers#show; it's just a little piece of extra information we want this page to have but without slowing down the rendering of the whole page.

What we can do here is remove the rental history for the server-side rendered view and populate the table with data we will fetch from the API using JavaScript. You can do this using Turbo or, as in the following example, using vanilla JavaScript:

```
rails-performance-book-completed/app/views/customers/show.html.erb
<h1>
  <%= @customer.name %>
</h1>
<div class="rentals">
    <h2>| Rentals</h2>
    <%= "#{@customer.rentals_count} rentals" %>
</div>

<script>
  <%= "var cId = #{@customer.id}" %>
    fetch("/api/v1/customers/" + cId + "/rentals.json").then(function(r) {
    r.json().then(function(content) {
      var table = "<table>"
      console.log(content);
      content.forEach((rental) => {
        console.log(rental);
        table += "<tr>"
        table += "<td>" + rental.movie_name + "</td>"
        table += "<td>" + (rental.rental_date || "") + "</td>"
        table += "<td>" + (rental.returnal_date || "") + "</td>"
        table += "</tr>"
      });
      var target = document.querySelector(".rentals");
      target.innerHTML += table;
    })
  })
</script>
```

While the previous example used SSR—as do most of the examples in this book—the general lesson is also applicable to systems using Single Page Applications (SPAs) for their front end. For example, if you have a slow endpoint that fetches a significant amount of data, you can consider breaking this process into multiple fetches so data can start being rendered earlier. This may imply changes on the back-end side, which may not be always possible; the back end may be owned by a different team with a very busy roadmap or even by a third party not belonging to your organization. Still, Rails is ideal for small teams (the unofficial motto of Rails is "the one-person framework"), so this may not be an issue for you. Moreover, even if you work in a huge organization, performance should be a priority for you; collaboration through multiple teams to achieve a faster experience for your customers is an ideal to be followed.

Learning Other Ways to Increase Your Page Speed

This chapter has triggered some old memories from the beginning of my career. Just out of college, I worked in some very small companies, companies that I joined almost entirely because they had Rails on their stack. Still, given the size of the company, the few engineers who worked there were expected to wear many hats, including assisting with non-engineering functions like SEO. This is how I started using PageSpeed Analyzer. Long story short, I had to spend time trying to make some of the company websites faster so Google would rank them higher. The trick here is that those sites were *static*: there were no SQL queries to finetune. How would I do it?

Well, the answer was all about the assets. We tend to think of websites as basically text files in HTML format, but this text file can summon many, many other files. In a static site, the time needed to generate the HTML document (I think about it as an entry point of sorts) is basically null. The game here is the *size* of the file—of this first HTML page (which will be typically small) and all of the assets downloaded by it: CSS files, JS files, and especially images. I'll be totally honest here: I have spent a significant number of hours compressing images so our sites could become a few milliseconds faster. For example, you can use one of the online services to optimize your images by recompression. Probably the most popular service to this day is TinyPNG.[16] They have an API and a Ruby client,[17] so you can use them to recompress any image uploaded to your application. You can also use an image optimizer gem like image_optim[18] to run your own recompressions without calling a third-party service. Take into account that compression can be lossless or "lossy": if you accept a small level of quality loss, you can reduce your image size much further. Still, even a lossless recompression can give great gains, particularly if you resize the image to the exact dimensions that you are going to be using.

Beyond reducing the size of the assets, you can also be more tactical around how you fetch them, so you only get what you need when you need it. The <img> element supports a loading attribute, so the image is only loaded at the moment that the user scrolls near them. In the following example, the first image will

16. https://tinypng.com/
17. https://github.com/tinify/tinify-ruby
18. https://github.com/toy/image_optim

be fetched as soon as the page loads, while the second will only be downloaded when the user viewport gets to it:

```
<img src="first.jpg" width="200px" height="200px" />
<img src="second.jpg" loading="lazy" width="200px" height="200px" />
```

What we just saw was powered by a native HTML attribute. Using JavaScript, we can go way more complex than this. For example, an interesting strategy is to host two versions of the same image: a first, very lossy one, so the user has something as fast as possible, and a second, lossless one. The page loads with the first image as default and moves on to load the second version as soon as the first is rendered:

```
<img src="lossy.jpg" high_res_image="lossless.jpg" />

$(document).on('turbo:load', function() {
  $('img').each(function() {
    loadHighResImage(this);
  });
});

function loadHighResImage(elem) {
  var highResImage = $(elem).attr('high_res_image');
  if(highResImage) {
    var image = new Image();
    image.addEventListener('load', () => elem.src = highResImage)
    image.src = highResImage;
  }
}
```

Summing Up

We're at the end of the chapter. I am sure you've noticed that this chapter has been a little bit different—a bit heavier on the narrative side and a bit lighter on the coding and engineering. Nothing that has been discussed can be implemented without alignment across all shareholders, as it heavily impacts the product.

The first concept we explored is product limits, and if I am being honest, this is the most important part. Nowadays, when I am discussing a new feature with a team, after having some understanding of what they are trying to build, I ask them about product limits and strongly suggest considering them before releasing their work to our users. Around this idea, we have also discussed making users pay to increase those limits so they have access to a more intense usage of your application.

Next, we discussed the cycle of data in an application. This section pairs closely with our discussion of cold storage in the Software Architecture chapter. Here, we tried to focus on how this would impact the user experience. Moreover, we have also commented on the most radical data solution of all: data deletion.

Then, we explored the idea of "doing things that don't scale," an attitude that is very healthy in companies at all stages, but particularly in small ones. Embracing this attitude will help you scale by both accelerating learning and laying the groundwork for scaling effectively.

Finally, we discussed the importance of increasing usability time. You have discovered PageSpeed Analyzer and learned about some of the basic metrics around page speed. In this section, we discussed the importance of being strategic around fetching: first, by doing smart data loading so the user can interact with the application as fast as possible, and second, by applying different techniques to minimize and optimize the downloading of the assets needed to experience the application.

Monitoring Performance to Build Scalable Systems

We are getting closer to the end of the book. So far, we have discussed all kinds of topics and techniques related to the scalability of a Rails application: database access, caching, software architecture, product design...we have even discussed the structure of the Internet in the previous chapter. Still, there is one step that I consider more important than anything we have discussed so far: monitoring. It's essential. There are three reasons for this:

1. If you don't have monitoring set up, you don't *really* know if you have a problem.

2. If you write a performance optimization, but you are not monitoring the change before and after, you don't know if what you did had an impact.

3. Performance is a feature. If your application becomes too slow, the user experience is degraded. A sufficiently slow endpoint is indistinguishable from a broken one.

If you inherit a slow Rails application, the first thing you need to do is not optimize queries, add a cache layer, or sign a CDN provider. It's implementing thorough monitoring to understand the slow endpoints and the bottlenecks of the application.

Choosing and Installing Your Observability Platform

You can choose from multiple observability services. Some of these platforms have even made things especially easy for Rails developers by building libraries to simplify the integration between their platform and your application. The most popular options are:

- Datadog: Easy to integrate, incredibly comprehensible

- New Relic: A classic because of its simplicity and easy integration with Rails applications[1]

- Grafana (with Prometheus): The open-source, self-hosted alternative. You can add Loki and Jaeger to include logging and tracing under the same platform.[2]

These are all strong options: I honestly do not think you can go wrong with any of them. At the beginning of my career, I used New Relic a lot. Part of my fascination with finetuning slow SQL queries came from their incredibly accessible UI, which pushed me, a clueless solo engineer running a startup, to improve the performance of the Rails application by pointing clearly to the database bottlenecks. To this day, New Relic would still be my option in very small startups and/or more junior teams. Its simplicity and ease of use are unbeatable advantages. Grafana is an open-source analytics and monitoring solution that can integrate with various data sources. It's extremely customizable and commonly used to monitor the health and performance of different kinds of systems. Choosing Grafana gives you a more personalized experience in exchange for requiring more work to integrate it with your application. A common solution for monitoring web applications is to integrate Grafana with Prometheus, an open-source time-series database, as a data source for metrics. Loki is a log aggregation system (developed by Grafana Labs) that can be used by Grafana as a logging source. Finally, Jaeger (developed by Uber) is an open-source distributed tracing system that can be connected to Grafana.

Still, the option I am going to use for this chapter is DataDog. Honestly, a big part of this pick is familiarity, as it has been the one I have been using for the last decade. It's relatively easy to set up, but at the same has great depth: it can be infinitely powerful when you adapt it to your desired purpose.

Installing Datadog

Setting up Datadog on your machine is a bit more complex than just installing a gem. Follow these steps:

1. Register and get your API key.

2. Install the Datadog agent. This software will collect events and metrics emitted by your application and eventually send them to Datadog.

---

1. https://github.com/newrelic/newrelic-ruby-agent
2. https://grafana.com/

3. Finally, add the `datadog` gem to your Rails application. With the gem installed, you will be able to emit metrics and report traces to Datadog via the agent.

Go to the Datadog website[3] and sign up. After signing up, you will be redirected to a page with instructions on how to install the Datadog agent on your machine. When I set up my application to write this chapter, I got something like this:

```
% DD_API_KEY=${MY_API_KEY} DD_SITE="datadoghq.com" bash -c
  "$(curl -L https://install.datadoghq.com/scripts/install_mac_os.sh)"
```

With this, you have the Datadog agent running in the background. You can check its state in the Web UI (http://localhost:5002). Now it's time to integrate the `datadog` gem with your Rails application. Start by adding it to your Gemfile:

rails-performance-book-completed/Gemfile
```
gem 'datadog', require: 'datadog/auto_instrument'
```

```
# Gemfile

gem 'datadog', require: 'datadog/auto_instrument'
```

Finally, create a configuration file in config/initializers/datadog.rb:

rails-performance-book-completed/config/initializers/datadog.rb
```
Datadog.configure do |c|
  c.service = 'rails-performance-book'
  c.env = Rails.env

  c.tracing.test_mode.enabled = (Rails.env == 'test')
end
```

Congratulations, you are ready to start monitoring your application.

Monitoring (Almost) All the Things!

Datadog offers many, *many* features. The purpose of this chapter is to give you a light introduction to it. However, I promise you will learn enough to monitor your performance really efficiently without having to understand all the functionalities of the platform.

Before learning how to monitor your application, you will need some requests to "seed" your metrics so you actually have something to monitor. I have prepared a Rake task that hits a different application endpoint every second. You can run it by writing the following in your terminal:

```
% rake seed_datadog
```

---

3.   https://www.datadoghq.com/

The task runs the following script that you can find in lib/tasks/seed_datadog.rake:

rails-performance-book/lib/tasks/seed_datadog.rake

```
require 'net/http'

desc 'Seed DD'

def call_url(url)
  Net::HTTP.get(URI(url))
  sleep 1
end

task seed_datadog: :environment do
  while true do
    store_id = Store.ids.sample
    customer_id = Customer.ids.sample

    call_url "http://localhost:3000/api/v1/stores/#{store_id}"
    call_url "http://localhost:3000/api/v1/stores/#{store_id}/audits"
    call_url "http://localhost:3000/api/v1/films"
    call_url "http://localhost:3000/films"
    call_url "http://localhost:3000/customers"
    call_url "http://localhost:3000/customers/#{customer_id}"
  end
end
```

Feel free to add more URLs if you want to monitor them, too.

Using the APM

Datadog comes with a native functionality designed to help you correctly monitor the performance of your application. You can find it on the left side of your screen. There should be a link with the name APM; hover over it, and then click Service Catalog. This will bring you to a list of all your services and many ways to filter them. Even if you have only explicitly added one, our Rails application actually involves multiple services that have been automatically added by Datadog. In my case, this included active_support-cache, mysql2, and net/http, apart from the Rails app itself, rails-performance-book. This last one is the one we mainly care about; click it to access the Service Page. If you are logged in and you gave your service the name rails-performance-book, you should be able to access it by hitting the URL https://app.datadoghq.eu/apm/services/rails-performance-book/ in your browser. This Service Page is divided into multiple sections. The first section, "Service Summary," should include the number of requests and errors, the percentage of the time that each request spends in each service (for example, how much in the Rails application itself vs. time waiting for a database response), and crucially, the latency. At the top right corner of the latency graph, you will find a button to make the graph full-screen (as shown in the images on page 195).

This latency graph shows the time delay between the start of a request and the response from the server. Checking latency is the main step to understanding the situation of your application. In the graph, you can see the evolution of latency through the last hour; you can change the amount of time checked in the top right corner. The graph is built using a metric: trace.rack.request. This will be useful later when you build your own dashboards using different metrics.

A very important piece of this graph can be found in the bottom part. You can see a list of metrics with the structure percentile:metric(env, service). Datadog offers us the max/slowest case and six percentiles: p50, p75, p90, p95, p99, and p99.9. The p50 percentile shows us the median request latency: 50 percent of the time, the request will be faster, and the other half it will be slower. With p75, 75 percent of the requests will be faster, and the remaining 25 percent will be slower. The same pattern applies to p90, p95, p99, and p99.9: 90/95/99/99.9 percent of the requests will be faster, and the remaining ones will be slower.

The most commonly used percentage in the industry probably is p95, followed by p50 and p99. This is because p95 captures edge cases where performance begins to degrade noticeably; these are often more critical for user experience.

The other interesting section of the APM is "Endpoints." The issue with the previous graph is in the context of a monolith, knowing the general latency may not be very useful. Yes, in some cases, the whole application can become slow. For example, if there is a massive bottleneck in a point used by most requests (like the database), all the endpoints and processes in your application will become slow since they will have to queue to pass through that bottleneck. This is a quasi-catastrophic situation, closer to reliability than to performance itself. Nevertheless, you'll usually want to be more granular and check the performance of each endpoint so you can optimize them.

Clicking on any endpoint will bring you to their "Resource Page." This page has an "Endpoint Overview" section with a similar structure to the one in the "Service Summary," including a latency graph. Check the "Resource Page" for Api::V1::FilmsController#index.

Using Traces

The previous dashboards, based on default metrics on request latency, will be very useful in understanding the "macro" tendencies of your application, even the tendencies in a particular endpoint. However, sometimes it's necessary to "zoom in"; traces will be the tool to use when you need to understand the details of what is happening with certain requests. You can think of a trace as a kind of "breadcrumb trail" left by each request in their journey through your application. Every time a request hits your application, markers will be generated for the steps taken. With them, a complete storyline of the life of the request in your application can be generated. Using traces, you will be able to investigate slowdowns by closely examining each of the steps that a slow request has followed to understand what happened and what needs to be optimized.

You can access traces in Datadog in multiple ways. If you are following from the previous section, you can just scroll down in the "Resource Page" for Api::V1::FilmsController#index: the Traces section is at the bottom. Here, you can already see information about each request that hit the action. To see even more, click the "View all in Trace Explorer" link. You can also access the Trace Explorer in the left sidebar under APM.

First of all, note that at the top of the page, the Trace Explorer is marking as if you were filtering by "Spans." While a trace is the entire journey of a request, a span is an individual unit within the trace, typically representing a single operation. A span can contain other spans, so you can "mark" different parts of the request in your application with the target of monitoring them better.

At the top of the Trace Explorer, you will see a search bar showing the current filters you are applying:

- env:development—Right now, you are running the application in development mode.

- operation_name:rack_request—The operation being monitored; in this case, the request that is being processed by Rack

- service:rails-performance-book—The service that is being monitored

- resource_name:"Api::V1::FilmsController#index"—The resource that we are filtering by; in this case, it's a combination of the controller (Api::V1::FilmsController) and the action(#index).

On the left side of the screen, you will see a list of facets. With those facets, you can change the filters currently applied to your trace search. For example, if you want to check your slowest requests, you can change the "Duration" filter to only see the ones that took over 100ms, for example. You can also check a different resource by changing the selection under "Resource"; try to check the traces for CustomersController#show.

Now, let's dive deeper into one particular trace. Check again the requests to Api::V1::FilmsController#index. On the right side, you will get a list of requests that hit that particular action. Click one of them, and a new panel full of information for that specific request will be displayed. Feel free to click "Open Full Page" to check this more comfortably.

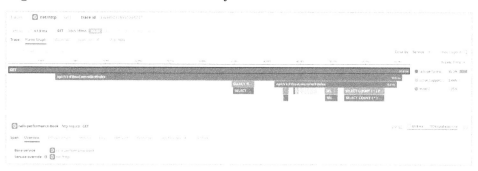

The first section is a flame graph. It represents the execution path of the request across multiple services (like MySQL or the cache layer). If you hover over some of the horizontal bars, you will see more granular information on all the steps executed during the request.

For example, in the trace shown, there was a check on a feature flag in the database (SELECT ... FROM flipper_features ...) that took 3.8 ms. Later, there was a query on the films table that took 922 microseconds. Further down the line, there is a set of accesses to active_support-cache; each one took around 70 microseconds. Those were accesses to fetch the cached JSONs corresponding to each object returned by the requests. Finally, there was a kind of big query at the end of the flame graph—SELECT COUNT (*) FROM films—taking 6.33 ms. If I wanted to optimize this endpoint further, I would take a look at improving that.

How to Read a Flame Graph

Flame graphs can look a bit confusing and feel a tad challenging. Fear not! These are some tips to get as much information as possible with a quick glance:

- Check the widest boxes first: The widest boxes are those in which the request is spending the most time. That means that they also offer the most opportunity to gain performance.

- Look for recurring patterns: If there are repeated "structures" in the flame graph, like a group of boxes of very similar sizes arranged next to each other, investigate further. You might find a loop of calls, n+1 style, that could be a prime candidate for optimization.

- Identify tall stacks: Look for unusually deep call stacks (boxes on top of each other). This suggests the existence of a pretty complex chain of calls. There might be a chance to simplify those calls.

Apart from "Flame Graph," Datadog offers you other ways to visualize the spans that make up the trace. "Span List" can also be quite useful for seeing data in a less visual but more textual way.

Under the flame graph (or the span list), you can see a list of information corresponding to the trace. In particular, the most interesting can be the list under "Span Attributes." You can see all kinds of data. Under http, you will see the method (GET), the status code of the response (200), and the path (api/v1/films). There is more low-level information in attributes, like the process

ID, the language of the service, and so on. All of this is automatically generated by Datadog's integration, and sometimes, it can be insufficient to properly understand what is happening in your application. Fortunately, you can customize traces further.

Customizing Traces

Traces and spans are highly customizable, so you can get exactly the information you need. In this section, you are going to customize the monitoring by adding two new elements:

- A new span attribute that will be added every time a user hits a request associated with a store, like (api/v1/stores/STORE_ID/audits). Adding this attribute can be crucial: if the application you have developed in this book is like a B2B, the store would be something like our customer. Adding the store ID as an attribute will allow you to filter requests by customer, which is basic to diagnosing issues happening in one specific account.

- A new service that will track the processes performed by the presenter layer. This is a way to separate the work done by the database from the one done by parts of our Rails application. Moreover, it's a clean example of how to further segregate the tasks executed by the application so it does not become an untraceable blob.

Let's start by adding a new attribute to the current span. To do so, I recommend you create a new middleware in your application. If you did the "Discovering Sharding" section in the "Thinking Architecture for Performance" chapter, you can inspire yourself with the ShardSwitcher middleware you created then. That middleware could look something like this:

rails-performance-book-completed/app/middleware/datadog_middleware.rb
```ruby
module Middleware
  class DatadogMiddleware
    def initialize(app)
      @app = app
    end

    def call(env)
      request = Rack::Request.new(env)
      request.path =~ /.*stores\/(\d+).*/
      store_id = $1

      Datadog::Tracing.active_span.set_tag("store_id", store_id) if store_id
      @app.call(env)
    end
  end
end
```

The key methods here are the call to Datadog::Tracing.active_span, which returns the current span, and the call to 'set_tag(key, value)', which sets the tag. Remember also to add the middleware to your application configuration in config/application.rb:

rails-performance-book-completed/config/application.rb
```ruby
require_relative '../app/middleware/datadog_middleware'
module Moviestore
  class Application < Rails::Application

    config.middleware.use Middleware::DatadogMiddleware

  end
end
```

With this done, restart your Rails application and test it out. Restart the rake seed_datadog task, or call an endpoint with a store_id parameter, like api/v1/stores/1 or api/v1/stores/1/audits. Now, go back to the Trace Explorer in your Datadog instance and check a trace for resources associated with a store: Api::V1::StoresController#show or Api::V1::AuditsController#index. Check the Span Attributes. At the bottom, you will see your new attribute, store_id. If you hover over it, an options menu should appear, and you should be able to "Filter by &store_id:X", selecting only traces associated with the desired store.

Next, you will create a new service to encapsulate all the presenter logic. Creating a new service in Datadog is simple: you just need to add new traces specifying this new service (as a string parameter). To create a new span, you will need to call the method Datadog::Tracing.trace(trace_name) and pass the logic that makes up the trace as a block. Let's apply this to the presentation layer. Fortunately, all the presentation classes share the same parent class: Api::V1::Presenter. Moreover, this class has only one method (beyond initialize): to_json. This simplifies our task a lot. You just need to wrap all the logic around that method with a new trace. This is a possible solution:

```ruby
# app/presenter/api/v1/presenter.rb

class Api::V1::Presenter
  [...]

  def to_json(exclude: [])
    return nil unless resource
    Datadog::Tracing.trace('presenter.to_json',
      service: 'presentation-layer', resource: resource&.class&.to_s) do

      [...]

    end
  end
end
```

Note that I also added the class of the object presented as the resource of the trace. Once you have created this new trace, call an endpoint a few times that uses the Presenter class (for example, Api::V1::FilmsController#index). Check the span list of any of its traces. You'll see a new service: presentation-layer.

The new service is also available in the Service Catalog and all other Datadog features. Remember that you can learn more about how to customize your traces by reading Datadog's documentation for its Ruby integration.[4]

Using Custom Metrics

Traces offer you the ability to follow the full trip of a request. On the other hand, metrics are numerical data points used to measure all the different aspects of our system. The Datadog integration generates metrics from traces and spans, like the latency of the requests, but you may be interested in generating your own.

There are multiple ways of generating metrics,[5] like generating custom metrics from spans.[6] You can also create your own metrics straight from your application code. Again, Datadog offers us plenty of flexibility. We could call Datadog's Metrics API[7] directly from the app; however, this can be impractical. Making a call to the API every time there is an event we want to measure

---

4. https://docs.datadoghq.com/tracing/trace_collection/automatic_instrumentation/dd_libraries/ruby/#integration-instrumentation

5. https://docs.datadoghq.com/metrics/custom_metrics/

6. https://docs.datadoghq.com/tracing/trace_pipeline/generate_metrics/

7. https://docs.datadoghq.com/api/latest/metrics/#submit-metrics

would not scale very well, and building our own balancing pipeline would take a lot of time. A popular option is using DogStatsD[8] for the task.

DogStatsD is a metrics collection and aggregation service built on top of the StatsD protocol. It will collect, aggregate, and transmit your custom metrics to your Datadog instance. You will need to install both the client in your Rails application (gem 'dogstatsd-ruby') and the server in your application host. Once installed, you will be able to submit a very diverse set of metrics, like counts, histograms, or timers.[9]

Building Your Own Dashboards

Now that you've learned about traces and metrics, it's time to put everything together in a good-looking dashboard—a place that the team can quickly access to understand the current state of the system. In this section, you will build your own performance dashboard.

Access the "Dashboards" section of Datadog (in the menu on the left side). You will see a list of dashboards generated by default by Datadog. Now, hit on "New Dashboard" and give it a good name—something like "General Performance Dashboard." With this, you should be looking at an empty dashboard with no widgets at all. A widget is each of the elements (like graphs) that compose the dashboard. A good dashboard is always full of informative widgets.

However, before creating your widgets, you need to set up the options you'll use to operate those widgets. For example, a widget can show you the p95 latency of your whole application, but that same widget could also show you the p95 latency for a particular endpoint and/or a particular environment if you use *variables*. Create a couple of variables by clicking "Add Variable." The first one should have the Variable tag "env" and that same Variable name. The second one should have the Variable tag "resource_name" and, yes, the same Variable name. With env and resource_name, you will be able to change the environment and the resource being exposed on your widgets dynamically. Note that the default value of all variables is *, that is, all possible values for that variable are enabled.

Next, let's add a widget. You can start by adding a time series that shows the evolution of the latency in our application. Click the window with a "+" and then choose "Timeseries." Here, start by choosing the metric you want to expose in this widget; the latency one is contained in the trace.rack.request metric.

---

8.   https://docs.datadoghq.com/developers/dogstatsd
9.   https://docs.datadoghq.com/metrics/custom_metrics/dogstatsd_metrics_submission/

To be able to use the variables you just created, you will need to add them next to the from space: add $env to it. With this, when you choose an env on the variable bar at the top of the dashboard, the widgets will filter out all the data corresponding to other environments. Finally, as we discussed previously, let's give preference to p95 instead of the average. Replace the avg by with the p95 by. We want to separate the performance of each action, so add resource_name next to the p95 by. You can also give your own title to the dashboard in the last section: I called it "Latency p95". Once you are done, click "Save."

Now, you are going to add a "Query Value" widget with the average latency. You can do so by clicking again on the window with a "+" and, this time, choosing "Query Value". Again, you want to build your widget around the trace.rack.request metric, but you want to have both $env and $resource_name on the from space and keep calculating the average (avg).

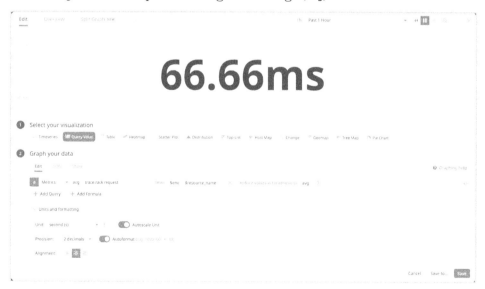

Finally, let's add a graph with something not directly related to latency. For example, it can be interesting to see which endpoints are the most used. You can do so by adding a "Top List" widget. The metric you need to choose is trace.rack.request.hits. You will also need to sum the results by resource_name. With this done, you can decide to expose the results as hits/second or as the absolute value of hits in a given time. For the absolute value, you will require the count (as count) and the sum of the results (reduce values in timeframe to sum). For the rate, you have to require the rate (as rate) and then average the results (reduce values in timeframe to avg). After that, you can also choose how many resources you want to expose and if you want to show the top or the bottom ones.

You have created three widgets, enough for a very basic dashboard. You can play with the size and position of the widgets to make it look as nice as possible.

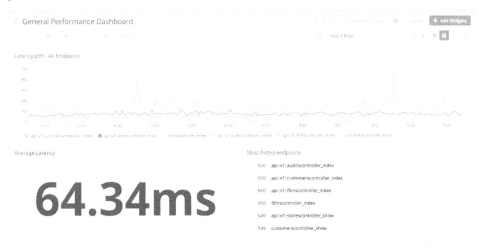

Done! I encourage you to experiment further with the metrics you currently have, to check all the other kinds of widgets that are available to you, and read the documentation[10] to learn more about the nuances and possibilities of the queries that populate your widgets.

Setting Up Performance Error Budgets

Now, you have multiple ways to visualize how performant your system is. But how can you use those tools to keep that performance on time? Well, the answer to that comes from reliability engineering. Its name: error budgets.

An error budget is a concept that defines the acceptable level of system unreliability over a period of time. It is assumed that having 100 percent uptime is neither realistic nor cost-effective. Instead, organizations define SLOs (Service Level Objectives). For example, Twilio maintains a staggering 99.999 percent (aka, five nines) of availability.[11] This means that every year, Twilio only has a *max* downtime of five minutes and 16 seconds, which is less than half a minute per month.

How can we apply this concept to performance? Well, SLOs do not only need to be associated with a working system. We can define thresholds as we desire. In particular, we can define an endpoint as performant if it's resolving requests in less than X milliseconds.

Defining SLOs

In this section, you will define a series of performance SLOs; they will materialize your error budget. You can create a new SLO by going to the left sidebar: Service Management > SLOs. There, when you create a new SLO, you will have to choose between three options:

- By Count: Measures reliability as a ratio of good/total events

- By Monitor Uptime: Measures the uptime of your monitors. A Monitor is a tool that continuously evaluates the state of the application. They are configured to alert the system stakeholders when a defined threshold of condition is breached.

- By Time Slices: Measure reliability using a custom uptime definition. This is ideal for our purpose, as we are going to give an alternative definition of uptime, one we could call "performant uptime."

---

10. https://docs.datadoghq.com/dashboards/querying/
11. https://aws.amazon.com/solutions/case-studies/twilio/

Choose "By Time Slices", and, as you did before with the widgets in the dashboard, you will need to configure a query. Try to set up an SLO that would be breached if Api::V1::FilmsController#index returns in more than 200 ms one percent of the time. To achieve this, you will need to use (again) our old friend, the trace.rack.request metric. You will filter the requests to the desired action by adding from resource_name:api::v1::filmscontroller_index. It's time to define the threshold itself; you can do so in the next section, "Set your target & time window." Set the window to 30 days, with a target of 99 percent. Feel free to add a slightly higher percentage as a warning threshold. Finally, choose a name for the SLO. Remember to add rails-performance-book as the service, as it will be useful later when you build the Error Budget dashboard.

Now, a challenge for you: create a few more SLOs, following the pattern of the one you just created. Try to do so for at least three other resources. You will notice that some resources are slower (like Api::V1::CustomersController#index), and therefore a higher uptime limit is reasonable.

SLOs, SLIs, SLAs

SLOs, SLIs, and SLAs. Three very similar terms define concepts in the same space but mean different things. Let's briefly define them:

- SLOs (Service Level Objectives): The goal for the service. In our case, this goal would be performance-related, like the maximum p95 latency for a given endpoint.

- SLIs (Service Level Indicators): The metric that measures the performance of the service

- SLAs (Service Level Agreements): An agreement between the provider of the service and the stakeholders/customers specifying the level of service. It's tied to a SLO.

For example, if the SLO for api/v1/films is a p95 latency of 200 ms, the service would achieve if the SLI (the indicator) is 180 ms, but it would breach if it was 220 ms. The SLA would also be a p95 latency of 200 ms, but it's something that was agreed upon with the customer and can have consequences if it's breached.

Building a Dashboard for Your Error Budget

With a few SLOs defined, it's time to build a dashboard that lets you monitor them comfortably. Datadog offers two widgets to work with Service Level Objectives: SLO List and SLO. SLO List exposes the most important information of all SLOs (up to 100) that match the query that defines the widget. The SLO widget focuses on one SLO, offering more information and being more customizable.

Create a new dashboard (I gave mine the name "Performance Error Budget"). First, add an SLO List widget. The only thing you need to do is add a filter; in this case, one that fetches all the SLOs of the service rails-performance-book.

Next, add two SLO widgets: one for Api::V1::FilmsController#index and another for Api::V1::Audits#index. You will have to select the SLO and, most importantly, the time windows that will be exposed. You can choose rolling time windows (the last 7, 30, or 90 days); calendar time windows (week to date, previous week, month to date, and previous month); and finally, you have the "Global time" option, that makes the window vary with the setting on the top of the dashboard, including a customizable limit percentage (as shown in the image on page 209). Choose whichever options feel more right for you, but I would recommend being consistent: don't monitor one endpoint by the last seven days and another by the calendar month if you don't have a very good reason to do so.

That's it! You have an Error Budget dashboard running! Now you will be able to check in real time how your SLOs are evolving.

Performance Alerts

Datadog provides you with many options to alert you when certain thresholds have been crossed. This is typically used to monitor errors, but if we agree that performance is a vital feature, shouldn't you set up alerts to warn you of degrading performance?

Well, surprise, surprise...my answer is a *cautious* no. The issue here is that performance alerts are particularly exposed to what I believe is the most rampant disease in monitoring in the industry: engineering teams getting drowned by false positives.

With alerts, more is not always better. Many have the understandable fear of missing a problem because of a lack of alerts; in my experience, experienced teams tend to fall more on the opposite side of the spectrum: missing issues because of an excess of alerting. Be conscious of this when setting up your alerts.

A noisy alerting system is as bad as, if not worse than, having no alerting system at all. This is particularly bad for performance, as the work has a more preemptive, easier-to-skip nature than fixing a broken application. Having an alerting system may end up replacing the periodical checks that, in my experience, work better with performance optimization.

Being Wary of How Much You Spend

Before closing this section, a word of caution: spending on monitoring can easily get out of hand. For example, in 2023, The Pragmatic Engineer reported that Coinbase (another company that uses Rails) spent 65 million dollars in one year on Datadog.[12] This, plus the sudden chill of Coinbase's main business (crypto), triggered the company to spin an effort to migrate to a different observability platform: one made in-house and built with a combination of Grafana, Prometheus, and Clickhouse.

While that sheer amount of money spent is uncommon, it's not uncommon for businesses to find themselves spending way more than they had imagined on monitoring platforms. Setting the autopilot on in your monitoring features can lead you to some nasty surprises.

Through the years, I have been involved in efforts to reduce our monitoring costs. The good news is that you should be able to set up thorough monitoring of your system without spending a fortune. One of the most common problems I have found is temporary metrics. You are driving an initiative (a new feature, an optimization...), so you do the right thing and create new metrics and even a dashboard to monitor the performance of your project. Great! The issue comes when time passes (months, years...) and all those metrics stay there. It's probable that you don't need such a level of monitorization anymore. You can probably leave the more general metrics of the new feature and integrate them with already existing dashboards.

Summing Up

You just completed the chapter on monitoring. I want to reiterate a couple of things: this was just an introduction to monitoring, something that should be more than enough for you to build the base of your monitoring system. Later, as your application grows, you will discover the most fitting practices to check on the performance of your own application.

Moreover, despite the fact that in this whole chapter you have been working with Datadog, do not feel that you *need* to use this platform. As I said before, I have chosen it for the book as it's the one that I am the most used to, but there are other very good options. What I would like you to keep in mind is not the specifics of setting up traces or building a dashboard on Datadog but the general philosophy of monitoring an application.

---

12. https://newsletter.pragmaticengineer.com/p/the-scoop-47

In fact, we started the chapter by presenting different options (Grafana with Prometheus, NewRelic, and Datadog) you can use to monitor your application. Later you integrated the Datadog client with your app and learned how to use some of its tools: the APM, traces, spans, and metrics.

Once we moved on from those basic elements, you built some dashboards that helped you visualize all the data generated by your app. Following this line, we have discussed the concept of SLOs and how they help us to build performance error budgets that, following concepts from reliability engineering, help developers to scale applications.

Time to move to the final chapter: we will discuss the implications of scaling, beyond performance.

Scaling, Beyond Performance

Welcome to the last main chapter! It has been quite a trip getting here, but you've made it! You've now seen everything strictly related to performance. However, this does not mean that you've reached the end. It turns out that scaling a Rails application and the business use case that typically accompanies it is not only about returning a response lightning fast. In this chapter, we will explore the difficulties associated with scaling a Rails application (and, more in general, a monolith) and what you can do to minimize those issues. I will call this set of problems "scaling teams."

Discussing how to scale teams is surprisingly different from discussing performance, so much so that even the tone of the discussion is quite different. In my experience, performance debates are a tad more aggressive, with nay-sayers of Ruby making quite extreme points. It seems to be an ideal area for software engineering influencers; bombastic statements, after all, make for a good show. I believe that this is because performance can seem like a deceptively simple part of software engineering. After all, the response time of a technology for a very specific use case in specific conditions can be measured objectively. Alas, building a system is more complex than stating that technology "x" can print "Hello World" five times faster than technology "y". Talking about scaling teams is more complicated and nuanced but, in my opinion, much less toxic. It's, in many ways, a human problem, and human problems are more obviously complex and subtle. The issues pointed out by Rails' detractors are typically about the difficulty of coordinating a large number of teams when all of them are working at the same time on the same codebase. Those are real problems, which don't exist (or are far less damaging) in microservice architectures. For example, who do you page when there is an incident in the monolith? On a microservice architecture, this is apparently more obvious: detect the service that is causing the problem and contact the team that owns it. There are similar problems associated with deployments, rolling out features, and so on. These are known issues, and in this chapter, you are going to explore the solutions.

Many of the techniques we are going to discuss are common among big players in the tech industry. In September 2024, I attended Friendly.rb, a Ruby conference in Bucharest, where I participated in a panel discussion on the scalability of Rails. I appreciated that in the panel, we not only debated about performance but a point was made about discussing how to scale *teams*. It turned out that Github (represented by Hana Harencarova) used very similar patterns and techniques to the ones we used at Zendesk (which I was representing). Now, your application can use the same techniques as the best in the field.

Setting Up Ownership for Your Application

It may be hard to imagine for people working in a startup with ten engineers, but major companies that use monolithic architectures (or monolith-ish, as in big applications that are accompanied by a few services) can have hundreds of engineers merging commits into the same Rails app.

The basic concept is brutally simple: *each and every file in your codebase should have an owner.* This does not mean that only the owner of that file can modify it. It just means that any change needs to be approved by the owner.

How do we enforce ownership? There are multiple ways, but maintaining the rules of the system can be difficult if you have to build something by yourself, with its only purpose being to enforce the rules. Fortunately, GitHub (the most popular repository hosting, also used in this book) provides a feature to declare ownership.[1] Other popular providers, like GitLab,[2] do the same.

While your application right now does not have any kind of ownership problems, we are going to set it up for the future, so when new engineers join, the boundaries are already defined. You can start by creating a .github folder in the root of your Rails application. Then, create a file named CODEOWNERS. In it, you will declare different patterns for files and folders,

---

1. https://docs.github.com/en/repositories/managing-your-repositorys-settings-and-features/customizing-your-repository/about-code-owners
2. https://docs.gitlab.com/ee/user/project/codeowners/

followed by the developer or team of developers that owns it. This is an example:

```
# .github/CODEOWNERS

app/controllers/admin_controller.rb @amikhaylov
app/controllers/admin @amikhaylov
app/controllers/* @Gawyn
app/models/* me@cristianplanas.com
*.js @frontend-org/js-team
.github/ @Gawyn
```

In the previous example, my friend (and reviewer of this book) @amikhaylov owns the file app/controllers/admin_controller.rb. He also owns everything under the folder app/controllers/admin, including subfolders. The next owner listed is @Gawyn, which is my GitHub username. I own all the files in the folder app/controllers/, but nothing in its subfolders; exactly the same applies to app/models, but this time, I used my email instead of my username to associate files to my GitHub user. Next, you'll find a line that serves as an example of giving ownership to a team instead of a particular developer. In it, we gave ownership of all our JavaScript files to the "js-team" in the "frontend-org" organization. Finally, we protected the CODEOWNERS file itself by giving owner-ship of the .github folder to me.

Once you push this CODEOWNERS file into the main branch, you will need to set up protection for the main branch,[3] with a rule to enforce the ownership. You can do so in the GitHub settings of your project in the "Rulesets" section as shown on page 216. Creating a new branch ruleset that should apply to your main branch. This new ruleset should require a pull request before merging (in my opinion, you should require that even if you are not setting file owner-ship). You should require at least one approval and that the review comes from the user(s) designated as a Code Owner. Note that the trade-off here is the reliability of the system in exchange for development speed. Requiring too many approvals can heavily hurt your capacity to ship code.

Reviewing and Accepting

How do these rules affect how we merge code? Well, you can check how the PR screen looks when the author is modifying a protected file. I have prepared an example on the public repository[4] that accompanies this book. Look at the figure on page 216.

---

3. https://docs.github.com/en/repositories/configuring-branches-and-merges-in-your-repository/managing-protected-branches/about-protected-branches
4. https://github.com/Gawyn/rails-performance-book/pull/5

✅ Require a pull request before merging

Require all commits be made to a non-target branch and submitted via a pull request before they can be merged.

Hide additional settings ∧

Required approvals

1 ▾

The number of approving reviews that are required before a pull request can be merged.

☐ **Dismiss stale pull request approvals when new commits are pushed**
New, reviewable commits pushed will dismiss previous pull request review approvals.

✅ **Require review from Code Owners**
Require an approving review in pull requests that modify files that have a designated code owner.

☐ **Require approval of the most recent reviewable push**
Whether the most recent reviewable push must be approved by someone other than the person who pushed it.

☐ **Require conversation resolution before merging**
All conversations on code must be resolved before a pull request can be merged.

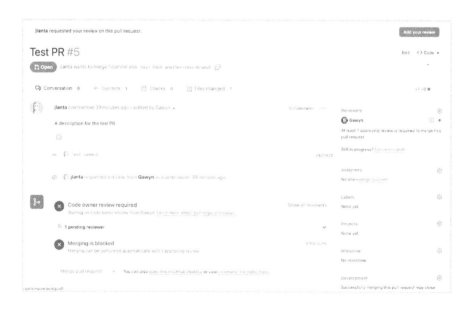

In our repository, the author of the PR, @jlanta, is one of the contributors. Still, she is not able to merge the PR. It requires a review by the owner of the modified files. Because the PR is modifying one of the controllers (app/controllers/customers_controller.rb), and all the controllers outside of the admin space are owned by @Gawyn, the PR requires approval from @Gawyn to be merged.

Modularizing Your Application

Defining clear ownership boundaries minimizes conflict between developers and teams, but it will not help to reduce the energy required to understand the application or even a piece of it. An onboarding engineer getting into an application with millions of lines of code will not be reading them all. Most probably, the newcomer will not be checking the CODEOWNERS file to read all the files owned by the team. Moreover, there are other problems related to having a large monolithic codebase. This kind of codebase typically lacks a clear structure, becoming the infamous "Big Ball of Mud." In a 1997 paper aptly titled "Big Ball of Mud,"[5] the authors, Brian Foote and Joseph Yoder, explore what they call "the most frequently deployed architecture":

> A BIG BALL OF MUD is haphazardly structured, sprawling, sloppy, duct-tape and bailing wire, spaghetti code jungle. We've all seen them. These systems show unmistakable signs of unregulated growth and repeated, expedient repair. Information is shared promiscuously among distant elements of the system, often to the point where nearly all the important information becomes global or duplicated. The overall structure of the system may never have been well defined. If it was, it may have eroded beyond recognition. Programmers with a shred of architectural sensibility shun these quagmires. Only those who are unconcerned about architecture and, perhaps, are comfortable with the inertia of the day-to-day chore of patching the holes in these failing dikes are content to work on such systems.

The paper is full of interesting insights on the nature of designing software; it's also really funny. I recommend you check it out if you haven't done so yet. Still, the issue is that Rails applications that support successful use cases have more chances of becoming "big balls of mud." A lot of times, it's because of an increase in the number of features provided by the system (aka feature bloat); other times, it's because the required speed of development makes it very hard to work with a clear architecture in mind. How can we stop the "promiscuous sharing of information among distant elements of the system"? Can we reduce the amount of coupling and reintroduce boundaries?

---

5.   https://www.researchgate.net/publication/2938621_Big_Ball_of_Mud

Enter the modular monolith. In a modular monolith, the codebase is divided into folders by logical domains that interact only when necessary and, in a structured way, provide functional isolation. This is a key advantage of microservices and one that, theoretically, we can keep while maintaining a monolith. Of course, it can be argued that microservice architectures are better at being modular, as they have a much harder constraint than almost anything we can add to a codebase. That's a valid point. However, this does not mean that we cannot establish certain modularization in the codebase of our monolith while keeping all the advantages of it: same infrastructure, same language, more consistency, no/less network usage, and so on.

In this section, we'll explore how to transform your Rails application into a modular monolith.

Adding Packwerk

In 2020, Shopify released the most popular gem to establish modules in a Rails app codebase: Packwerk.[6] It is currently being used by many large companies, including Zendesk, GitHub, and Shopify itself.

Again, I ask you to add a gem to your project. Add Packwerk to your Gemfile (gem 'packwerk') and then run bundle install. To run Packwerk, you will need to have Zeitwerk[7] enabled; it comes by default since Rails 6. After running bundle install, you will have to run bundle binstub packwerk in the terminal; this will generate a packwerk file in the bin folder of your application. Finally, to generate the configuration files, you will use that new file by executing bin/packwerk init.

Note that Packwerk uses identity_cache. If you have been following the book, your project already has it configured. However, to use all the features in Packwerk, you will have to configure identity_cache in all environments, including production and test. You can do that by adding the following to your environment configuration files in config/environments/:

```
# config/environments/development.rb
# config/environments/production.rb
# config/environments/test.rb

config.identity_cache_store = :mem_cache_store, {
  expires_in: 6.hours.to_i,
  failover: false,
}
```

---

6.   https://github.com/Shopify/packwerk
7.   https://github.com/fxn/zeitwerk

At this point, everything should be ready for you to build your first package. Packwerk offers you two tools to validate and check that your application structure and dependencies are correct: bin/packwerk validate and bin/packwerk check. Before moving on, you can run check to confirm everything is OK:

```
% bin/packwerk validate

Finished in 1.06 seconds

Validation successful
```

Everything seems to be in place, so now we can run our first dependency check in between packages:

```
% bin/packwerk check
Packwerk is inspecting 133 files
................................................
Finished in 2.43 seconds

No offenses detected
No stale violations detected
```

No offenses and no violations were detected. Of course, that was expected; there are no packages yet, so no offenses of undeclared dependencies are possible.

Building Your First Package

Let's start modularizing the application by creating one package. It may be a good idea to start with a piece of code that is naturally isolated from the rest of the application: all the functionality related to audits, which you created earlier in this book, is an ideal candidate.

Create a components folder in the root of your Rails application. In it, create a subfolder with the name audit. This subfolder will mimic the structure of a Rails application. Given that the logic for audits is divided into three different kinds of classes (a model, a controller, and a presenter), you will have to copy the same folder structure that currently holds audit.rb, audits_controller.rb and audit_presenter.rb. This also implies copying the api/v1 part of the structure, as it is required to keep our namespacing. This is the structure you want:

```
components/
  audit/
    app/
      controllers/
        api/
          v1/
      models/
      presenters/
        api/
          v1/
```

To get it, you can use mkdir with the -p flag:

```
% mkdir -p components/audit/app/controllers/api/v1
% mkdir -p components/audit/app/models
% mkdir -p components/audit/app/presenters/api/v1
```

Now, move those three files to the folders you just created for them:

```
% mv app/controllers/api/v1/audits_controller.rb
   components/audit/app/controllers/api/v1/.
% mv app/models/audit.rb components/audit/app/models/.
% mv app/presenters/api/v1/audit_presenter.rb
   components/audit/app/presenters/api/v1/.
```

By removing all these files from the app/ subfolders, they are not being autoloaded anymore. You will need to modify config/application.rb so the classes located under components/ are also loaded:

rails-performance-book-completed/config/application.rb
```
module Moviestore
  class Application < Rails::Application

    Dir["./components/*"].each do |path|
      next unless File.directory?(path)
      component = path.split("/").last

      config.autoload_paths +=
        Dir[Rails.root.join('components', component, 'app', '**')]
    end
  end
end
```

Note that we are adding all the first-level subfolders of components/[component]/app: subfolders like controllers, models, and presenters. We do it like this because we need to respect the folder that defines the namespacing. If we loaded components/audit/app/controllers/api/v1 directly, Zeitwerk (Rails default code loader) would expect a class without the Api::V1 namespacing.

The last step is to formally define the package by creating a package.yml file in the components/audit folder. It should follow a similar structure to the one you can find in the root folder. In my case, I just added some metadata defining ownership and, crucially, enforced checking dependencies:

```
metadata:
  stewards:
    - "@Gawyn"
enforce_dependencies: true
```

You have your first package! Does it have dependencies?

```
% bin/packwerk check
Packwerk is inspecting 133 files
................................................
................EEE............................
Finished in 1.36 seconds

components/audit/app/controllers/api/v1/audits_controller.rb:1:34
Dependency violation: ::ApplicationController belongs to '.',
  but 'components/audit' does not specify a dependency on '.'.
Are we missing an abstraction?
Is the code making the reference, and the referenced constant,
  in the right packages?

Inference details: this is a reference to ::ApplicationController
  which seems to be defined in app/controllers/application_controller.rb.
To receive help interpreting or resolving this error message, see:
  https://github.com/Shopify/packwerk/blob/
    main/TROUBLESHOOT.md#Troubleshooting-violations

[...]
```

You will see that Packwerk detects dependencies with four classes: ApplicationController, ShardRecord, Api::V1::Presenter, and Store. In my opinion, you can divide these four classes into two groups. The first group is formed by the classes that are "building blocks" for the whole application (ApplicationController, ShardRecord, and Api::V1::Presenter). The second group is the one class that should be part of a different business logic component, Store. In fact, the first group could also be its own component, something with a name like platform.

Next, you will check the undeclared dependencies across components. Note that, before doing this, you will need to make sure that all packages (the one in audit and the one in the root folder) are enforcing dependencies. This means that they have the option enforce_dependencies set to true in their package.yml.

Packwerk helps you to keep track of these undeclared dependencies by generating a TODO file. You can do it by executing bin/packwerk update-todo. This will create two package_todo.yml files: one in the Root folder for the default (".") package, and another in components/audit for the audit package. The former looks like this:

```
# This file contains a list of dependencies that are not part
# of the long term plan for the '.' package.
# We should generally work to reduce this list over time.
#
# You can regenerate this file using the following command:
#
```

```
# bin/packwerk update-todo
- - -
components/audit:
  "::Audit":
    violations:
    - dependency
    files:
    - app/models/rental.rb
    - app/models/store.rb
```

Still, for the time being, we should declare these dependencies. You can do so by adding a dependencies attribute in both package.yml. The one for "." at the root folder should include this:

```
dependencies:
  - components/audit
```

The one for the audit component should include this:

```
dependencies:
  - "."
```

If you run bin/packwerk check, you will have no violations; running bin/packwerk update-todo will remove both package_todo.yml files. Done? Well, not really. Remember the validate function you used in the beginning? It may have something to say about this frenzied adding of dependencies. Run bin/packwerk validate, and you should get something like this:

```
% bin/packwerk validate
Packwerk is running validation...

Finished in 1.02 seconds

Validation failed

Expected the package dependency graph to be acyclic,
  but it contains the following circular dependencies:

        - . → components/audit → .
```

It turns out that you just defined a cyclical dependency! Having dependencies like this basically beats the purpose of having modularization set up in the first place. If you had to extract them into different applications, how could you do it? There are a couple of solutions here: one, to merge them back into one bigger package, and two, which makes more sense in this case, moving the circularly referenced code into a new intermediary package on which both other packages can depend.

Setting Privacy Boundaries

Dependency delimitation is incredibly useful but is not the only usage of modularization. Another useful feature of this process is defining public interfaces for the packages, so a dependency does not imply that anything can be directly required. Until Packwerk 3, there was an out-of-the-box feature (enforce_privacy) to declare public elements of a component and mark everything else as private. Now, you'll need to add an extension to do so.

Let's do it. Start by adding a new gem to your Gemfile: gem "packwerk-extensions".[8] This gem not only provides the Privacy Checker functionality, which was extracted from Packwerk, but also includes others like Visibility Checker, Folder-Visibility Checker, and Layer Checker. Still, today, we only want to add the Privacy Checker, so edit the packwerk.yml file in the root folder and add the following:

```
# packwerk.yml

require:
  - packwerk/privacy/checker
```

Enforcing privacy is disabled by default, so let's enable it for our audit component. Do so by adding the following to components/audit/package.yml:

```
enforce_privacy: true
```

With this option, running check will return multiple violations despite the factthat the root component and the audit component are dependencies of each other:

```
% bin/packwerk check
Packwerk is inspecting 134 files
................................................
...............E.............................
Finished in 1.4 seconds

app/models/store.rb:7:2
Privacy violation: '::Audit' is private to 'components/audit'
  but referenced from '.'.
Is there a public entrypoint in 'components/audit/app/public/'
  that you can use instead?

Inference details: this is a reference to ::Audit which seems
  to be defined in components/audit/app/models/audit.rb.
```

---

8. https://github.com/rubyatscale/packwerk-extensions

```
To receive help interpreting or resolving this error message, see:
  https://github.com/Shopify/packwerk/blob/
    main/TROUBLESHOOT.md#Troubleshooting-violations
[...]

1 offense detected

No stale violations detected
```

In my case, Packwerk found only one violation, which came from the Store class. This corresponds to the invocation of the Audit class on the generate_audit method:

```
# app/models/store.rb

class Store

  [...]

  def generate_audit(event, subject, actor)
    ActiveRecord::Base.connected_to(shard: shard) do
      Audit.create(
        event: event,
        subject: subject,
        actor: actor,
        store: self
      )
    end
  end
end
```

You are going to fix this problem so there are no privacy issues anymore, and you will do it in a way that will solve future issues, too. You are going to have to declare a public API so other packages can use the features from audit without incurring privacy issues. By default, all classes declared in files located under the public folder in a package will be fair game for our privacy checker. With that purpose in mind, create a public folder under components/audit/app and write a class that will allow other components to execute Audit.where and Audit.create. My extremely simplified solution looks like this:

```
rails-performance-book-completed/components/audit/app/public/audit_interface.rb
class AuditInterface
  def self.create(params)
    Audit.create(params)
  end

  def self.where(params)
    Audit.where(params)
  end
end
```

Now, replace the call to Audit.create in the Store class with calls to AuditInterface.where and AuditInterface.create. With this, only methods that have been intentionally defined as public by being added to AuditInterface are available for external packages. Test this by calling bin/packwerk check again:

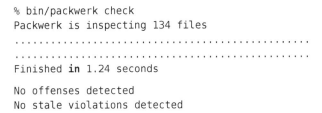

```
% bin/packwerk check
Packwerk is inspecting 134 files
..............................................
..............................................
Finished in 1.24 seconds

No offenses detected
No stale violations detected
```

No offenses, no violations. I would call this a win!

Most importantly, Packwerk is a very flexible tool: one can be more or less strict about adding new dependencies. You can use it as something exclusively informative or as a hard limit around which you create the complete design of your application. It is your call, and it is an important one. Next, we will discuss this and other theoretical issues around modularization.

The Limits of Modularization

While I was writing this chapter in 2024, Rails World took place in Toronto. When the agenda was announced, there was one talk that particularly got my attention. It was the keynote for the second day, "The Myth of the Modular Monolith,"[9] by Rails Core and Shopify Staff Engineer Eileen Uchitelle. I have been a big fan of her talks since I saw her keynote[10] about Rails scalability at RailsConf 2018 in Pittsburgh. Moreover, the topic was obviously interesting to me at that point, given that I was writing this section, which is basically a recommendation for the usage of modules in Rails applications to tame the complexity inherent in large Rails apps. The fact that a Rails Core member working at Shopify (creator of Packwerk) would have a keynote suggesting that modular monoliths were not the way obviously interested and worried me.

In the presentation, Eileen points to six goals that modularity (and, more particularly, the implementation of Packwerk into the codebase of Shopify) was set to achieve. She divides them into three categories: architectural, operational, and organizational. Those objectives were:

- Lack of organization and structure (Architectural)
- Tight coupling and no boundaries (Architectural)

9.   https://www.youtube.com/watch?v=olxoNDBp6Rg
10. https://www.youtube.com/watch?v=8evXWvM4oXM

- Flaky tests and slow CI (Continuous Integration) (Operational)
- Scalability of deployments (Operational)
- Difficult to assign and find owners (Organizational)
- Onboarding new hires takes too long (Organizational)

CI: Continuous Integration

CI, or Continuous Integration, is a development practice where code changes are automatically built, tested, and integrated into a shared repository. Thanks to CI, issues can be detected earlier, before they escalate and affect stakeholders.

In the context discussed here, we are primarily referencing the test suite, which is automatically executed in response to events like new pull requests, commits, or merges.

Of the objectives, I must admit that I had never expected modularization to help with operational issues. Theoretically, you could speed up your CI by only executing the tests of the modified components, but on a CI level, you typically want to be conservative and run the whole suite. I do not see a clear path to deploy components in the context of a monolith, and I do not see how modularization would help with flaky tests.

However, I do find value in modularization for the other two categories: architectural and organizational issues. For example, openly declaring owners of components helps to find the right person to take care of certain areas. This is the way I find out who to talk to about specific problems in the organization. Reducing the visible amount of code to be learned helps, in my opinion, new hires to be more successful. Finally, while trying to remove any kind of coupling between components is an exhausting task that may not be worth it, setting up components and keeping an eye on the structure of the code does help to improve the quality of the code and make its complexity more tractable. Of course, I do admit that modularization is no silver bullet, but neither is any architectural solution; even in microservice architectures, finding the "owner" of a bug can be complicated, as services interact with each other in very complex ways.

The conclusion of the keynote was that the shortcomings of modularization are not an issue of the technique itself, but that their target was unachievable by technical means. Modularization was set to fix complexity problems that are innate to any large human enterprise and, quoting her, *"You cannot solve human problems with modularity"* (another great quote in that same tone from the presentation is *"You can't engineer yourself out of a large org"*).

I do agree that modularity is not able to solve these problems—there is certainly no silver bullet for those, and even less so at the technical level. Nevertheless, I do believe that certain techniques, like modularity, deliver value by reorganizing that complexity in ways that make it easier for a human being to understand. The applications used by large organizations are complex because the use case those organizations serve is complex in itself. There is no way to erase that complexity that doesn't mutilate the purpose of the org. We should not aspire to remove that complexity; what we need to do is find better ways to manage it. And for that purpose, I believe that modularization works.

Using Feature Flags for Better Rollouts

Another common source of problems with a big monolithic codebase id the deployment pipeline. Deploying is, in general, slow. Moreover, if something goes wrong with your newly deployed code, having to execute an unexpected deployment in the middle of the day can disrupt the whole engineering team. And, as your application grows, it becomes harder to be completely sure that your brand-new code will not hit some edge case—a circumstance that can force you to roll back the whole deployment altogether.

What if you could switch on and off parts of your application logic at will, making deployments a no-risk matter? What if you could enable a feature only for a group of selected users and add or remove users from that feature at will, using a UI? What if you could slowly roll out a feature, making sure that the freshly baked design is able to scale for all your users? This is exactly what feature flags allow you to do.

Think of feature flags like remote controls for your code: small switches embedded in your application, tied to data in your database (or, in certain designs, in an external service), that allow you to decide, in real-time, whether you want to turn certain features on or off. Modern feature flag systems allow you to roll out new features slowly. You can start by enabling the feature for 10 percent of your users, wait a few days, do 25 percent, wait a few days…giving yourself enough time to detect anything that can go wrong. You can also target specific users, like customers who offered themselves as beta testers, or you can write some ad hoc logic that will include or exclude users of that particular code path.

Again, the Ruby community has built good tools that you will find at your disposal if you want to add feature flags to your application. This said, the most popular feature flag implementation in Ruby is Flipper.[11] Flipper also comes with some nice features that other libraries currently lack (like a UI), so I recommend you pick Flipper.

Understanding the Structure of a Feature Flag

Let's start by adding a new gem (almost the last one!) to your project. Add Flipper (gem 'flipper') to your Gemfile. Flipper also requires you to install a storage adapter. For this exercise, you need to install the ActiveRecord one (gem 'flipper-active_record'), but Flipper also supports others, like Mongo, Redis, and Sequel.

At this point, you have to choose if you want to have your feature flag hosted in the cloud or locally. I strongly recommend you go for the local option. One of the best characteristics of having a monolith is that we do not need to deal with the network as much as in other kinds of architectures. To enable the "cloudless" version of Flipper, you are going to have to prepare your database. Do so by executing rails g flipper:setup and rails db:migrate:

```
% bin/rails g flipper:setup
  create  db/migrate/20241021232036_create_flipper_tables.rb
% rails db:migrate
== 20241021232036 CreateFlipperTables: migrating ==
-- create_table(:flipper_features)
   -> 0.0103s
-- add_index(:flipper_features, :key, {:unique=>true})
   -> 0.0103s
-- create_table(:flipper_gates)
   -> 0.0041s
-- add_index(:flipper_gates, [:feature_key, :key, :value],
  {:unique=>true, :length=>{:value=>255}})
   -> 0.0036s
== 20241021232036 CreateFlipperTables: migrated (0.0284s) ==
```

You just created two tables: flipper_features and flipper_gates. flipper_features is basically a list of all the features in the system, while flipper_gates holds the key to the logic. Let's explore the structure of this last table a little bit further, as it describes how feature flags are implemented. This can be useful if, in the future, you want to extend the existing behavior or even implement your own feature flag system. The flipper_gates table has three main columns:

- Feature Key (feature_key): The name of the feature that you want to control. For example, if you want to add a new search feature to your application, you can create a feature called search.

---

11. https://github.com/flippercloud/flipper

- Key (key): This is the way that the feature is enabled. Next, we will comment on the six different ways that Flipper offers to enable a feature, but for example, just enabling a feature will create a feature_gate with boolean as a key.

- Value: The value associated with the previous key. Depending on the key, it can be a number, a Boolean, a combination of a class, or an ID. Going back to the previous example, if the feature has been enabled, the value would be true.

The following are the six different ways to control features provided by Flipper. You can read more in the chapter dedicated to features in Flipper's documentation:[12]

Key	Value	Description
Boolean	true/false	Enable a feature for all users
expression	An Arel-like expression	Enable a feature for all actors that match a certain query
actor	A combination of class and ID ("User;10")	Enable a feature for a specific actor. Any model can be an actor.
percentage_of_actors	A percentage	Enable a feature for x percent of the members of the actor class
percentage_of_time	A percentage	Enable a feature x percent of the time, regardless of the actor
group	The name of the group	Enable a feature for actors that belong to a group. A group needs to be defined in the code, typically by declaring a block that returns a Boolean.[13]

Here are some examples of how to use them:

```
# Boolean
Flipper.enable(:search)

# Expression
new_year_actors = Flipper.property(:created_at)
  .lte(Time.now.beginning_of_year.to_s)
Flipper.enable(:new_year_feature, new_year_actors)

# Actors
Flipper.enable_actor(:feature_for_first_user, User.first)
```

---

12. https://www.flippercloud.io/docs/features
13. https://www.flippercloud.io/docs/features/groups

```
# Percentage of Actors
Flipper.enable_percentage_of_actors(:experimental_design, 10)

# Percentage of Time
Flipper.enable_percentage_of_time(:experimental_feature, 50)

# Groups
# The following block needs to be included in an initializer
Flipper.register(:heavy_users) do |actor, context|
  actor.respond_to?(:rentals_count) && actor.rentals_count > 100
end
Flipper.enable_group(:heavy_users_feature, :heavy_users)
```

All feature gates can be removed by using exactly the same method, but replacing enable with disable.

To check if a feature is enabled, you need to call Flipper.enabled?. If the created feature does not depend on any actor, you only need to pass one parameter, the name of the feature (Flipper.enabled?(:search)). In most cases, though, you want to pass the name of the feature and the actor to see if the feature is enabled for that specific case (Flipper.enabled?(:new_year_feature, current_user)).

All these different types of feature flags have different use cases. In my experience, the most used one may be "Percentage of Actors"; you can start with a zero, and slowly increase the percentage until you get to what is called GA (General Availability): the feature is released to 100 percent of the actors. Typically, your actor is going to be a very specific kind of class. In a B2B company, it would be the account of your customer. In a B2C, it would be the registered user. They are the basic elements on top of which you should build your feature release flow. Another two that are commonly used are "Expression" and "Groups," which serve the same purpose: to target a feature for a specific type of actor. For example, you can enable a feature for customers depending on their characteristics, like country of origin, amount of usage of the application, or others. "Actors" can also be used permanently. For example, if you write an optimization targeted to a limited set of customers, you can enable it so only they can use this kind of feature. Finally, "Percentage of Time" is not so much directed to enable product features, but to experiment with the characteristics of the platform. For example, you may want to compare the performance of two different code paths that do the same thing. With this feature, you can take a more truly random sample.

Releasing a Feature Under a Flag

To experiment with feature flags, you are going to make a small change in your application; this change will be under a feature flag. It will be a small one, but it will be a breaking change. You will add a new attribute to an API response.

You are going to add a new attribute to the store object returned by endpoints like api/v1/stores/%id. This new attribute would be the total number of items in the inventory. You can do so by editing the StorePresenter. Start by adding the new attribute without worrying about the feature. It should look like this:

```
# app/presenters/api/v1/store_presenter.rb

class Api::V1::StorePresenter
  [...]

  def to_json
    {
      id: resource.id,
      name: resource.name,
      most_rented_film: Api::V1::FilmPresenter
        .new(resource.most_rented_film).to_json,
      inventory_count: resource.inventories.count
    }
  end
end
```

Take a look at http://localhost:3000/api/v1/stores/1: the new attribute inventory_counter should be there. If it's not, it may be because you have been following the book, completed the "Tracking the Lifecycle of a Request" chapter, and now you are getting a 304, as the resource itself has not changed. If this happened to you as it happened to me when I was preparing the chapter, temporarily remove the call to stale? in the controller (app/controllers/api/v1/stores_controller.rb) and let this be a lesson on the increased complexity that usually comes with performance optimizations.

Going back to the exercise, now you need to make sure that the inventory_count key-value pair is only returned if a certain feature flag (let's call it inventory_count_in_store_presenter) is enabled. A straightforward way to do so is the following:

```
rails-performance-book-completed/app/presenters/api/v1/store_presenter.rb
class Api::V1::StorePresenter
  attr_reader :resource

  def initialize(store)
    @resource = store
  end

  def to_json
    body = {
      id: resource.id,
      title: resource.name,
      most_rented_film: Api::V1::FilmPresenter
        .new(resource.most_rented_film).to_json
    }
```

```
    if Flipper.enabled?(:inventory_count_in_store_presenter, resource)
      body[:inventory_count] = resource.inventories.count
    end

    body
  end
end
```

If you hit the endpoint again, you will see that the inventory_count attribute has disappeared. That's normal: all features are disabled by default. Let's enable the feature for everyone! You can do so by entering the Rails console bundle exec rails c and calling Flipper.enable_feature!(:inventory_count_in_store_presenter). Now, inventory_count should be returned by the API endpoint again. I would recommend you play a bit with different ways of enabling and disabling your new feature. For example, enable the feature for half of the stores by calling Flipper.enable_percentage_of_actors(:inventory_count_in_store_presenter, 50). Now check the response you get for different store IDs (api/v1/stores/1, api/v1/stores/2, etc...); is it around 50 percent?

Now that you have learned how to add feature flags to your application, I want to give you a tip about their usage: once a feature has been completely rolled out and has achieved general availability, remember to remove it. If you don't do so, you may eventually end up with hundreds of feature flags that have stayed in your codebase for years, and that will make your code more complex and dirtier.

Congratulations, you have completed the exercise. What do you think about feature flags? You may be thinking that being able to control the code paths with feature flags is pretty cool, but having to access the console to change the sliders feels quite clunky, particularly if you need to do so on production. Well, it turns out that there is a better way.

Controlling Your Feature Flags from the UI

Feature flags are a very powerful tool, but to unlock their full potential, you need to make them accessible. By accessible, I do not mean "a bit easier to use by my fellow engineers," but something that anyone, including non-technical members of the organization, can use with confidence. Ideally, you can have a project manager complete the rollout of a feature on production, or enable a flag for a customer with a special requirement. To do all this, you need an interface that everyone can understand and utilize. One of the reasons why I picked Flipper for this example is that it comes with its own web interface—no need to build your own.

To include this UI in your application, you will need to add Flipper UI to your Gemfile (gem flipper-ui). Next, you will need to add a route to your new endpoint, similar to what you did with Sidekiq earlier in the book.

rails-performance-book-completed/config/routes.rb
```ruby
Rails.application.routes.draw do

  if !Rails.env.production? # Replace this with an authentication check
    mount Flipper::UI.app(Flipper) => '/flipper'
  end
```

Like with other Rails engines that get access to sensitive data, remember to protect this on production so no one can mess around with your feature flags. This example is coded so /flipper will not work on production; change it with something that requires authentication.

Open your browser and go to http://localhost:3000/flipper. You will access a site with all your current features listed:

If you click one of the features, you will be able to see the conditions in which it is enabled and edit them. You will also be able to remove the feature; remember that feature flags are disabled by default, so if you remove a rolled-out feature, and the check is still in the code, you will be removing it.

If you have been following the example in this section, you will have a feature flag named inventory_count_in_store_presenter enabled for 50 percent of the actors as shown on page 234.

Before completing the chapter, I would like to comment on a very common use case: enabling a feature for one specific actor. In this case, we will enable it for the store with ID 1. To do so, you will need to click "Add an actor" and write the following String: "Store;1". This is how Flipper saves the feature gate value for actors: "#{object.class};#{object.id}"; in other words, the class of the

Features   Settings   Docs • Version: 1.3.1

inventory_count_in_store_presenter   ☑ Conditionally enabled

No actors enabled   Add an actor

No groups enabled   Add a group

Enabled for 50% of actors   Edit

Enabled for 0% of time   Edit

        Fully Enable   Disable

Danger Zone

Deleting a feature removes it from the list of features and disables it for everyone.

Delete

actor, a semicolon, and the ID of the actor. This way of introducing new actors to the feature can feel a bit awkward. Flipper offers a better UI in their pro solution. You should also feel free to build a solution that better fits your needs. For example, some B2B companies that use feature flags have set up a system so flags can be enabled just by using the subdomain or the name of the account. This makes it much more manageable, as you will not need to check which customer corresponds to ID 424242 in your database. You can build many other kinds of abstractions to facilitate the use of flags, for example, by enabling a feature for the whole database shard in which the account data is located. The possibilities are endless.

Summing Up

You've made it to the end of this chapter! In it, we have discussed a different kind of scalability problem that has nothing to do with a high volume of requests but with managing large codebases and big engineering teams.

The pains associated with big organizations cannot be cured, but they can be mitigated. You have played around with three resources that, I am convinced, will help you in the following ways:

- Defining clear ownership boundaries. These boundaries are not just words on a piece of (digital) paper but have real effects on how your codebase is managed.

- Modularizing your codebase. Continuing the previous point, a modular codebase can mimic some of the advantages (readability, maintainability) of microservices, with none of their drawbacks.

- Setting up feature flags. Thanks to them, you should be able to deploy in a much more safe and confident way. They will also give you and the rest of your team a huge amount of control over the release cycle.

It's time to say goodbye. But first, allow me a few words.

The Next 20 Years with Rails

I write this chapter, the conclusion of this book, at the end of November 2024. According to rubygems.org,[1] the first version of Ruby on Rails was released on the 25th of October, 2004. Twenty years have passed. I have been working professionally with Rails for most of this time. I have lived the hype era, in which Rails was the new cool kid on the block powering the Web 2.0 revolution. I lived through times when the pendulum of software design had moved heavily to favor microservices, years in which many self-proclaimed serious software architects looked down on Ruby on Rails and its core ideas. And here we are now when there is a renewed interest in monolithic architectures and a perceived "Rails renaissance."[2,3]

A lot has happened, and yet, quoting Dr. Manhattan, "Nothing ever ends." New technologies will emerge, and new patterns will rise. How will the next 20 years treat Ruby (and Rails) and, beyond that, the ideas that they represent in the technological landscape?

Scaling with Human-First Technology

I will be honest with you and state the obvious: I do not know what the future of Ruby on Rails, and software engineering in general, will look like in 2044. Still, I would bet that certain evolutionary patterns will continue, at least while the bases of traditional computing are not replaced with something like quantum computing. I believe that we will keep building higher levels of abstraction on top of the ones that we already have. These new abstractions could take any kind of form: maybe they will be similar to our current programming languages, but there is the chance that they may not.

---

1. https://rubygems.org/gems/rails/versions
2. https://hashrocket.com/blog/posts/the-rails-renaissance
3. https://www.youtube.com/watch?v=nrgaeiDlQbl

In 2023, I was invited to participate in a panel in the context of RubyConf Taiwan. The title of the panel was "The Path to Engineer Happiness in the Age of AI." The four panelists agreed the future looked exciting but, at the moment, more full of questions than of real solutions. I played around with the idea of a collaboration between AI and humans that would go beyond the "copilot pattern." Programming languages are already abstractions that help us "talk to the machine"; can AI help us cross these layers of abstractions, from the human brain to the chip, in a more efficient way?

In any case, there will be a debate on the shape of the tools that we will use to rule over technology. What should they look like? What should they care about? This debate will be as fundamental then as it is now. That's why I hope that in the future, we'll embrace the Ruby way even more.

What is the "Ruby way"? In my opinion, it's trying to "tame" the complexity of technology to make it as friendly as possible for as many people as possible. After all, Ruby is famously optimized for developer happiness. The following two excerpts are from the first point of the Rails doctrine:[4]

> There would be no Rails without Ruby, so it's only fitting that the first doctrinal pillar is lifted straight from the core motivation for creating Ruby.

> Ruby's original heresy was indeed to place the happiness of the programmer on a pedestal. Above many other competing and valid concerns that had driven programming languages and ecosystems before it.

In other words, Ruby's philosophy is caring about the UX of the developer. We, as software builders, understand how important this is, as UX is also a very significant factor in making our products successful. That's why our user experience as developers is paramount to determining the success of programming language. A tool that puts humans first is a more productive tool; this is, I believe, why Ruby on Rails was behind the creation of some of the most popular and successful companies of the 21st century. Rails allowed humans to do a lot with very little.

And this, my reader, is also scalability. Ruby on Rails is a fantastic tool to mitigate complexity, and complexity does not scale. Scalability is not only about handling millions of requests and managing petabytes of data. It's also about empowering humans to reach their full potential for creativity and innovation. Rails embraces this idea at its core—an idea that has allowed me and many others to make our dreams come true. Here's to the Ruby community and to all the other fools who dream. Here's to the mess we make!

---

4.   https://rubyonrails.org/doctrine#optimize-for-programmer-happiness

Index

DIGITS

304 Not Modified responses, 114, 116, 119–122

37signals, 180

429 Too Many Requests response, 164

A

abuse, 162, 180

action caching, 75–79

actionpack-action_caching, 76

actionpack-page_caching, 76, 79

Active Store, 84

Active Support, 6, 194, 199

active_record_shards, 130

active_span, 201

ActiveJob
 archiving data with, 171
 asynchronous processing, 140–151
 performance, 145
 setup, 140

ActiveRecord
 about, 12
 cache layer, 80–82
 EXPLAIN and, 30–38
 fetching, 21–30, 34
 indexes, 38–45
 preloading data, 16–21
 removing n+1s, 13–21
 running pure SQL, 33
 storage adapters, 228
 transforming queries into SQL strings, 33

actor, feature flags with Flipper, 229

actual_time, 33

after_save, creating background jobs, 142

AI (artificial intelligence), 238

AJAX, 184

alerts, performance, 209

Alexander the Great, 178

Amazon S3, 177

AOF (Append Only File) option, 171

Apache Kafka, see Kafka

API
 design and pagination, 89–100
 GraphQL, 106–112
 sideloads, 105
 splitting model data, 100–105

Api::V1::Presenter, 221

APM systems and n+1s detection, 15

Append Only File (AOF) option, 171

appendonly, 171

ApplicationController, 221

applications, see also API
 companion application, loading dataset, 7
 companion application, setup, 1–9
 database setup, 2
 databases, switching between MySQL vs. PostgreSQL, 2
 defined, 1

modularization of, 217–227

ownership and, 214–217, 226

architecture
 archiving data and, 169–180
 asynchronous processing, 138–151
 microservices, xv, 151–160, 218
 modularization, 217–227
 sharding, 127–138, 182

archiving data
 with ActiveJob, 171
 cold/hot, 176–178
 communication and, 170
 data store selection, 170
 destroying data, 178–180
 features and, 170, 174
 pagination and, 175
 scheduling, 173
 understanding, 169–180
 user access and, 173–180

args key, configuring tasks, 149

arrays
 fragment caching, 60
 lean fetching with pluck, 25

artificial intelligence (AI), 238

as_json, 65

asdf, 4

assets, page speed and, 187

associations
 caching objects with identity_cache, 82

GraphQL and, 109
preloading data, 16–21
assumed requirements, 179
asynchronous processing
    asynchronous loading,
        184–187
    with background jobs,
        140–151
    microservices and, 152
    performance, 138–151
    transition challenges, 139
authentication
    action caching and au-
        thenticated users, 76
    Warden and, 164

B
backfills
    running, 52
    sharding example, 134
background jobs
    asynchronous process-
        ing, 140–151
    creating, 142–144
    monitoring, 146
    setting priorities and
        queues, 145
    Sidekiq, 140–147
    Solid Queue, 147–151
base64, 97
Basecamp, 84, 180
batch_size, 29, 150
Batched Key Access join
    buffer type, 32
Big Ball of Mud, 217
Block Nested Loop join buffer
    type, 32
Booleans, feature flags, 229
bounce rates, 184
buffers
    EXPLAIN ANALYZE with Post-
        greSQL, 36
    Using join buffer, 32
Bullet, 15
Bundler, 6
bunny, 140

C
cache, 58–61
cache keys
    caching collections, 67
    caching objects, 65
    fragment caching, 59

including expiration on,
    69
pattern, 59
cache stores
    auto-expiration, 70
    Cache-Control header direc-
        tives, 115
    comparison of Solid
        Cache, Memcached,
        and Redis, 84–86
    installing, 5
    :null_store as default, 57,
        83
    options, 57, 83–86
    write-through caching, 74
cache version, 59–60
Cache-Control header
    about, 57
    CDN configuration, 124
    performance and, 115–
        122
cache_has_many, 82
cache_has_one, 82
cache_index, 82
cache_key
    caching collections, 67
    caching objects, 65
    defining, 69
cache_path, 78
cached_response, 67
caches_action, 77–79
caches_path, 77–80
caching
    action caching, 75–79
    ActiveRecord cache layer,
        80–82
    arrays, 60
    asymmetry in data ac-
        cess, 48
    auto-expiration, 70
    cache version, 59–60
    collections, 59, 66–69
    with counter_cache, 50–55
    defined, 47, 49
    enabling, 57
    expiration, 65, 67, 69,
        79, 106, 124
    fan-out writing, 72–75
    fragment caching, 58–61
    hit ratio, 47
    HTTP headers and, 114–
        122
    JOIN and, 19
    memory use, 53, 69
    objects, 59, 64–66, 82
    page caching, 76, 79

pagination and, 95
performance, 51–55, 61,
    63, 72, 76, 79, 83–86
renewal triggers, 59
Russian doll, 61–70
setup, 55–57
sideloads, 106
steps in, 47
write-through, 70–75
writing own, 63–70
cardinality, 42
CDNs (Content Delivery Net-
    works), 114, 122–124
Chaos Engineering, 24
chaos monkeys, 23
check, 219, 222
chruby, 4
class key, configuring tasks,
    149
clients, request lifecycle
    overview, 113
cloud computing
    feature flag hosting, 228
    scheduling archive jobs,
        173
code for this book, xvii
Coinbase, 210
collections, caching, 59, 66–
    69
columns, order of and index-
    es, 42
command key, configuring
    tasks, 149
commands, tasks as, 149
communication
    archiving data and, 170
    microservices, 152–154
    product limit messages,
        167
complexity
    event-driven architecture,
        153
    fan-out writing, 75
    increase in app complexi-
        ty over time, 138
    of large organizations,
        227
    microservices and, 151,
        153
    Ruby way and, 238
    scaling and, xv, 238
    sharding and, 130, 137
    sideloads, 106
    write-through caching, 72
connected_to, 132, 136

connecting_to, 132

consumers, Karafka, 155–158

Content Delivery Networks (CDNs), 114, 122–124

convention over configuration paradigm, xiv, 21, 61, 127, 151

Copeland, David Bryant, 144

cost attribute, EXPLAIN with PostgreSQL, 35

counter_cache, 50–55

counts, SLOs (Service Level Objectives), 206

created_at, 98

creative destruction, 179

cron jobs, archiving data, 171

crontab, 173

Cumulative Layout Shift, 183

cursor-based pagination, 94–100

custom caching, 63–70

cyclical dependencies, 222

D

Dalli, 85

dashboards
error budget, 208
monitoring, building, 203–206

data, *see also* ActiveRecord; caching; pagination
archiving, 169–180
asynchronous loading, 184–187
CDNs (Content Delivery Networks) and, 114, 122–124
companion application dataset, loading, 7
data structures and cache storage options, 85
denormalization, 49, 51, 86–88
destroying data, 178–180
economic importance of, 12
fetching, 21–30, 34
GraphQL, 106–112
life cycle management, 168–180
linking vs. embedding, 101–105
n+1s, removing, 13–21

n+1s, size of dataset and, 14
n+1s, splitting model data, 102
preloading, 16–21
rate limits, 163–166
record limits, 166
redundancy and denormalization, 86
sideloads, 105
splitting model data, 100–105
throttling, 165
usage and number of licenses, 168

--database shard_one, 132

databases
application setup, 5
archiving data, 169–180
companion application dataset, loading, 7
creating, 6
denormalization, 49, 51, 86–88
EXPLAIN, 30–38
indexes, 38–45
migrations, 41, 132
MySQL vs. PostgreSQL, 2
normalization, 49
setup, understanding, 2
sharding, 127–138, 182
switching between MySQL vs. PostgreSQL, 2
switching, sharding by subdomains and, 136

Datadog
about, 192
APM, 194–202
creating new services, 201
custom metrics, 202
dashboards, building, 203–206
error budgets, 206–210
Metrics API, 202
monitoring basics, 193–203
performance alerts, 209
setup, 192
SLOs (Service Level Objectives), 206–210
spans, 197, 199–202
traces, 197–206

dates, cursor-based pagination with, 98

DB_MODE, 2

:default (queues), 146

Delayed::Job, 140

deleting, fragment caching and, 59

denormalization
counter_cache and, 51
defined, 49
using, 86–88

dependencies
checking, 220
cyclical, 222
installing, 6
package managers, 6
packages, building with Packwerk, 219–222
privacy boundaries, 223–225

deployment with feature flags, 227–234

design
archiving data and, 169–180
convention over configuration paradigm, xiv, 21, 61, 127, 151
data life cycle management and, 168–180
GraphQL, 106–112
pagination, 89–100
product limits, 161–168
sideloads, 105
splitting model data, 100–105

destroying data, 178–180

destruction, creative, 179

Devise, 164

disable (Flipper), 230

dispatchers (Solid Queue), 150

DNS Lookup, 113

Docker, 154

DogStatsD, 202

domains
CDNs, 123
sharding based on, 136–138

duplication of data
counter_cache, 53
denormalization and, 86
splitting model data, 104

E

eager_load, 18–21

ECMAScript, 184

edge servers and CDNs, 122–124

embedding vs. linking, 101–105

enable (Flipper), 229

enable_feature! (Flipper), 232

enabled? (Flipper), 230

enforce_privacy, 223

engineering
career success and, xv
defined, 1

entity tags, 116, 119–122

environment
monitoring with traces and, 198
scheduling tasks with Solid Queue and, 149

error budgets, 206–210

ETags, 116, 119–122

event-driven microservices, see microservices

eviction policies, cache storage options, 85

exclude, 104

experience and career success, xv

expiration_key
caching collections, 67
caching objects, 65
including on cache key, 69

expire_page, 79

Expires header, 116

expires_in, 79, 118

EXPLAIN, 30–38

.explain, 30

EXPLAIN ANALYZE, 33–38

expression, feature flags with Flipper, 229

Extra
EXPLAIN, 31
indexes, 40

F

Facebook, 106

facets, traces, 198

fan-out reading, 75

fan-out writing, 72–75

feature flags, 182, 227–234

feature_key, 229

features
archiving data and, 170, 174

feature bloat, 138, 217
supporting non-sharded, 135

fetching
ActiveRecord, 21–30, 34
in batches, 28
narrow, 24–30
wide, 21–24, 28–30, 34

file system as cache storage, 83

filtered, 31

.find_in_batches, 28

First Contentful Paint, 183

flame graphs, 199

Flipper, 228–234

Flipper UI, 233–234

Foote, Brian, 217

fragment caching, 58–61

fresh_when, 121

FULL JOIN, 19

FULL OUTER JOIN, 19

G

garbage collection and n+1s, 15

General Availability (GA), 230

GitHub
companion application, downloading, 3
ownership, enforcing, 214–217
scaling teams and, 214

GitLab, 214

Google
loading time tools, 183
SEO rankings, 183, 187

Gordian Knot, 178–180

Grafana, 192

Graham, Paul, 181

graphiql-rails, 107

GraphQL, 106–112

graphql, 107

GraphQL for Rails Developers, 112

graphs
flame graphs, 199
monitoring dashboards, building, 205

group, feature flags with Flipper, 229

H

Harencarova, Hana, 214

has_many, 82

has_one, 82

hashing, modular, 134

Heinemeier-Hansson, David, 69

HEY.com, 84

hiredisgem, 85

hit ratio, 47

horizontal sharding, see sharding

HTTP requests
lifecycle overview, 113
performance and HTTP headers, 114–122

HTTP responses
304 Not Modified, 114, 116, 119–122
429 Too Many Requests, 164
manipulating directly, 118
performance, 114, 117, 119–122

I

id
cursor-based pagination with, 95–100
EXPLAIN, 30
indexes, 39

identity_cache, 80–82, 218

If-None-Match header, 114, 116, 119

image_option, 187

images, loading, 187

immutable Cache-Control header directive, 115

includes
preloading data, 16–21
sideloads, 106
splitting model data, 103

inconsistency and denormalization, 86

indexes
adding, 40–42
advantages, 42
defined, 38
EXPLAIN, 31
forcing for queries, 43
identity_cache, 81
keys, 31, 39
order of columns, 42
order of keys, 42

overhead, 39
performance, 43–45
possible_keys, 31, 39, 42
storage needs, 39
understanding, 38–45
Information Technology (IT)
term, 12
INNER JOIN, 18
IP address, 113

J
Jaeger, 192
JavaScript, 184
JOIN
decomposition, 19
defined, 18
EXPLAIN, 31–32
EXPLAIN ANALYZE, 34
fetching and, 34
preloading data with ea-
ger_load, 18
types of, 19
joins, 18
Justin Bieber problem, 75,
181

K
Kafka, 154–160
Kaminari, 90–94
Karafka, 154–160
Karlton, Phil, 106
key
EXPLAIN, 31
feature flags, 229
indexes, 39, 42
key_len
EXPLAIN, 31
indexes, 39
keys
archived data, 175
cache keys, 59, 65, 67,
69
EXPLAIN, 31
feature flags, 229
indexes, 31, 39, 42

L
Largest Contentful Paint, 183
latency
improving with CDNs,
122
monitoring with Datadog,
194
LEFT JOIN, 19
LEFT OUTER JOIN, 19

linking vs. embedding, 101–
105
lists, pagination, 105
loading
asynchronous loading,
184–187
images, 187
loading time and perfor-
mance, 182–188
preloading data, 16–21
sideloads, 105
loading HTML attribute, 187
locking, 54
logging, Write-Ahead, 3
Loki, 192
loops, archiving data, 171

M
manual rebalancing, 182
Mastodon, 75
Matsuda, Akira, 90
max-age Cache-Control header directive, 115, 124
max-stale Cache-Control header
directive, 116
McBreen, Donal, 84
Memcached
auto-expiration, 70
identity_cache, 80
installing, 5
Solid Cache and Redis
comparison, 84–86
memory
cache store option, 57, 83
caching and memory use,
53, 69
fetching and, 29
indexes and, 44
n+1s and, 15, 20
preloading data with ea-
ger_load, 19
mentoring, xv
message brokers, 153–160
metrics, see also monitoring
custom metrics with
Datadog, 202
loading time, 183
percentiles and, 195
microservices
communication, 152–154
complexity and, 151, 153
creating, 157
financing and, xv, 151
modularization and, 218
monitoring, 158

popularity of, xv
producing and consum-
ing messages, 155–158
using, 151–160
migrate, 41
migrate_shards folder, 132
migration, 41
migrations
creating, 41
sharding, 132
min-fresh Cache-Control header directive, 116
mkdir, 220
modular hashing, 134
modularization
applications, 217–227
goals, 225
limits of, 225–227
packages, building, 219–
222
packages, privacy bound-
aries, 223–225
monitoring, see also Datadog
background jobs, 146
basics, 193–203
dashboards, building,
203–206
error budgets, 206–210
importance of, 191
microservices with Karaf-
ka, 158
performance alerts, 209
platform selection, 191
SLOs (Service Level Objectives), 206–210
spending on, 210
with traces, 197–206
monkey-patching term, 82
monoliths
advantages of, 152
feature flags, 227–234
latency metrics and, 196
modularization and, 217–
227
renewed interest in, 237
must-revalidate Cache-Control
header directive, 115
must-understand Cache-Control
header directive, 115
MySQL, see also databases
EXPLAIN, 30–35
EXPLAIN ANALYZE, 33–35
installing, 5
vs. PostgreSQL, 2

N

n+1s
  defined, 13
  detection tools, 15
  GraphQL, 111
  removing, 13–21
  size of dataset and, 14
  splitting model data, 102
narrow fetching, 24–30
Netflix, 24
New Relic, 13, 15, 192
next_page_url, 92
no-cache Cache-Control header directive, 115
no-store Cache-Control header directive, 115
no-transform Cache-Control header directive, 115
normalization, defined, 49
:null_store, 57, 83

O

object-oriented programming (OOP) language, Ruby as, 12
object-relational mapping (ORM), 12, see also ActiveRecord
objects, caching, 59, 64–66, 82
octopus, 130
offsets
  offset pagination, 94, 99
  pagination with Kaminari, 92
one-to-many associations and GraphQL, 109
only-if-cached Cache-Control header directive, 116
OOP (object-oriented programming) language, Ruby as, 12
ORM (object-relational mapping), 12, see also ActiveRecord
ownership
  applications and components, 214–217, 226
  career success and, xv

P

-p flag, 220
PaaS, dividing accounts, 182
package.yml file, 220

packages
  building with Packwerk, 219–222
  checking dependencies, 220
  package managers, 6
  privacy boundaries, 223–225
Packwerk, 218–227
packwerk-extensions, 223
page, 91
page caching, 76, 79
page-based pagination, 94, 99
pagination
  archived data, 175
  caching and, 95
  cursor-based, 94–100
  design and, 89–100
  fetching and, 22, 28
  with Kaminari, 90–94
  lists, 105
  offset pagination, 94, 99
  page-based, 94, 99
  performance, 95, 99
  setup, 91
  splitting model data and, 105
partials, Russian doll caching, 62
partition, EXPLAIN, 31
per, 91
percentage_of_actors, feature flags with Flipper, 229
percentage_of_time, feature flags with Flipper, 229
percentiles and monitoring metrics, 195
perform, 143
perform_later, 143
performance, see also monitoring
  action caching, 76
  ActiveJob, 145
  alerts, 209
  asynchronous processing, 138–151
  cache store options, 83–86
  caching, 51–55, 61, 63, 72, 76, 79, 83–86
  CDNs (Content Delivery Networks), 114, 122–124
  counter_cache, 51–55

cursor-based pagination, 95, 99
denormalization, 49, 86–88
error budgets, 206–210
forcing indexes, 43, 45
fragment caching, 61
GraphQL, 111
HTTP headers, 114–122
HTTP responses, 114, 117, 119–122
indexes, 43–45
loading images, 187
loading time, 182–188
n+1s detection, 15
offset pagination, 99
page caching, 76, 79
page-based pagination, 99
pagination, 95, 99
read/write tradeoff, 70, 72, 76
Russian doll caching, 63
Sidekiq, 145
Solid Queue, 147
usability time and, 182–188
Using temporary and Using filesort, 32
write-through caching, 72
persistence options, Redis, 171
Playfulbet, xiii, 75
PlayfulGaming, xiii
pluck, 25–30, 34
polling_interval Solid Queue option, 150
possible_keys, 31, 39, 42
PostgreSQL, see also databases
  EXPLAIN, 35–38
  installing, 5
  vs. MySQL, 2
  TEXT data length, 23
preload, 18–21
prev_page_url, 92
priorities, background jobs, 145
priority attribute, tasks, 149
privacy, modularization and privacy boundaries, 223–225
Privacy Checker, 223
private, Cache-Control header directive, 115

processes Solid Queue option, 150

producers, Karafka, 155–157

products
  abuse, 162, 180
  archiving data and, 169–180
  data life cycle management and, 168–180
  product limits, 161–168
  rate limits, 163–166
  record limits, 166
  requirements and specificity, 162

Prometheus, 192

Prosopite, 15

proxy-revalidate Cache-Control header directive, 115

public
  Cache-Control header directive, 115
  packages, privacy boundaries, 224

Q

queries
  EXPLAIN, understanding, 30–38
  forcing indexes for, 43
  transforming into SQL strings, 33

QueryType (GraphQL), 108

queue attribute, tasks, 149

queues
  background jobs with Sidekiq, 145
  background jobs with Solid Queue, 147–151
  monitoring, 146
  weighted, 146

queues (Solid Queue option), 150

Quintus Curtius Rufus, 179

R

racecar, 154

Rack::Attack, 163–166

Rails
  advantages, xiv, 127
  convention over configuration paradigm, xiv, 21, 61, 127, 151
  future of, 237
  Rails doesn't scale myth, xiii, 11, 38

setup, 1–9
versions, 6

rails-sharding, 130

rails_cursor_pagination, 95

rate limits, 163–166

rbenv, 4

RDBMS (relational database management system), 12

read_fragment, 78

reads
  fan-out reading, 75
  read/write performance tradeoff, 70, 72, 76

rebalancing, manual, 182

recalculate!, 143

record limits, 166

Redis
  archiving data, 171
  configuration file, finding, 171
  installing, 5
  Memcached and Solid Cache comparison, 84–86
  persistence options, 171
  write-through caching, 74

redis gem, 85

ref
  EXPLAIN, 31
  indexes, 39

relational database management system (RDBMS), 12

requests
  asynchronous processing diagram, 154
  CDNs (Content Delivery Networks) and, 114, 122–124
  HTTP headers, 114–122
  lifecycle overview, 113
  product limits, 161–168
  rate limits, 163–166
  record limits, 166
  synchronous processing diagram, 152

requirements
  assumed requirements, 179
  specificity and, 162

reset_counters, 52

resolvers, 111

resources for this book, xvii

response.headers, 118

responsibility and career success, xv

Resque, 140

Resque Scheduler, 173

rollouts with feature flags, 227–234

rows
  EXPLAIN ANALYZE and, 33
  EXPLAIN and, 31, 35
  indexing and advantages of fewer rows, 45

rows (EXPLAIN ANALYZE), 33

rows (EXPLAIN), 31, 35

Ruby
  as object-oriented programming (OOP) language, 12
  setup, 4

Ruby on Rails Background Jobs with Sidekiq, 144

ruby-build, 4

Russian doll caching, 61–70

rvm, 4

S

s-max-age Cache-Control header directive, 115

S3, 177

SaaS
  dividing accounts, 182
  product limits and, 167

_save_fragment, 78

scaling, see also caching; monitoring; teams, scaling
  complexity and, xv, 238
  problem solving and, 181
  Rails doesn't scale myth, xiii, 11, 38
  startups' focus on, 180
  when to ignore, 180–182

schedule attribute, tasks, 149

scheduling
  archiving data, 173
  tasks with Solid Queue, 148–151

schema, GraphQL and, 107

Schierbeck, Daniel, 154

Scout, 15

SELECT, understanding, 30–38

select
  fetching with, 25, 29
  removing n+1s, 13–21

select_type, EXPLAIN, 31

SEO rankings, 182, 187

serialization, large TEXT fields and, 24
servers
  edge servers and CDNs, 122–124
  Karafka server, starting, 156
  request lifecycle overview, 113
Service Level Agreements (SLAs), 208
Service Level Indicators (SLIs), 208
Service Level Objectives (SLOs), 206–210
set_tag, 201
setup
  ActiveJob, 140
  caching, 55–57
  companion application, 1–9
  databases, understanding, 2
  Datadog, 192
  GraphQL, 107
  identity_cache, 80
  Karafka, 154
  pagination with Kaminari, 91
  Rails, 1–9
  Ruby, 4
  Sidekiq, 140
  Solid Queue, 148
sharding
  cautions, 137
  creating shards, 131
  domain-based shards, 136–138
  horizontal, 128
  horizontal vs. vertical, 130
  manual rebalancing, 182
  supporting non-sharded features, 135
  using, 127–138
  vertical, 130
ShardRecord, 132, 221
Shopify, 80, 218, 225
Sidekiq
  background jobs, 140–147
  modifying configuration, 146
  performance, 145
  scheduling archive jobs, 173
  setup, 140

Sidekiq Scheduler, 173
sideloads, 105
SIMPLE SELECT type, 31
SLAs (Service Level Agreements), 208
SLIs (Service Level Indicators), 208
SLO List widget, 208
SLO widget, 208
SLOs (Service Level Objectives), 206–210
social networks and Justin Bieber problem, 75, 181
Solid Cache, 6, 84–86
Solid Queue
  about, 140
  background jobs, 147–151
  scheduling archive jobs, 173
spans, traces, 197, 199–202
Speed Index, loading metrics, 183
SQL, see also databases; MySQL; PostgreSQL
  cache version construction, 61
  EXPLAIN, understanding, 30–38
  running pure from ActiveRecord, 33
  SQLite, 3
SQLite, 3
stale-if-error Cache-Control header directive, 115
stale-while-revalidate Cache-Control header directive, 115
stale?, 120, 122, 231
StatsD, 203
storage, see also cache stores
  archiving data, 170
  indexes and, 39
storage adapters, 228
Store, 221
strong ETags, 120
synchronous processing
  diagram, 152
  expectations of, 139
  microservices, 152

T
table, 31
tables, see also sharding
  table field and EXPLAIN, 31
  temporary, 32, 42
tasks
  configuring, 149
  scheduling with Solid Queue, 148–151
TCP connections, 113
teams, scaling
  challenges of, 213
  feature flags, 227–234
  modularization of applications, 217–227
  ownership and, 214–217, 226
TEXT columns, fetching problems, 23–24, 27
threads Solid Queue option, 150
thresholds, SLOs (Service Level Objectives), 206–208
throttle, 164–166
throttled_responder, 165
throttled_response_retry_after_header, 165
throttling, 163–166
time
  EXPLAIN ANALYZE, 33
  EXPLAIN with PostgreSQL, 35
  feature flags with Flipper, 229
  indexes, 44
  SLOs by time slices, 206
  usability time, 182–188
time slices, 206
timestamps, cursor-based pagination with, 98
TinyPNG, 187
to_json
  caching individual objects, 64–66
  splitting model data, 104
  write-through caching, 70
to_sql, 33
TODO file (Packwerk), 221
Total Blocking Time, 183
total_pages, 92
traces
  customizing, 200–202
  facets, 198

monitoring with Datadog, 197–206
spans, 197, 199–202
type, EXPLAIN, 31–32
types
GraphQL, 107
JOIN types, 31–32

U

Uchitelle, Eileen, 131, 225
UNION SELECT type, 31
update-todo, 222
updated_at, 98
usability time, 182–188
users
action caching and authenticated users, 76
archived data access, 173–180
large TEXT fields and, 23
usability time and, 182–188
Using filesort, 32, 40
Using join buffer, 32
Using temporary, 32

V

validate (Packwerk), 219, 222
validation, Cache-Control header directives, 115
variables, monitoring dashboards, building, 203
versions
cache version, 59–60
Rails, 6
Ruby, 4
vertical sharding, 130

W

WAL (Write-Ahead Logging), 3
Warden, 164
Warner, Jason, 151
weak ETags, 120
weighted queues, 146
whenever, 173
where_conditions, 97
wide fetching, 21–24, 28–30, 34
widgets, monitoring dashboards, 203–206
width attribute, EXPLAIN with PostgreSQL, 35

will_paginate, 90
workers (Solid Queue), 150
Write-Ahead Logging (WAL), 3
write-through caching, 70–75
writes
fan-out writing, 72–75
index overhead, 39
page caching and, 76
read/write performance tradeoff, 70, 72, 76
serialization by SQLite, 3

X

X
fan-out writing, 75
Justin Bieber problem, 75, 181
XING, 95

Y

Yoder, Joseph, 217

Z

Zeitwerk, 218, 220
Zendesk, scaling success, xv, 214

Thank you!

We hope you enjoyed this book and that you're already thinking about what you want to learn next. To help make that decision easier, we're offering you this gift.

Head on over to https://pragprog.com right now, and use the coupon code BUYANOTHER2025 to save 30% on your next ebook. Offer is void where prohibited or restricted. This offer does not apply to any edition of *The Pragmatic Programmer* ebook.

And if you'd like to share your own expertise with the world, why not propose a writing idea to us? After all, many of our best authors started off as our readers, just like you. With up to a 50% royalty, world-class editorial services, and a name you trust, there's nothing to lose. Visit https://pragprog.com/become-an-author/ today to learn more and to get started.

Thank you for your continued support. We hope to hear from you again soon!

The Pragmatic Bookshelf

SAVE 30%!
Use coupon code
BUYANOTHER2025

Agile Web Development with Rails 7

Rails 7 completely redefines what it means to produce fantastic user experiences and provides a way to achieve all the benefits of single-page applications – at a fraction of the complexity. Rails 7 integrates the Hotwire frameworks of Stimulus and Turbo directly as the new defaults, together with that hot newness of import maps. The result is a toolkit so powerful that it allows a single individual to create modern applications upon which they can build a competitive business. The way it used to be.

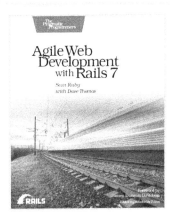

Sam Ruby
(474 pages) ISBN: 9781680509298. $59.95
https://pragprog.com/book/rails7

Agile Web Development with Rails 7.2

Rails 7.2 completely redefined what it means to produce fantastic user experiences and provides a way to achieve all the benefits of single-page applications—at a fraction of the complexity. Rails 7.2 integrated the Hotwire frameworks of Stimulus and Turbo directly as the new defaults, together with that hot newness of import maps. The result is a toolkit so powerful that it allows a single individual to create modern applications upon which they can build a competitive business. The way it used to be.

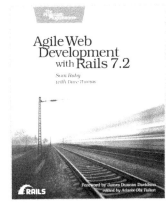

Sam Ruby
(472 pages) ISBN: 9798888651049. $67.95
https://pragprog.com/book/rails72

High Performance PostgreSQL for Rails

Build faster, more reliable Rails apps by taking the best advanced PostgreSQL and Active Record capabilities, and using them to solve your application scale and growth challenges. Gain the skills needed to comfortably work with multi-terabyte databases, and with complex Active Record, SQL, and specialized Indexes. Develop your skills with PostgreSQL on your laptop, then take them into production, while keeping everything in sync. Make slow queries fast, perform any schema or data migration without errors, use scaling techniques like read/write splitting, partitioning, and sharding, to meet demanding workload requirements from Internet scale consumer apps to enterprise SaaS.

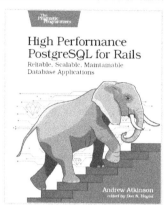

Andrew Atkinson
(454 pages) ISBN: 9798888650387. $64.95
https://pragprog.com/book/aapsql

Programming Ruby 3.3 (5th Edition)

Ruby is one of the most important programming languages in use for web development. It powers the Rails framework, which is the backing of some of the most important sites on the web. The Pickaxe Book, named for the tool on the cover, is the definitive reference on Ruby, a highly-regarded, fully object-oriented programming language. This updated edition is a comprehensive reference on the language itself, with a tutorial on the most important features of Ruby—including pattern matching and Ractors—and describes the language through Ruby 3.3.

Noel Rappin, with Dave Thomas
(716 pages) ISBN: 9781680509823. $65.95
https://pragprog.com/book/ruby5

Ruby Performance Optimization

You don't have to accept slow Ruby or Rails performance. In this comprehensive guide to Ruby optimization, you'll learn how to write faster Ruby code—but that's just the beginning. See exactly what makes Ruby and Rails code slow, and how to fix it. Alex Dymo will guide you through perils of memory and CPU optimization, profiling, measuring, performance testing, garbage collection, and tuning. You'll find that all those "hard" things aren't so difficult after all, and your code will run orders of magnitude faster.

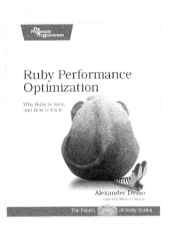

Alexander Dymo

(200 pages) ISBN: 9781680500691. $36

https://pragprog.com/book/adrpo

Modern Front-End Development for Rails, Second Edition

Improve the user experience for your Rails app with rich, engaging client-side interactions. Learn to use the Rails 7 tools and simplify the complex JavaScript ecosystem. It's easier than ever to build user interactions with Hotwire, Turbo, and Stimulus. You can add great front-end flair without much extra complication. Use React to build a more complex set of client-side features. Structure your code for different levels of client-side needs with these powerful options. Add to your toolkit today!

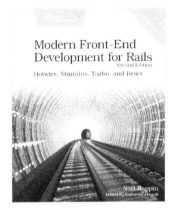

Noel Rappin

(408 pages) ISBN: 9781680509618. $55.95

https://pragprog.com/book/nrclient2

The Pragmatic Bookshelf

The Pragmatic Bookshelf features books written by professional developers for professional developers. The titles continue the well-known Pragmatic Programmer style and continue to garner awards and rave reviews. As development gets more and more difficult, the Pragmatic Programmers will be there with more titles and products to help you stay on top of your game.

Visit Us Online

This Book's Home Page
https://pragprog.com/book/cprpo
Source code from this book, errata, and other resources. Come give us feedback, too!

Keep Up-to-Date
https://pragprog.com
Join our announcement mailing list (low volume) or follow us on Twitter @pragprog for new titles, sales, coupons, hot tips, and more.

New and Noteworthy
https://pragprog.com/news
Check out the latest Pragmatic developments, new titles, and other offerings.

Save on the ebook

Save on the ebook versions of this title. Owning the paper version of this book entitles you to purchase the electronic versions at a terrific discount.

PDFs are great for carrying around on your laptop—they are hyperlinked, have color, and are fully searchable. Most titles are also available for the iPhone and iPod touch, Amazon Kindle, and other popular e-book readers.

Send a copy of your receipt to support@pragprog.com and we'll provide you with a discount coupon.

Contact Us

Online Orders:	*https://pragprog.com/catalog*
Customer Service:	*support@pragprog.com*
International Rights:	*translations@pragprog.com*
Academic Use:	*academic@pragprog.com*
Write for Us:	*http://write-for-us.pragprog.com*

www.ingramcontent.com/pod-product-compliance
Lightning Source LLC
LaVergne TN
LVHW081338050326
832903LV00024B/1198